Outstanding Dissertations in

ECONOMICS

A Continuing Garland Research Series

The Differential Effects of Changing to a Value-Added Tax in an Open Economy

Dennis R. Leyden

Foreword by Carl S. Shoup

Garland Publishing, Inc.
New York & London, 1982

Library of Congress Cataloging in Publication Data

Leyden, Dennis R.
The differential effects of changing to a value-added tax in an open economy.

(Outstanding dissertations in economics)
Originally presented as the author's thesis (Ph.D.—University of Virginia, 1976) under the title: An economic analysis of a tax alternative to the current turnover tax on business in West Virginia : a simulation study, 1967–1969.
Bibliography: p.
1. Value-added tax—West Virginia. 2. Turnover tax—West Virginia. I. Title. II. Series.
HJ5715.U6L48 1982 336.2'714'09754 79-53643
ISBN 0-8240-4168-2 AACR2

All volumes in this series are printed on acid-free, 250-year-life paper.

Printed in the United States of America

Foreword

It is a pleasure to have this opportunity to commend Professor Leyden's study to the attention of public finance scholars and policy formulators, and indeed to a broader group of economists as will be indicated below. In addition to those who have a particular interest in value-added taxation and the turnover tax, this work should appeal especially to at least four groups (with overlapping memberships).

First, there are those especially interested in the use of input-output analysis for ascertaining the differing effects of a tax change on different producing sectors of the economy. In this respect, Professor Leyden's monograph extends the work of Aaron, and of Dresch, Lin, and Stout by applying the analysis at the state level and by encountering and solving further problems of application.

Second are those concerned with the results of a tax change in an open economy, where the openness is so great that it cannot be ignored. Professor Leyden directly attacks this problem, dealing as he does with taxation in a single state of the United States.

Third, and a very broad group, are those puzzling over the choice between partial equilibrium and general equilibrium analysis when studying the the incidence and other effects of a broad-based tax. In general, a broad-based tax requires a general equilibrium framework. The present study deals with the chief instance where something can be said about the incidence of that kind of a tax in a partial-equilibrium analysis.

Fourth, a still broader group consists of those who want to see how the generalizations of tax theory can be employed to derive specific, quantitative statements about a particular taxing jurisdiction.

On all four counts Professor Leyden pushes back the frontiers of our knowledge. His imaginative, yet careful, approach and his conclusions will, we may hope, inspire others to continue with the arduous task of obtaining concrete answers, or at least reasonable quantitative conjectures, for a given time and place.

Incidentally, those who wish to refresh themselves on, or become acquainted with, the development of the value-added tax concept in public finance literature should find the second chapter of particular interest.

In sum, we are all indebted to the author for accepting so challenging a task and for accomplishing it in so illuminating a manner.

Carl S. Shoup

McVickar Professor of
Political Economy Emeritus,
Columbia University

June, 1979

AUTHOR'S PREFACE TO GARLAND EDITION

This dissertation was originally titled "An Economic Analysis of a Tax Alternative to the Current Turnover Tax on Business in West Virginia: A Simulation Study, 1967-1969" and submitted to the University of Virginia in 1975. Aside from its ponderous syntax, the title does not reveal clearly the nature of the study; hence, the current title. In addition, the reader should be aware that there are a number of pages which were revised from the original as a consequence of the careful review provided to me by Professor Carl Shoup. This Garland edition, therefore, is an improved version of the original work. I am indebted to Professor Shoup for his contribution to the substance of the work as well as his generosity in writing an introduction. My debt is greater than this, however, for it was his thoughts on open economy analysis which led me to undertake the research and guided its design.

DRL
June 1979

ACKNOWLEDGMENTS

This study could not have been accomplished without the cooperation, resources, and support of a number of agencies and individuals to whom I owe a debt of gratitude.

My thanks to the West Virginia State Tax Department, especially to Chief Justice Charles H. Haden, former Tax Commissioner; Richard L. Dailey, his successor; William Cobb, former Research Director; Arnold Margolin, current Research Director; and Arthur Blakeslee, Research Analyst, who by their commitment to the goals of the study made extraordinary efforts to insure the quality of the empirical data.

At West Virginia University, where this study was executed, I wish to express my thanks to the following: Jack T. Turner, Dean of the College of Business and Economics for his support and encouragement throughout the course of the study; Wayne A. Muth, Director of the Computer Center, and Phillip D. Stark, Assistant Director, for their support in many hours of computer time, programming, and keypunch services; James A. Kutsch, former Systems Analyst and Programmer, who translated my data processing and analysis instructions into program language; Professors Kenneth L. Shellhammer and Gregory J. Yi for their helpful advice on the input-output phase of this study; Miss Patricia Gurtis for translating my hieroglyphics into typewritten form and who saw the study through many drafts and re-drafts; Miss Nancy Greene and Miss Carla Uphold for their typing assistance; Mrs. Eleanore Getz for her proofreading assistance; Ralph Hofer, Dianna Ringer, Edward Portaro, and Larry Jackson--work-study students--and my son and daughter, Dennis and Julia, for their help in the data processing.

A special note of thanks is due my committee members, Professors Roland N. McKean and Edgar K. Browning, for their critical evaluations throughout the study and to Professor Warren G. Nutter for his evaluation of the final draft.

Because of her special qualities, I wish to thank my wife, Anne--a friend of long standing--who took the time to be concerned, offer support and criticism, and act as a soundingboard for ideas.

To all of the above and others who helped me on the way, my thanks and sincere appreciation.

D. R. L.

TABLE OF CONTENTS

TABLE OF CONTENTS (Continued)

TABLE OF CONTENTS (Continued)

LIST OF FIGURES

LIST OF TABLES

LIST OF TABLES (Continued)

LIST OF TABLES (Continued)

LIST OF TABLES (Continued)

CHAPTER I

INTRODUCTION

This thesis investigates the economic effects of changing the principal business tax in West Virginia from a general sales (turnover) tax to a value-added tax. Thus the study explores a matter that has had comparatively little attention--the effects of a value-added tax at the sub-national level. The principal contribution is a set of pioneering, though inevitably speculative, estimates. Needless to say, the propositions derived from economic theory and the empirical measurements rest on assumptions that greatly restrict their applicability. It is hoped nonetheless that this work will advance our understanding of using a value-added tax in an open economy.

In Chapter II, a survey of the literature describes the development of the concept of value-added taxation and describes past efforts to evaluate such a tax when applied at national and state levels. Chapter III provides an historical review of business tax policy in West Virginia, especially with respect to the debate over the value-added and turnover taxes. This review, coupled with the spelling out of the specific provisions of the two taxes, provides the institutional background for the economic analysis contained in Chapters IV through VI.

Chapter IV attempts to estimate the price effects and incidence of the turnover tax, under certain conditions, and the corresponding differential effects with the shift to a value-added tax. The chapter reviews some alternative analytical models for the analysis of incidence and price effects in a closed economy (e.g., the United States) and an open economy (e.g., West Virginia). The first approach used is a partial equilibrium competitive model limited to exploring short-run incidence and the impact on prices. Alternative assumptions are used, and some of the restrictive assumptions are subsequently relaxed to permit analysis of the longer-run effects of the turnover tax. To the extent possible, we offer observations about the general equilibrium implications of a turnover tax in an open economy. Following this, we look at the differential incidence of the change to a value-added tax. The same general assumptions as with the turnover tax are used, and both short- and longer-run implications associated with the tax change are developed. Finally, some of the short-run theoretical effects are simulated through the use of a sample of corporate tax returns, stratified by size and industry. In these calculations an input-output matrix for West Virginia is employed, and alternative assumptions are introduced in an effort to convey some idea of the range of plausible outcomes.

Chapter V focuses on efficiency and excess burden considerations. Using models consistent with the previous chapter, we explore the effects of the tax on efficiency both theoretically and empirically. Estimates are developed, using extreme assumptions, of possible effects on output, consumption, and employment of the factors of production, including estimates of certain components of the excess burdens or welfare losses under each of the two taxes.

Chapter VI uses the corporate tax data to explore the adequacy, stability, and growth of the state tax revenue under the two taxes. Total tax collections, by industry, are provided for the turnover tax for 1967-1969 and are contrasted with simulated amounts of revenue that would have been generated by the value-added tax in the same time period. These estimates are made under the restrictive assumption that no adjustments in the underlying value-added relationships would have occurred over the period 1967-1969. This gives "rough clues" to the responsiveness of the two taxes to changes in aggregate economic activity in West Virginia in the short run. In addition, estimates are made of revenue yields under the two taxes through the year 1980.

Chapter VII summarizes the study and provides some tentative conclusions. Finally, there are five appendixes which indicate more fully the methods employed in the data collection and analysis.

CHAPTER II

INTEREST IN, AND LITERATURE ON, VALUE-ADDED TAXATION AT THE NATIONAL AND SUB-NATIONAL LEVEL

Early History and Forms of Value-Added Taxation

Early History

Although the concept of value added has been used for over a century, its use as a basis for defining a tax base has been of relatively recent origins. By all accounts Kurt Von Siemens, a German industrialist and tax advisor to the German goverment seems to be the "father of the idea," having recommended its adoption to the German government in 1918 to replace their turnover (cascade) tax.[1] In the United States, the idea is generally attributed to T. S. Adams who suggested it, although not by that name, as a replacement for the federal corporate income tax. He argued, as did others at that time, that there was a case for business taxation but the specific form it should take should not be the corporate income tax. Specifically, he proposed a tax on sales with credits granted for taxes paid on "goods bought for resale or for necessary use in the production of goods for sale."[2] Senator Smoot (R. Utah) in 1921 offered a similar proposal in the midst of a debate on a national sales tax[3]

---

[1]John F. Due, "Value-Added Tax Proposals in the United States," Essays in Honor of C. Ward Macy, ed. by Paul Kleinsorge (Eugene, Ore.: University of Oregon Books, 1966), p. 113.

[2]Thomas S. Adams, "Fundamental Problems of Federal Income Taxation," Quarterly Journal of Economics 35 (September 1921):553.

[3]Due, "Tax Proposals in the U.S.," p. 113.

as did J. F. Zoller, an attorney for the General Electric Company, as a replacement for the corporate net income tax.[1] In 1932 it was considered by the House Ways and Means Committee as an alternative to a proposed manufacturing sales tax.[2]

In 1935, Gerhard Colm joined the growing list of advocates by suggesting that a value-added tax be used to finance the unemployment compensation bill which was then being debated. Two years later, Roscoe Arant proposed it as a replacement for all business taxes and in 1939 a committee of the National Tax Association recommended its use as a tax on corporation.[3]

Although attention was primarily directed to the national levels during this pre-World War II period, some proponents suggested its adoption at the state level. C. J. Tobin recommended it in 1929 at the National Tax Association Annual Conference as a tax for the state of New York, while in 1932 and 1933 the Brookings Institution recommended it to the Alabama and Iowa governments, respectively.[4] In addition in the mid-30's, Connecticut modified its tax on corporations by writing it up as a tax on profits, interest, and rents.[5] With the exception of Connecticut, none of these efforts (national or state) were successful.

---

[1]Paul Studenski, "Toward a Theory of Business Taxation," Journal of Political Economy 48 (October 1940):651.

[2]Ibid. [3]Ibid., pp. 651-52.

[4]Due, "Tax Proposals in the U.S.," p. 116.

[5]Ronald V. Welch, "Equity, Administration and Compliance, and Intergovernmental Fiscal Aspects: Comment," in The Role of Direct and Indirect Taxes in the Federal Revenue System, A Conference Report of the National Bureau of Economic Research and the Brookings Institution (Princeton, N.J.: Princeton University Press, 1964), p. 212.

With the advent of World War II, interest in the tax subsided and did not reappear until the late 40's when the Shoup Mission to Japan recommended it's adoption at the prefecture (state) level as a replacement for the existing enterprise tax.[1] The tax was adopted with the date of implementation set for two years later. During the two-year period, opposition developed and the tax was finally voided,[2] not so much on its merits, however, as on the relative amount of power it would have placed at the prefecture level.[3]

At the national level, the first implementation of value added took place in France during the period 1953-55, when it was adopted to replace the French Production Tax of 1936. The tax was limited to manufacturing and wholesaling activities, but, in lieu of the value-added tax, wholesalers could choose to be taxed under a gross business tax.[4] In the United States, at about the same time, Michigan found itself in need of revenue, but in disagreement as to how it should be obtained. A "Business Activities Tax" was passed which was, in fact, a value-added tax but did injustice to the concept. Among the provisions which violated the concept of value added were the following: (1) deduction from gross receipts of up to 50 per cent, plus an additional 10 per cent if payrolls were in excess of 50 per cent of gross sales; (2) exemption of

---

[1]Shoup Mission, Report on Japanese Taxation (4 vols., Tokyo: Supreme Commander for the Allied Powers, 1949) II, pp. 197-204.

[2]Hanya Ito, "The Value-Added Tax in Japan," The Annals of the Hitotsubashi Academy, 1 (October 1950):43-59.

[3]Motokazu Kimura, "An Unrealized Plan: The Value-Added Tax in Japan," The Annals of the Hitotsubashi Academy 13 (April 1958):123.

[4]Robert H. Floyd, "The Very Controversial Tax on Value-Added," Monthly Review (Atlanta: Federal Reserve Bank, July 1972):111.

the first $12,500 of value added; (3) depreciation limited to real property; and (4) an adjustment to the tax due based on the ratio of net income to value added where the tax due varied inversely with the rate of profit.[1] The Michigan Business Activities Tax endured until 1967 as the only tax application of the value added concept below the national level. In 1967, it was repealed, the cost of getting agreement on the adoption of a personal income tax in Michigan.

Such were the beginnings of the idea that value added--an indicator of economic activity, measured in income flows to the factors of production--should be used as the basis for business taxation.

Variants of Value-Added Taxation

When value added was first discussed and for some thirty years afterwards, it was not generally understood that the tax might take more than one form. This insight emerged gradually in the course of the consideration of the Shoup VAT proposal to the Japanese following World War II. In the first of two reports, Shoup's Mission recommended as part of the overall tax reform package a value-added tax whose base was the algebraic sum of gross receipts minus purchases (including capital goods), or the sum of payroll, rent, interest, and profits not to include adjustments for depreciation or inventory changes.[2] In the 1950 report, however, Shoup recognized that this definition of the tax base would be ". . . unfair to concerns that finish capital equipment program[s] shortly before the tax takes effect."[3] He suggested, therefore, that firms

---

[1]Due, "Tax Proposals in the U.S.," pp. 117-8.

[2]Shoup Mission, 1949, pp. 201-2.

[3]Shoup Mission, Second Report on Japanese Taxation (Tokyo: Japan Tax Association, 1950), p. 17.

either take, as a deduction, depreciation on existing assets on the effective date of the tax and full deduction of capital purchases afterwards, or take depreciation as a deduction on all assets whether acquired before or after the tax, but not take new capital purchases as a deduction in the year of purchase. While Ito is credited with having pointed out the discriminatory effects of this option against existing capital,[1] the analytical distinction between the two methods was not resolved until 1955 when Shoup so reported his findings to the National Tax Association.[2] In fact, we have now come to distinguish the two methods as the consumption and income forms of the tax. Carl Shoup coined the terms used to identify these two forms of the value-added tax, and identified the distinction between them as well as their equivalencies with other forms of taxation. An explanation of these forms follows.

Conceptually, value added is created in the process of providing goods and services for sale, and is seen as the difference between the sale prices and the input purchases of materials and supplies. In a two-factor economy the value-added tax is based upon the contribution of labor and capital to the value of the product. The treatment of capital purchases dictates the distinction amongst the three forms of the tax. If the firm is permitted to deduct capital purchases in the year of acquisition, it is said to be a consumption form of value-added tax (CVAT).

---

[1]See Ito, "Value-Added in Japan," pp. 57-58 and Kimura, "Unrealized Plan," pp. 119-20.

[2]Carl S. Shoup, "Theory and Background of the Value-Added Tax," Proceedings of the Forty-Eighth Annual Conference on Taxation of the National Tax Association, 1955 (Sacramento, Calif., 1956), "Consumption Tax, and Wages Type and Consumption Type of Value-Added Tax," National Tax Journal 21 (June 1968):153-61, and private correspondence between the author and Carl Shoup.

In symbolic terms, assuming a two-factor closed economy, this would be:[1]

$$C = W + P + D - I$$

where W = Wages

P = Profits

D = Depreciation

I = Investment

C = Consumption

Further, ignoring time considerations and assuming that investment is equal to profits plus depreciation, then the consumption form of value-added tax is seen as a tax on the wage component. In present value terms, this equivalence holds even if for the period in question, $I \neq P + D$. If, however, capital is deducted only as it is used up (depreciation), it is termed an income form of the tax (IVAT) and may be expressed as follows:

$$W + P = C + I - D$$

which, by our previous assumption of equality between investment and profit plus depreciation, renders the income value-added tax, a tax on income or a tax on consumption plus net investment.

Finally, if capital purchases are not deductible, either upon acquisition or as consumed (depreciation), it is termed a gross product value-added tax (GVAT) and in symbolic terms is equal to:

$$W + P + D = C + I$$

Thus, under a uniform levy a

Consumption value-added tax = proportional consumption or wage tax.

Income value-added tax = proportional tax on income.

Gross value-added tax = proportional tax on gross income.

---

[1]See Shoup, "Consumption Type of Value-Added Tax."

Operationally, there are three methods for calculating the value-added base. For the consumption value-added tax, the addition method requires summing up all the payments to the factors of production plus decreases in inventory minus capital purchases. The subtraction method takes total receipts and deducts from that figure all business purchases. The invoice method requires that firms total their gross sales and calculate their value-added tax liability by subtracting all invoiced purchases. Permitted as a deduction, however, are the value-added taxes which are separately stated on their purchase invoices and, of course, capital purchases.

Current Interest

Though the Common Market adopted the recommendation of the Neumark Committee to establish a tax on value added as a common business tax for all of the member countries,[1] it was not until 1967 in Denmark that a comprehensive form of the tax which extended through the retail level was adopted. Denmark was, then, not yet a member of the EEC. Adoption of comprehensive value-added tax systems by several nations followed in rapid succession--France and Germany in 1968, Sweden and the Netherlands in 1969, Luxemburg and Norway in 1970, Belgium in 1971, and Italy, Austria, and Great Britain in 1973. The 1954 French form of the value-added tax is now in use in Algeria, Ivory Coast, Malagasay Republic, Morocco, Senegal, Tunisia, and Viet Nam. It has also been introduced in modified form in Finland, Greece, Brazil, and Mexico and is used in the Phillipines as well.[2] By 1969, the

---

[1]Hans Smit and Peter E. Herzog, The Law of the European Economic Community; A Commentary on the EEC Treaty (New York: The Matthew Bender and Company, Inc., 1976) Vol. 3, pp. 425ff.

[2]John F. Due, "Proposal for a Federal Value-Added Tax," Illinois Business Review 27 (Jan.-Apr. 1970):6; Richard W. Lindholm, "The Value-Adde Tax: A Short Review of the Literature," Journal of Economic Literature 12 (December 1970:1179; Floyd, "Controversial Tax on Value-Added;" and George Lent, "Value-Added Taxes," IMF Survey 1 (August 1972), p. 30.

tax had become a significant source of revenue for France, Germany, and the Netherlands, where it represented 42, 23, and 19 per cent of their respective tax revenues.[1] In Brazil, all of the states use VAT right through the retail stage.[2]

In the United States, interest appears to be increasing once more at both the federal and state level. In 1966, it was suggested by the widely known and respected Committee for Economic Development as a replacement, at least in part, for the corporate income tax.[3] In 1970, however, the President's Task Force on Business Taxation opposed its adoption unless additional revenue became necessary.[4]

At the state level, a tax of this type was introduced (but not adopted) in California, Illinois, and Oregon. In 1971 an unsuccessful effort was made by the Governor of Michigan who suggested it along with an increase in personal income taxes to replace reliance on property taxes to finance schools.[5] Michigan continued to press for its adoption, however, and in 1975, the governor proposed and the legislature adopted a consumption form of value-added tax as a replacement for the business portion of the intangibles tax and the property tax on inventories.[6]

---

[1]Lent, "Value-Added Taxes."

[2]See Michele Guerard, "The Brazilian State Value-Added Tax, IMF Staff Papers, 20 (March 1973):118-169.

[3]Committee for Economic Development, Research and Policy Committee, Better Balance in Federal Taxes on Business (New York: Committee for Economic Development, 1966).

[4]Business Taxation, Report of the President's Task Force on Business Taxation (Washington, D.C.: U.S. Government Printing Office, 1970).

[5]"Michigan Governor Seeks Value-Added Tax," State Tax Review 32 (April 21, 1971).

[6]House Taxation Committee Substitute for House Bill No. 4640, House of Representatives (East Lansing, Mich.: State of Michigan, April 1975).

In West Virginia, an income value-added tax was introduced in 1967 and again in 1970. In 1970 it was passed by a Democratic legislature and vetoed by a Republican governor. Even though no state now has a true value-added tax, some states have it in a modified form. We have already noted Connecticut's experience. In addition, Louisiana applies it at the wholesale and retail level with a tax credit extended to the retailer if the wholesale tax appears on the retailers' purchase invoices. The constant emergence of this method for taxing business and its slow but seemingly inexorable adoption by more and more governments attests to the durability and tenacity of the idea in the face of repeated efforts to thwart its adoption and implementation.

Economic Effects of Value-Added Taxation

Concomitantly with these developments at the practitioner level, a body of professional literature on the subject has emerged. A conscientious bibliographer would have no trouble in locating more than 200 books and articles directly related to the tax, the variety and scope of which range from short polemics to scholarly treatises at both the theoretical and policy-making levels. Such numbers are misleading, however. In the screening of the literature, the bibliographer would find that there are relatively few articles which deal with value-added taxation in analytically precise terms, where the underlying assumptions are presented, and where the analysis is conducted within the confines of a specified model. There are even fewer which deal with the entire range of the effects of a public finance measure. These less precise articles seem to have as their goal the task of informing others of the nature of the tax and its possible effects. As such, rigorous analysis was probably neither required nor desired.[1]

What follows is a review of the more complete analytical discussions which make a contribution to the understanding of the effect of this tax measure. The conclusions drawn with respect to this tax are critically dependent on the form of the tax, the model of analysis, and the specific assumptions made with respect to the relevant variables.

We have classified the literature as national and sub-national, since these two geographic levels have involved different considerations requiring different models, which yield different conclusions as to the merits of the tax.

At the international level the principal concern has been the competitive impact of the balance of payments effects on different countries, such as among the common market countries and between the common market and the United States. No attempt will be made here to

---

[1]For the flavor of these articles see Richard E. Slitor. "The Value-Added as an Alternative to Corporate Income Tax," Alternatives to Present Federal Taxes (Princeton, N.J.: Tax Institute of America, 1964) pp. 35-54; Dan T. Smith, "The Value-Added Tax as an Alternative to the Corporate Tax," Proceedings of the Fifty-Seventh Annual Conference on Taxation of the National Tax Association, 1963 (1964), pp. 424-30; Arnold C. Harberger, "Let's Try a Value-Added Tax," Challenge (November-December 1966); Richard W. Lindholm, "Adaption of Tax Policy to International and Great Society Requirements (Especially the Value-Added Tax)," Tax Changes for Shortrun Stabilization, Subcommittee for Fiscal Policy, Joint Economic Committee (Washington, D.C.: Government Printing Office, 1966), pp. 288-291; Earl R. Rolph, "The Economic Effects of a Federal Value-Added Tax," Public Finance and Fiscal Policy, ed. by Joseph Scherer and James A. Papke (Boston: Houghton Mifflin Co., 1966), pp. 143-53; Walter Missorten, "Some Problems in Implementing a Tax on Value Added," National Tax Journal 21 (December 1968):396-411; Lindholm, "A Short Review," pp. 1178-89; Mel Krauss and Richard M. Bird, "The Value-Added Tax: Critique of a Review," Journal of Economic Literature 9 (December 1971):1167-1173; and Dan T. Smith, "When-if-we-have the VAT," Harvard Business Review 51 (January-February 1973):6-18ff.

review of this body of literature, most of which deals with the European experience and is adequately documented in a number of sources.[1]

At the national level attention has focused on the consumption form of the tax, its equivalence to other kinds of taxes, and the effects its adoption would have in a closed economy when compared with the corporate income tax.

At the sub-national level, with the exception of Michigan's current consideration of a value-added tax of the consumption type, concern has focused on the income form of the tax and its effects in an open economy when compared with a number of alternative taxes.

---

[1]Otto Eckstein, "Comparison of European and United States Tax Structures and Growth Implications," The Role of Direct and Indirect Taxes in the Federal Revenue System, A Conference Report of the National Bureau of Economic Research and the Brookings Institution (Princeton, N.J.: Princeton University Press, 1964), p. 217; Neumark Report of the Fiscal and Financial Committee on Tax Harmonization in the Common Market (Chicago: Commerce Clearing House, 1963); Clara K. Sullivan, The Search for Tax Principles in the E.E.C., Harvard Law School International Program in Taxation (Chicago: Commerce Clearing House, 1963); Clara K. Sullivan, The Tax on Value-Added (New York: Columbia University Press, 1965); Great Britain, Commission on Turnover Taxation, Report, 1964 (Richardson Report), (London: Her Majesty's Stationery Office, March 1964); Smith, "Alternative to the Corporate Tax"; Nathan N. Gordon, "Tax Harmonization in the Common Market and U.S. Tax Policy," Proceedings of the Fifty-Eighth Annual Conference on Taxation of the National Tax Association, 1965 (1966), pp. 393-400; Francesco Forte, "On the Feasibility of a Truly General Value-Added Tax: Some Reflection on the French Experience," National Tax Journal 19 (December 1966):337-61; E. B. Butler, "Britain and the Continental Value-Added Tax--III," Bankers' Magazine of Australasia (July 1968):39-45; Richard W. Lindholm, "The French Value-Added Tax," Oregon Business Review (February 1968); Carl S. Shoup, "Experience with the Value-Added Tax in Denmark and Prospects in Sweden," Finanzarchiv (March 1969):236-52; Mel Krauss and Peter O'Brien, "Some International Implications of Value-Added Taxation," National Tax Journal 23 (December 1970):435-40; and Edwin J. Cohen, "Foreign Experience with a Value-Added Tax," National Tax Journal 24 (September 1971):399-402.

Economic Effects at the National Level

Although this topic had been discussed in earlier years, and despite the fact that the tax had been proposed to different levels of government, it was not until 1963 that a sophisticated analysis appeared in the professional literature. In that year, a conference was held under the joint sponsorship of the National Bureau of Economic Research and the Brookings Institution. Along with other issues, the conference examined the effect and appropriate role of value-added taxation in the federal tax structure.[1]

Among the papers presented was one by Musgrave and Richman which dealt with the excess burden effects of substituting a consumption or income value-added tax for a profits tax on business.[2] They argue that, if the profits tax is not shifted in the short run and the profits tax applies to all firms, the incidence of the profits tax is on the profit sector and the move to an income value-added tax will have the effect of redistributing income from the wage sector to the profit sector. To the extent that an excess burden was created through the imposition of the profits tax, the move to an income value-added tax will reduce the excess burden; however, the income value-added tax creates another excess burden in that the differential incidence of the tax on wages creates an excess burden in connection with the work-leisure choice. No *a priori*

---

[1]National Bureau of Economic Research and Brookings Institution, *The Role of Direct and Indirect Taxes in the Federal Revenue System*, A Conference Report of the National Bureau of Economic Research and Brookings Institution (Princeton, N.J.: Princeton University Press, 1964).

[2]Richard A. Musgrave and Peggy Brewer Richman, "Allocation Aspects, Domestic and International," *The Role of Direct and Indirect Taxes in the Federal Revenue System*, A Conference Report of the National Bureau of Economic Research and Brookings Institution (Princeton, N.J.: Princeton University Press, 1964), pp. 81-131.

efficiency case can be made, therefore, for a tax on all factor incomes as opposed to a tax on a single factor universally applied. Modifying their assumption to one in which the profits tax is shifted in the short run, Musgrave and Richman conclude that excess burdens would in fact be reduced. Their reasoning is that under a profits tax relative prices must change in order to maintain the level of profits and that these "differ with the characteristics (turnover, margin, financial structure, etc.) of firms and industries."[1]

> In short, without short-run shifting, the substitution is regressive, raises investment incentives and may or may not reduce or raise excess burdens. With short-run shifting the equity and investment effects of the substitution are insignificant, but the presumption is that excess burden is reduced.[2]

These conclusions, only stronger, are applicable to the case in which a consumption value-added tax is substituted for a general profits tax with an additional argument that it would favor savers over consumers, given that the tax is shifted forward.

When the assumption of a general profits tax is dropped (with the concomitant recognition of an unincorporated sector to which the profits tax does not apply), the so-called "Harberger effect" takes place if no short-run shifting takes place. Capital flows are likely to move out of the corporate and into the non-corporate, causing excess burdens; but this excess burden can be removed by imposing an income value-added tax in both the incorporated and unincorporated sectors. If shifting of the profits tax is assumed, excess burdens arise from the distortion of relative consumer prices and/or factor incomes between the corporate and unincorporated sectors, and again the shift to an income value-added tax applying to both sectors will reduce that excess burden.

---

[1]Ibid., p. 94. [2]Ibid., p. 95.

Earl Rolph, who attended the NBER-Brookings Conference noted above, testified before the House Ways and Means Committee in 1964. His concern was with the equivalence of value added with other forms of taxation. In that testimony he concludes that there is no difference in the welfare position of factor owners when a proportional income tax is compared with an income form of value-added tax.[1] According to Rolph, this conclusion obtains if one assumes that (1) all of the effects of the income tax are worked out, (2) money demand conditions do not change, and (3) the relative market power of every individual and business does not change. Under these assumptions, Rolph suggests that adoption of a value-added tax imparts neutral price and allocation effects within the domestic economy. Moving on to a more realistic analysis, he argues that the value-added tax as a replacement for existing excises would make more sense and that this would provide a basis for modifying the personal income tax exemptions in the lower income brackets. Though his analysis of the effects of the tax is less sophisticated than that of Musgrave and Richman, he does make an important observation, i.e., a consumption value-added tax is not identical to a retail sales tax, but is a tax on sources of income as opposed to uses of income. That being the case, a sale is not required in order for a tax liability to exist.[2] He goes on to argue that it is also unlike a traditional income tax with its exemptions and preferential rates.

---

[1]U.S., Congress, House, Committee on Ways and Means, "The Economic Effects of a Federal Value-Added Tax," Excise Tax Compendium, by Earl R. Rolph (Washington, D.C.: U.S. Government Printing Office, 1964), p. 101.

[2]Ibid., p. 144. We should note parenthetically that this conclusion holds true only when the tax is calculated by the addition or subtraction method and not when the tax is calculated by the invoice method. (supra, p. 10)

Due, however, took issue with these general conclusions on equivalence and argued that capital should be viewed in Austrian terms, i.e., as an intermediate product and as such any tax imposed on capital is likely to be shifted forward in the form of higher prices. If he is correct, a tax on capital is in effect like a tax on consumption goods, in that they both result in forward shifting of the tax through higher prices. If that is true, then an income value-added tax is equivalent to a general retail sales tax on consumption.[1] One should add that this implies a sufficiently long period of time for all of these elements of "embodied capital" tax changes to be worked through the system.

By 1967, Harberger's general equilibrium model[2] was brought to bear on this tax issue with the publication of Mieszkowski's general equilibrium work on tax incidence theory[3] and Oakland's general equilibrium differential incidence analysis of the effects on income distribution with the shift from a profits tax (applied to the entire business sector) to a value-added tax.[4] Noting that Due stands alone in his conclusion on equilibrium between the different consumption and income forms of value-added taxation, Mieszkowski argues that

> Due's position is inconsistent with the theory of marginal product pricing for, . . . this theory implies that a general sales tax on

---

[1]John F. Due, "The Value-Added Tax," Western Economic Journal, Vol. 3, No. 2 (1965):165-71.

[2]A detailed discussion of Harberger's model, and also of one developed by McLure, is deferred until Chapter IV, because these models pertain directly to the assumptions and analysis employed in this study.

[3]Peter M. Mieszkowski, "On the Theory of Tax Incidence," Journal of Political Economy 75 (June 1967):250-262.

[4]William H. Oakland, "The Theory of the Value-Added Tax: II, Incidence Effects," National Tax Journal 20 (September 1967):270-81.

final goods is not equivalent to a general sales tax on final sales of consumption goods, since a general sales tax is equivalent to the latter tax plus a general sales tax on final sales of investment goods.[1]

Focusing on the effect of general taxes on resource allocations and relative prices, Mieszkowski argues that "general [value-added] taxes have no effect on the allocation of resources and relative commodity prices except insofar as the pattern of government expenditures differs from the pattern of private expenditures."[2] This conclusion, however, is dictated by the constraints of his model, in which he assumes that supplies of the factors of production are fixed and that payments to these factors completely exhaust total product. Thus, his model ignores any variation in the quantity of labor or savings supplied in response to the imposition of a general tax.

He concludes by arguing that the question of whether taxes are shifted backward or forward may be immaterial and that it is more important to trace out the effects of the tax change to include the factor-substitution and the factor-intensity effect. However, these effects exist only in the case where "commodity taxes [are] imposed at differential rates on different commodities and taxes on wages and/or profits in particular sectors [which] affect consumption choice and the demand for factors of production."[3] The discussion as such goes beyond the scope of our interest here.

Oakland's general equilibrium model for investigating the income distribution effects of substituting a value-added tax for a profits tax

---

[1]Mieszkowski, "Theory of Tax Incidence," p. 252.

[2]Ibid., p. 250. [3]Ibid., p. 252.

does not take into account the effects of a corporate profits tax per se. Using a Harberger model, Oakland concludes that with constant prices, net real wages will be greatest under a gross value-added tax and lowest under a consumption value-added tax. Net rentals are greatest under an income value-added tax followed by a gross value-added tax, consumption value-added tax, and a profits tax, respectively. (Under the model, all capital is rented from a rentier class).[1]

His overall conclusion is that in the short run with fixed factor supplies and constant prices the tax will be shifted onto the factors of production, a not unexpected conclusion.[2] Departing from the constraints of the formal analytical model, Oakland argues that the model may not adequately describe what would happen in practice for a number of reasons, e.g., wages are not in the short run determined by marginal productivity, money wages are sticky in the downward direction, and wages could increase so as to wipe out any increase in profit.[3]

Returning to the model, Oakland argues that if savings are made interest elastic, then an increase in after-tax profits in the long run will lead to greater productivity, greater productivity giving rise to an increase in real wages thus ameliorating the short-run effects on wage income. Oakland, though, is skeptical about such an outcome and concludes that the tax under any form ". . . increase[s] the degree of income inequality in both the short and the long run."[4]

The next significant theoretical piece was Shoup's treatise on public finance in 1969 wherein he set forth his views of the effects of

---

[1]Oakland, "Incidence Effects," p. 271. [2]Ibid., p. 279.

[3]Ibid. [4]Ibid., p. 280.

taxes and changes in differential incidence terms.[1] In contrast to Mieszkowski's formal analytical synthesis of tax incidence cited above, Shoup's work is a less formal but wider ranging synthesis and extension of the entire range of effects of public finance measures at both the micro and macro levels of analysis. The importance of the work is reflected in its orientation, for Shoup uses the value-added tax as the base from which other taxes are to be judged as to their economic effects. Thus, Shoup says: "Analytically it might be more convenient to start with the value-added tax, which exerts a uniform impact, and appraise the others as deviants from this archetype [of general sales tax]."[2] Though Shoup's analysis is from a consumption value-added tax to a corporate income tax, we will present his argument as if the changes were from a corporate income tax to a consumption value-added tax so that it may be compared with the other studies reviewed here.

Shoup dealt only briefly with the movement from a corporate income tax to a consumption value-added tax.[3] Confining his analysis to the differential incidence of the movement in a general equilibrium setting, he argues that the immediate effect will be an increase in tax liability for the unincorporated sector and an increase in corporate profits, accompanied by a flow of capital out of the unincorporated sector into the corporate sector and consequently away from the non-corporate dominated fields of construction, personal services, repair services, and

---

[1]Carl S. Shoup, Public Finance (Chicago: Aldine Publishing Company, 1969).

[2]Ibid., p. 207. For similar reasons he uses the value-added tax to compare the differential incidence of income taxes as well. See his comments on p. 293 and Chapter 1 for an elaboration on this latter point.

[3]Ibid., pp. 300-302.

wholesale trade. The capital outflows will lower marginal productivities of specialized resources to these industries. The outflows will continue until the rates of return after tax are equalized. As a consequence, Shoup concludes that we should see a rise in corporate dominated production of goods and a corresponding decline in the provision of professional services and repairs.

Shoup is less sure of the distributional implications of such a move, arguing that the move to a value-added tax is likely, but not certain, to be regressive because capital comes chiefly from the middle- and upper-income brackets; however, the consumption pattern of low-income families could cause this conclusion to be reversed if low-income families consume more in the way of corporate than non-corporate products. He suggests, but without evidence, that low-income families probably buy more of non-corporate products. If this is true, the differential incidence of the value-added tax probably _is_ more regressive than the corporate income tax.

Assuming that capital is not perfectly price-inelastic, the amount of capital will increase and this will over time increase the marginal productivity of labor, with corresponding increases in wage rates. The improvement in the wage rate may with growth ameliorate the regressivity of the tax shift. In the long-run period, prices of labor-intensive industries are likely to rise and hence impact on consumers of labor-intensive products.

In another section of his book, Shoup explores the differential incidence between an income value-added and a universal income tax.[1]

---

[1]Ibid., pp. 298-99.

The differential incidence of the movement from a progressive universal income tax to an income form of value-added tax is conducted in general equilibrium terms. In this part of his analysis, Shoup argues that the change will induce firms to lower the price they pay to the factors of production employed or to raise prices of products sold or both.

Depending on the monetary policy employed, the overall outcome will be one of the following:

1. Product prices and money income rise by the amount of the tax, the latter as a consequence of the repeal of the income tax.

2. Factor income and product prices remain the same but after tax disposable income is unchanged in the aggregate.

3. Product prices rise by less than the amount of the tax and factor incomes do not rise as much as the repeal of the income tax would suggest.

Apart from the effects of the dynamic process, ". . . the relation between product money prices and disposable money incomes is unchanged in the aggregate."[1] The distributional implications are the same as in the shift from a corporate profits tax to a value-added tax. Large families and low-income individuals will incur the greatest loss in real income, while high-income small families will enjoy a gain in real income. The case is more striking if a consumption form of value-added tax is used as the substitute equal-yield tax.[2]

From a growth point of view the substitution of a consumption value-added tax for a universal income tax is likely to lead to increases in real growth since the move would lead to an increase in the rate of return to capital. The positive income effect will act in the same way

---

[1]Ibid., p. 299. [2]Ibid.

as an increase in the interest rate, thus inducing greater savings and investment. The substitution effect also acts to diminish consumption and increase savings which give some elasticity to the investment function, thus leading to an increase in investment.[1]

In a tone almost identical to the Shoup view and the Musgrave-Richman short-run shifting view, Bossons eschews consideration of long-run shifting, arguing that this is a question which lacks interest, since in the long run everything is shifted. He argues that in the very long run, the impact of a tax substitution on real disposable income, relative prices, and capital flows gradually brings about reallocation of the stock of real capital that causes further adjustments in income and prices. All taxes are thus shifted in the long-term sense of the word, though such long-term "shifting" merely reflects normal behavioral adjustments to changes in profitability of investment regardless of the causes of such changes. Changes in climate that affect the agricultural productivity of a region are also "shifted in exactly the same sense."[2]

Beyond the question of the time period involved, Bossons also argues that

> . . . though they may have macroeconomic effects, their more important effects are concerned with their impact on the distribution of income and wealth and on relative prices. . . . What is of basic interest in a structural change is what has been altered at the microeconomic level.[3]

---

[1]Ibid., p. 332.

[2]John Bossons, "The Economic and Redistributive Effects of a Value-Added Tax," Proceedings of the Sixty-First Annual Conference on Taxation of the National Tax Association, 1971 (Kansas City, Missouri, 1972), p. 260.

[3]Ibid., p. 256.

Assuming competitive conditions, Bossons argues traditionally that the incidence of the corporate income tax will be on the corporate ownership and will be reflected in both the income and wealth positions of the ownership. This income will take the form of reduced after-tax profits, retained earnings, and corporate dividends, while wealth will be diminished by a decline in the market value of corporate common stock. As a consequence of these actions, we should expect a reduction in investment in corporations.

Bossons goes on to argue, however, that the competitive model may not be wholly applicable, since there is some evidence that short-run shifting can occur when monopoly power is not fully exploited, as may happen under oligopoly with barriers to entry. Under these latter conditions, Bossons suggests that as much as 10 per cent of a corporate income tax may be shifted forward in the short run. The other 90 per cent remains on corporate ownership and has the effects described earlier.

If a consumption value-added tax were substituted for the corporate income tax, we should expect a redistribution of real income to high income (corporate ownership) from low-income individuals. This would come about largely as a result of the increased tax on consumption. Qualitatively the effects are much the same as one would expect from the substitution of a consumption value-added tax for a general income tax. Although he does not mention it, Bossons is assuming here that the corporate income tax is not shifted and that the value-added tax is.

The most recent entrant into the theoretical arguments presented on value added at the national level are Ture and McLure, who attempt to delineate the effects of a value-added tax when used to replace a corporate income tax.[1] Using alternative assumptions, McLure argues that if the corporate income tax is not shifted, it favors debt over equity capital, discriminates against the corporate form of organization and corporate products, and because it is levied on capital only, is non-neutral with respect to the employment of capital. On the other hand, if the corporate income tax is shifted to consumers, it will discriminate against corporate products and if it is shifted backward, it will discriminate against the employment of labor in the corporate sector. A consumption value-added tax as a substitute exhibits some favorable characteristics in this regard, but only if there are no provisions for the exemption of specific terms from the tax base (e.g., food and drugs) or for the application of differentiated rates. Further, he notes that unless retained earnings are taxed, the substitution of a consumption value-added tax for a part of the corporate income tax will create an advantage for high profit firms and will be an inducement to have corporate income show up in the form of capital gains rather than ordinary income.

Regarding growth, McLure argues that "substitution of VAT for part of the corporation income tax would increase private savings substantially perhaps by as much as 80 per cent of the tax change. . . ."[2] Whether this results in increased investment and improvement in the rate of growth depends on overall budget policy. The likelihood is that

---

[1]Norman B. Ture, "Economics of the Value-Added Tax," Value Added Tax: Two Views, (Washington, D.C.: American Enterprise Institute for Public Policy Research, 1972) and Charles E. McLure, Jr., "The Tax on Value Added: Pros and Cons," Value Added Tax: Two Views, (Washington, D.C.: American Enterprise Institute for Public Policy Research, 1972).

[2]McLure, "Value Added: Pros and Cons," p. 41.

it would. Finally, McLure argues that as far as stabilization is concerned, substitution of the consumption value-added tax for part of the unshifted corporate income tax would lead to an increase in prices by the amount of the tax, but that it would give the government a better tool of discretionary fiscal policy than the corporate income tax.

Ture criticizes the usual identification of the consumption value-added tax with a consumption tax. It is not, strictly speaking, a consumption tax because it exempts the purchase of capital goods. On the contrary, he continues, when the product is produced and the capital used up in the process, the effect is to make the consumption value-added tax neutral with respect to the purchase of consumption goods and capital goods. The only extent to which it may be considered discriminatory against saving is in the case in which factor payments include a return to human capital.[1] Since returns to human capital are taxed doubly, neutrality would argue that the income value-added tax is closer to being a neutral tax since it taxes both human and physical capital at the point of creation and the point of consumption.

The concentration on theory is reflected by the fact that only one author has made a serious attempt at empirically estimating some of the effects of the adoption of a value-added tax in the United States. In 1968, Aaron attempted to trace out the price effects of a move from the existing corporate income tax to a gross value-added tax using an input-output model of the United States.[2] In this article Aaron makes a comparison of tax liabilities for major industries and estimates the

---

[1]Ture, "Economics of the Value-Added Tax."

[2]Henry A. Aaron, "The Differential Price Effects of a Value-Added Tax," National Tax Journal 21 (June 1968):162-75. Stephen Dresch of the National Bureau of Economic Research has done exhaustive work in this area, but it is not yet available in published form. See National Bureau of Economic Research, 54th Annual Report (September 1974):44-45.

amount of change in payments to the factors of production. His input-output model assumes fixed physical input-output coefficients as well as exogenous final demand and zero elasticity of final demand. With these assumptions, Aaron finds that the price effects depend upon the assumption of "unshifting"[1] of the corporate income tax and the shifting of the value-added tax.

Recognizing that it is not possible to spell out the precise extent and direction of shifting, Aaron explores some ranges of possibilities, which are summarized in Table 1. Assuming that none of the

TABLE 1

PRICE EFFECTS OF A GROSS VALUE-ADDED TAX OF 6.2 PER CENT UNITED STATES, 1962

Assumptions		Effects on Final Prices in Index Terms	
Unshifting of Corporate Income Tax	Shifting of Gross Value-Added Tax	Average	Range
0	100	106.2	---
50	50	101.5	101.8- 96.8
100	100	99.9	93.2-103.5
	150[a]	101.6	94.8-108.1
	50[b]		

[a]Concentrated industries--metal mining, oil and gas, ordnance --food, tobacco, chemical, rubber, metals, machinery, home appliances

[b]Non-concentrated industries.

Source: Derived from: Aaron, "Differential Price Effects," Table 1, p. 167.

---

[1]Our interpretation of the term "unshifting" used by Aaron is that if, for example, the corporate income tax was shifted forward 100 per cent to consumers through price increases, the removal of the corporate income tax in the absence of any other change would result in a reduction in prices equivalent to the amount of original price increases.

corporate income tax is unshifted (i.e., the tax saving associated with the removal of the corporate income tax is retained by the firm) and 100 per cent of the gross value-added tax shifted, he finds that prices will rise uniformly by the amount of the gross value-added tax--6.21 per cent. On the other hand, if one assumes that some portion of the profits tax is unshifted forward (price decline), the price effects are no longer uniform and the change is a function of the intra- inter-firm and industry profit levels of the suppliers to the various sectors as the creation of products and services moves to the final demand sector.

Aaron also observes in an analysis of the separate price effects of the corporate income tax and the gross value-added tax that under varying assumptions about shifting and unshifting, the price effect differs (See Table 2 below). The reason for the failure to register a

TABLE 2

EFFECTS ON PRICES ATTRIBUTABLE TO CORPORATE INCOME TAX REMOVAL AND GROSS VALUE-ADDED TAX REPLACEMENT UNITED STATES, 1962

	Per Cent Change	
Assumption for Unshifting of Corporate Income Tax and Shifting of Gross Value-Added Tax	Price Fall Per 5 Per Cent Drop in Corporate Income Tax	Price Rise Per 1 Per Cent Change in Gross Value-Added Tax
0	0.00	0.00
50	0.28	0.50
100	0.57	1.00
150	0.85	1.50

Source: Aaron, "Differential Price Effects," p. 169.

one-for-one equivalence in price change for a given per cent change in the corporate income tax rate is that profits may range from some finite negative or positive sum for any one firm for any one year. What is presented, therefore, is the composite effect of these forces. On the other hand, the gross value-added tax is uniform and consequently under a uniform shifting assumption it would exhibit a comparable change in price, given the assumptions of the model.

On the matter of factor adjustments and tax effects, Aaron finds that, under any assumption of less than complete shifting of either the corporate income tax or gross value-added tax, the effects "will require adjustment in prices or factor remunerations by widely different amounts in different industries."[1] The average change in tax liability would be 123.2 per cent if agriculture is included and 76.6 per cent if excluded. According to Aaron, 17 industries would experience a decline in tax liabilities. With the exception of agriculture, the largest increase would occur in auto repairs.[2] This is typical of the impact made by the combination of low profit and high value-added margins in particular industries and firms.

The effect of shifting a portion of the tax forward leads to increases or decreases in value added depending on the net effects of prices received and prices paid for inputs and outputs. If value added rises, then one or more factor shares will gain.[3] Under the profits tax the largest size of the base is 54 times higher than the lowest. By contrast the largest size of the base for the value-added tax is only three tim that of the lowest.[4] Whether one sees this as a significant factor or

---

[1]Ibid., p. 169. [2]Ibid., pp. 169-71. [3]Ibid. [4]Ibid.

not depends on one's view of the appropriate or permissible range for a business tax amongst industries.

Predictably, Aaron argues that major changes would occur under any of the shifting assumptions other than that of complete forward shifting of both taxes. If the assumption is no unshifting of the profits tax and complete forward shifting of the gross value-added tax, all of the firms would experience a gain in money value added and at least in the short run an increase in money profit margins; for those whose money value added rose by less than 6.2 per cent, however, there would be a decrease in real value added.

Economic Effects at the Sub-National Level

While the professional literature at the national level has been largely of a theoretical nature, dealing with the corporate net income tax in comparison to a consumption value-added tax, the focus at the sub-national level has been on a limited set of empirical questions and on the income form of the tax.[1] This difference in focus has not been

---

[1]The principal studies which have dealt with these issues in a value-added tax context are as follows: James A. Papke, "The Theory and Practice of Value-Added Taxation" (Ph.D. dissertation, Cornell University, 1959); James A. Papke, "Michigan's Value-Added Tax After Seven Years," _National Tax Journal_, 13 (December 1960):350-63; Charles F. Bonsar, "Analysis of Major Business Taxes Levied by Indiana," _Business Taxation in Indiana_ (Indianapolis: Indiana Commission on State Tax and Financing Policy, 1966), pp. 9-135; Cadwell L. Ray, "An Analysis of Value-Added Taxation with Special Reference to the State of Texas" (Ph.D. dissertation, University of Texas, 1967); Robert D. Ebel, _The Michigan Business Activities Tax: Value-Added Taxation in the Subnational Economy_, MSU Business Studies (East Lansing, Mich.: Division of Research, Michigan State University, 1972); Robert D. Ebel, _An Evaluation of a Value Added Tax for the State of Hawaii_ (Honolulu, Hawaii: University of Hawaii, 1973); Papke, "Objectives of a Tax Program for West Virginia," and others, 1966; and Leyden, "Some Empirical Observations."

accidental for analysis of taxation at the state level involves issues which are to a large extent non-existent at the national level. These issues deal with the: (1) open-economy implications for shifting and incidence analysis; (2) effects of taxation on industrial location; (3) allocation and apportionment of multistate business income; (4) revenue adequacy; and (5) equity of treatment of business enterprises.

Open-Economy Implications for Shifting and Incidence Analysis

Analysis of the economic effects of taxation at the sub-national level requires an open-economy model, a requirement which raises the complexity of the task to formidable, if not impossible, dimensions except under the most simplifying assumptions. With the exception of McLure's theoretical work on the interregional incidence of taxes, no open-economy general equilibrium model has been used in the analysis of value-added taxes at the state level.[1] Thus, analysts have avoided attempts to be definitive about the incidence or differential incidence of value-added taxes except in the most general way, utilizing "conventional wisdom" about forward shifting of non-general sales taxes and backward shifting of profits and income taxes. The most comprehensive, yet still limited, treatments are Ebel's monographs on the Michigan experience and the exploration of the adoption of a value-added tax in Hawaii.[2]

---

[1]This study is reviewed in Chapter IV, p. 90ff in our discussion of possible general equilibrium approaches to incidence analysis at the state level. Also reviewed in Chapter IV is Shoup's partial equilibrium discussion of incidence in an open economy.

[2]Ebel, <u>Michigan Business Activities Tax</u> and <u>Evaluation of a Value Added Tax</u>.

Drawing on an earlier work of McLure,[1] Ebel notes that the question of whether a business tax may be shifted forward to consumers or backward to factor-suppliers is a function of several determinants. These determinants, some of which are also pertinent at the national level, are the assumptions about the maximization goals of firms and individuals, price elasticity of final demand, price elasticities of factor supplies, state of technology, share of the market, variable or fixed-cost nature of the tax, and size of the tax base.[2]

Ebel analyzes the effects of three of these variables in a short-run partial equilibrium context, holding all other determinants constant. In particular, he analyzes the variable or fixed-cost nature of the tax, size of the tax base, and share of the market determinants. With respect to the cost nature of the tax, Ebel argues that inasmuch as the Michigan value-added tax is a variable cost, it is more easily shifted forward than one which is of lump-sum variety. The degree of forward shifting, however, depends on the price elasticity of demand and resource supply.

With respect to the size of the tax base, Ebel argues that the more general the tax, *ceteris paribus*, the less likely a tax will be shifted backward rather than forward. This is so since the more general the tax, the more limited the availability of untaxed alternatives and, therefore, the easier it will be for firms to pass the tax forward.[3] On both counts, Ebel concludes that the Michigan Business Activities Tax and the Hawaiian value-added tax could easily be shifted forward. The extent

---

[1]Charles E. McLure, "Commodity Tax Incidence in Open Economies," *National Tax Journal* 17 (June 1964):187-204.

[2]Ebel, *Michigan Business Activities Tax*, p. 124. [3]Ibid., p. 136.

to which it will depends on the third factor--share of the market--identified above. This strength may be a factor of the dominance in national markets and/or the degree of competition found by firms in local markets. Thus, Ebel judges that the industries of construction, utilities, wholesale trade, and retail trade in Michigan and Hawaii and services in Hawaii would have little difficulty in passing the tax forward. Agriculture in both Hawaii and Michigan and the services trades in Michigan are likely to have (had) more difficulty because of the existence of competing products from outside the state and in Michigan, the existence of a larger part of the state's agriculture sector which was exempt by reason of statutory exemption or by virtue of their size.[1] With respect to market domination in manufacturing, either because of locational advantage enjoyed by the stone, clay and glass, primary metal, and electrical machinery industries or to the national dominance of the transportation equipment industry, the Michigan Business Activities Tax would, in all likelihood, be passed on to final consumers,[2] but in Hawaii producers face strong competition and, therefore, would not be able to pass the tax forward.[3]

Effects of Taxation on Industrial Location

While sub-national governments are not capable of dealing with the problems of economic stability and monetary-fiscal policy, they are very much concerned with the effects of taxation on the decision to

---

[1]Ibid., pp. 137-38 and Evaluation of a Value Added Tax, pp. 72-74.

[2]Ebel, Michigan Business Activities Tax, pp. 138-39.

[3]Ebel, Evaluation of a Value Added Tax, p. 73.

locate and/or expand plants and the consequent effects on employment and economic growth in the states.

As a consequence, a great deal of study has been made of the impact of taxation on industrial location, but with the exception of Ebel's work on Michigan and Hawaii, no writer has addressed himself to the question of the possible effects of a value-added tax on industrial location decisions. In general, those who have attempted to ascertain the effect of taxes on plant location have concluded that taxes are not among the major determinants of the plant location decisions, but are rather part of a wider assortment of determinants.[1] As Table 3 demonstrates, state and local taxes are only 2 of 24 factors currently provided to plant location specialists as being important. Though the order in which these factors are listed bears only a very rough relationship to their importance,[2] the ordering is consistent with the conclusions drawn by analysts who have attempted to assess the influence of different factors on plant location decisions. For each factor, there is also

---

[1]The earlier works are summarized in John F. Due, "Studies of State-Local Tax Influence on Location of Industry," National Tax Journal 14 (September 1961):163-173. Subsequent studies frequently cited are Eva Mueller and James N. Morgan, "Location Decisions of Manufacturers," American Economic Review: Papers and Proceedings of the Seventy-Fourth Annual Meeting, 1961 52 (June 1962):206-17; Melvin D. Greenhut and Marshall Colberg, Factors in the Location of Florida Industry, (Tallahassee, Fla.: The Florida State University, 1967); William V. Williams, "A Measure of the Impact of State and Local Taxes on Industry Location," Journal of Regional Science 7 (March 1967):49-59; and Advisory Commission on Intergovernmental Relations, State-Local Taxation and Industrial Location, Report A-30 (Washington, D.C.: Government Printing Office, April 1967), pp. 59-70.

[2]Telephone conversation on May 25, 1975 with an official of Conway Research, Inc., publishers of the "17th Annual Site Selection Handbook, 1974," Industrial Development and Manufacturers Record, September 1974.

provided a detailed list of sub-factors that are currently considered important in the plant location decision. For example, in the category

TABLE 3

FACTORS TO BE CONSIDERED IN PLANT LOCATION DECISIONS

I.	Markets
II.	Basic Materials and Services
III.	Labor
IV.	Transportation
V.	Local Government and Taxes
VI.	State Government and Taxes
VII.	Environmental Considerations
VIII.	Power and Fuel
IX.	Telecommunications
X.	Water and Waste Disposal
XI.	Financing
XII.	Climate
XIII.	Community Facilities
XIV.	Education
XV.	Cultural Aspects
XVI.	Recreational Facilities
XVII.	Churches
XVIII.	Medical and Hospital Facilities
XIX.	Police and Fire Protection
XX.	Planning and Zoning
XXI.	Federal Activities in Area
XXII.	Representation in Congress
XXIII.	Individual Sites
XXIV.	Overseas Factors

Source: Site Selection Handbook, Sept. 1974, Vol. 19, No. 3. Conway Publications, Inc., Atlanta.

of state and local government taxes, Table 4 reveals that in addition to taxes and rates, such factors as fiscal soundness of the government, official attitudes, regulations, local unrest, and balances between taxes and services rendered are important parts of the information asked of local developers.

TABLE 4

DETAILED INFORMATION REQUESTED BY PLANT LOCATION SPECIALISTS ON STATE AND LOCAL GOVERNMENT AND TAXES IN 1974

V. LOCAL GOVERNMENT AND TAXES

- A. Structure of Municipal Government
  1. Elected and Appointed Officials
  2. Background of Incumbents
  3. Local Political Structure
  4. Record of Local Government
- B. Financial Condition
- C. Civic Attitudes
  1. Toward Industry
  2. Toward Bordering Jurisdictions
  3. Problem Areas
     - a. New Revenue Sources
     - b. Public Improvements
     - c. Redevelopment of Private Property
     - d. Urban Plans to Rehabilitate "Ghetto" Areas
     - e. Annexations
- D. Civil Disorders
- E. Local Taxes
  1. Property Taxes
  2. School Taxes, if Separate
  3. Local Sales or Use Tax
  4. Local License Taxes
  5. Comparison of Local Tax Load with Services Rendered

VI. STATE GOVERNMENT AND TAXES

- A. Structure, Financial Condition and Attitudes (Same Factors as Local Government)
- B. State Regulations and Legislation (see also "Labor--Legislation")
  1. Private Use of Natural Resources
  2. Laws Affecting Incorporation of Businesses
  3. Laws Affecting Out-of-State Corporations
- C. State Taxes
  1. Personal Income Tax
     - a. Rate, Exceptions and Deductions
     - b. Method of Collection
  2. Corporate Income Tax
  3. Sales, Use or Payroll Taxes
  4. Unemployment Compensation Tax--Rates, Administration
  5. Workmen's Compensation Tax
  6. Inventory, Machinery and Equipment Taxes
  7. Franchise and Incorporation Taxes
  8. Gasoline, Liquor and Tobacco Taxes
  9. Vehicle and Other License Taxes
- D. Comparison of Total State and Local Tax Load with Services Rendered
- E. Future Tax Prospects in the Area in View of Needs for Major Capital Improvements

Source: Condensed in part from _Site Selection Handbook_, p. 298.

We may easily discern from this detailed list of factors relating to taxation and government that industrial developers are concerned with the economies of spatial resource allocation, equity in the treatment of business enterprises, and effect on growth. Thus, under resource allocation we find questions related to measures of interstate tax differentials and tax costs (including compliance cost). Under distribution issues, we may note questions of tax climate, distribution of taxes among industries, and the treatment of small business enterprises. Finally, from a growth viewpoint, there are questions of the tax treatment of capital as well as those related to the relationships between tax revenue productivity and predictability of future tax liability.

Spatial Resource Allocation and Plant Location. There does not appear to be any empirical evidence that existing interstate tax differentials deter industrial development: The most recent effort in this regard is the work of the Advisory Commission on Intergovernmental Relations[1] cited earlier. They found that the tax differential argument is not an important factor until the decision comes down to a particular area in a region which has been selected because of other considerations such as proximity to market, availability of labor force, and access to raw and intermediate suppliers. Once the regional decision has been made, the existence of a tax differential may influence plant location decisions and the principal determinant in this regard is more often than not likely to be the local property tax.[2] In a specific test of the influence of

---

[1]State and Local Taxation and Industrial Location.

[2]Thompson, for example, found that property taxes in particular and their long-range stability were extremely important. In fact, one

interstate total tax differentials on economic growth, they conclude

> As between neighboring States, there appears to be no direct relationship between industrial growth and tax differentials due largely to the fact that States are careful not to get "too far out of line" with their immediate neighbors. As among local governments. . ., tax differentials exert discernible plant location pull--the industrial tax haven stands out as the most conspicuous example.[1]

This may also be explained in part by the argument advanced by Williams, who suggests that

> A _prima facie_ case exists for the proposition that, _other things being equal_, taxes will have a substantial locational impact. However, in the more plausible situation of varied profit opportunities, the importance of taxes is diminished to the extent that they represent the appropriation of a locational rent.[2]

On the basis of this evidence, it seems safe to conclude that if taxes in general are not an important influence in plant location decisions, then a single tax levied at the state level is even less likely to be an important factor in the plant location decision. Thus, if we assume that value-added taxes at the state level are to be viewed as replacements of equal-yield existing taxes, their contribution to a tax differential among states would be extremely small, especially when it is seen in terms of its contribution to overall tax costs. Ebel notes in his evaluation of the Michigan value-added tax, which was considered quite high when compared with other states:

> . . . that for the highest BAT industries--construction and manufacturing--the figure was less than one-half of 1 per cent of the

---

company was found to have made a study of local property taxes over a 25-year period before making their decision on the location of a particular plant. See James H. Thompson, _Methods of Plant Site Selection Available to Small Manufacturing Firms_, Small Business Management Research Reports (Morgantown, W.Va.: West Virginia University for the Small Business Administration, 1961), p. 55.

[1]_State-Local Taxation and Industrial Location_, pp. 78-79.

[2]Williams, "Impact of State and Local Taxes," p. 49.

> total cost measure. . .[I]t can be concluded that the BAT was not one of the high cost elements in the Michigan tax system. . . .[1]

Distributional Equity and Plant Location. Tax climate in the parlance of industrial location specialists is a term used to describe the fairness of state and local taxes on business enterprises. Unfavorable tax climate can arise over what are considered unfair administrative regulations or the consequence of significant differentials in the taxes paid by various industries in the geographic area which cannot be justified on economic and equity grounds. The charge of unfavorable tax climate may also be used to whipsaw legislators into effecting more favorable tax treatment as much as to describe the reality of existing tax treatment.[2] Further, ACIR reports that once a state has developed a reputation for a bad tax climate it is often difficult, if not impossible to change ". . . even though the state changes its laws and administrative practices."[3]

In this regard, Ebel considers the Michigan value-added tax as being

> . . . superior to both the gross receipts and corporate net income tax levies, but . . . inferior to a [pure] value-added or net income tax on total (corporate and noncorporate) business. The policy implications [in this regard] are that the [tax] either

---

[1]Ebel, Michigan Business Activities Tax, p. 148.

[2]See Due's admonishment of business representatives who use these and other tactics to oppose any change in business taxation that does not result in a lowering of their tax impact. "Studies of State-Local Tax Influence," pp. 172-73.

[3]State-Local Taxation and Industrial Location, p. 72.

> should have been repealed in favor of a net income levy, or amended to conform [more closely] to the value-added tax [concept].[1]

A final "equity" criterion affecting industrial location is the treatment of the "no profit" firm. When business taxes are levied without regard to the profitability of the taxed enterprise, they serve to discourage low or no-profit firms from locating in the taxing jurisdiction. In effect, it takes on the character of the infant industry argument of international trade, with one difference. There is no argument advanced that these firms should at some point be asked to bear their "fair share" of the business tax load. Rather their argument is that whenever a firm has no or low profits, it should not have to pay business taxes to the state or local jurisdiction in which it is located. The argument is inconsistent, therefore, since firms once established are not likely, in the short run, to move their plant and if, in the long run, there are no profits earned, the firm will in all likelihood cease to exist. Unfair treatment of no-profit firms was charged particularly against the Michigan value-added tax, but Ebel's empirical work indicates that because of ". . . the specific dollar exemption and statutory deduction combination, most small firms were excluded from the scope of the tax."[2] The small firms, coincidentally, also ". . . account for the bulk of the no-profit business in Michigan."[3]

Economic Growth and Plant Location. A final element in the plant location decision deals with the effect of taxation on growth through the tax treatment of investment goods and the ability of firms to plan for

---

[1]Ebel, Michigan Business Activities Tax, p. 149

[2]Ibid. [3]Ibid.

future tax liabilities. Taxes which impact more heavily on investment capital or which lead to uncertainty about future tax liabilities are said to discourage firms from making long-term investments. In this regard, the Michigan value-added tax was particularly vulnerable to criticism. Though it had the potential for non-discriminatory treatment of capital vs labor, the "inconsistent statutory treatment of real versus personal property and of interest versus dividend payments . . . reduced the potentially favorable effect of the [Michigan value-added tax] on state economic development."[1] Though subject to criticism on the inconsistent treatment of types or sources of investment capital, the Michigan value-added tax was judged to be a good contra-cyclical tax instrument inasmuch as it was elastic on the upside of the business cycle and inelastic on the downside. This meant that the tax contributed favorably to the stability of Michigan state revenue and lessened the need for changes in rate and/or taxes with changes in economic activity. This meant, therefore, that businessmen could be more certain of their future tax liabilities and that was favorable to long-run investment decisions.[2]

Allocation and Apportionment of Multistate Business Income

The problem of the tax treatment of business income and sales among the states from business enterprises which operate in more than one state as a consequence of the Interstate Commerce Clause of the United States Constitution is a controversial subject which has been in the courts and the subject of considerable debate at both the federal and state legislative level. This controversy seems no closer to settlement

---

[1]Ibid., p. 151. [2]Ibid., p. 150.

today than in the past. While the issues raised include tax base definitions, tax jurisdiction of states, and the treatment of related taxpayers, the most controversial issue has to do with the conflict among the states as to the appropriate methods for allocation and apportionment of the business tax base. We will only deal with this latter issue as it relates to value-added taxation both because the broader issues are beyond the scope of our investigation and because they are adequately documented elsewhere.[1]

The essential argument advanced before the courts has been and is: "How should the defined business tax base be divided among the states in which a particular business enterprise operates?" The positions advocated may be seen as a continuing debate between those who argue for a "sources of business income rule" and those who advocate a "uses of business income rule."[2] According to the "sources of income rule," the

---

[1]See for example the works of U.S., Congress, House, Committee of the Judiciary, Special Subcommittee on State Taxation of Interstate Commerce, State Taxation of Interstate Commerce, 88th Cong., 2nd Sess., 1964-1965, vols. 1-4; Elliot R. Morss, "An Evaluation of the Report on State Taxation," National Tax Journal 18 (September 1965):297-303; Charles F. Bonsar, "State Taxation of Interstate Commerce," Business Taxation in Indiana (Indianapolis, Ind.: Indiana Commission on State Tax and Financing Policy, 1966), pp. 69-96; John G. Cragg, Current Problems and Issues in State Taxation of Interstate Commerce, Government Finance Brief No. 3 (new series) (New York: Tax Foundation, Inc., 1966); C. Lowell Harriss, "State-Local Taxation of Interstate Commerce: Progress and Problems," Proceedings of the Fifty-Ninth Annual Conference on Taxation of the National Tax Association, 1966 (1967), pp. 294-307; Jerome R. Hellerstein, "State Taxation, Interstate Business: Reflections on Legislative Directions," Federal-State-Local Fiscal Relationships, (Princeton, N.J.: Tax Institute of America, 1968), pp. 257-267; Leonard E. Kust, "A New Venture in Federalism," Tax Review 31 (December 1970):51-54; Tax Foundation, "Taxation of Interstate Business," Proceedings of the Tax Foundation Seminar (New York: Tax Foundation, Inc., 1970); and Oliver Oldman and Ferdinand P. Schoettle, State and Local Taxes and Finance (Mineola, N.Y.: The Foundation Press, Inc., 1974), pp. 550-665.

[2]Oldman and Schoettle, State and Local Taxes, pp. 557-558.

division of the tax base is determined by where the base being taxed is generated. Thus, a firm subject to sales taxes and employing resources in two states but with sales only in one of the states would pay taxes only in the state where the sales occurred. Those who advocate a "uses of busines income rule" would argue that if a firm employs resources in two states, it should pay taxes to the states involved based upon the value of the resources employed. The justification for this latter position is based on the argument that the state furnishes public goods and services to the firm as a consequence of the resources employed and not according to whether or not it results in income to the firm. Using the same example, the firm would be taxed on the sales in the one state, but the tax would be apportioned by the value of resources employed in both states.

Oldman and Schoettle point out that "to the extent that the states' choices of division-of-income rules reflect theoretical considerations, the rules in use today generally appear to embody the sources of income approach."[1] This, of course, implies that many states use other than theoretical considerations in deciding on how to divide multistate tax bases for taxing purposes. The three means by which they accomplish the division of multistate business income in the taxing process are: (1) separate accounting; (2) formula apportionment; and (3) specific allocations.[2] Separate accounting requires that the multistate firm separately account for its activities in a particular state. Formula apportionment is used when separate accounting is not possible and involves the allocation of specific tax bases by some proxy measures

---

[1]Ibid., p. 557. [2]Ibid., p. 559.

which presumably will apportion non-separable tax base activity to the states concerned.[1] Specific allocation is a device by which certain types of tax base, principally income, are allocated directly to a specific state, i.e., not apportioned by formula. This latter method is used in conjunction with the formula apportionment technique, but wide disagreement exists among the states as to the tax base items to be apportioned or allocated.[2]

In the three studies which attempted to deal with the allocation and apportionment issues, the main emphasis was on examining the impact of alternative apportionment formulas on multistate industry, but they did not answer the question of whether or not the alternative formulas contributed to the resolution of the controversy over the treatment of multistate businesses. In 1966, Bonsar reported on a three-factor formula apportioning value-added income to the state of Indiana, and suggested that the shift to a value-added tax would bear most heavily on multistate manufacturing corporations when compared with their liability under the prevailing gross-net income tax on corporations in Indiana.[3] In 1967, Ray compared alternative single-factor formulas using gross receipts and assets and their combination as a two-factor formula. In the comparison between the two single formulas, Ray finds that the amount of value added in Texas goes from $9.9 billion under a gross receipts formula to $16.5 billion under an asset formula. Also the combined two-factor formula gave a $13.1 billion estimate of value added in one state--Texas--by corporations operating in the state. The large increase

---

[1]Ibid. [2]Ibid., p. 575.

[3]Bonsar, Business Taxation in Indiana, pp. 130-34.

of the assets over the gross receipt apportionment is due to the fact that manufacturing corporations in Texas are highly capitalized, representing 59 per cent of corporate assets in the state but only 32.5 per cent of gross receipts.[1] Using the two-factor formula and comparing the value-added yield with a corporate net and gross receipts tax, he finds that the gross receipts tax generates the largest yield for the transportation, communication, and utilities, and the wholesale and retail trade industries, and reduces the contribution of the mining and manufacturing industries. The shift to a value-added tax or a net income tax results in a shift to manufacturing and mining as the dominant contributor to tax revenue.[2]

Ebel's work, in 1972, compares the three-factor formula used in Michigan with three hypothetical alternatives: (1) sales (destination basis); (2) equally weighted payroll and property, weighted payroll and property (ratio of 3:1); and (3) sales (destination basis) payroll, and property. In comparison with the three-factor formula, a single factor sales formula reduces total tax liability by approximately 1/3 with significant declines in tax liability among the high export industries such as manufacturing (-55 per cent) and mining (-34 per cent). Of those industries which sell primarily to Michigan residents, only wholesale trade would have experienced a significant increase in tax liability (+26 per cent) while all others would have experienced increases of no more than 3 per cent.[3] Within the manufacturing sector, with the

---

[1]Ray, "Analysis of Value-Added Taxation," p. 141.

[2]Ibid., pp. 147-49.

[3]Ebel, <u>Michigan Business Activities Tax</u>, p. 108.

exception of primary metal, stone, clay and glass, and electrical machinery, which have high proportions of in-state versus multistate sales, manufacturing tax bills would decline.[1] Changing from the existing three-factor formula to the two-factor formula of payroll and property (unweighted or weighted) results in an approximate 18 per cent overall increase in multistate business tax liability with the largest increase in the manufacturing sector, followed by mining and the wholesale trade sector. There would be little change for all the other industry sectors.[2] Within the manufacturing sector, Ebel found that the stone, clay and glass, primary metals, and electrical machinery would have had reductions while all other manufacturing sectors would have experienced increases.[3]

In general, these findings are consistent with what one might have expected of the different apportionment formulas, namely that a single-factor formula based on sales destination would favor the multistate firms and industries which are large exporters, while the two-factor formula will reflect the importance of property and payrolls in the production process. What is not intuitively obvious, however, is the fact that giving extra weight to payrolls to reflect their importance in the national income accounts makes little difference in tax liability. We suspect that this may be attributed to the canceling effects arising from wide variations in the property-payroll mix of individual firms. The three-factor formula on the other hand serves to mitigate the payroll-property mix in a state and gives weight to the destination of sales.

---

[1]Ibid., p. 110. [2]Ibid., p. 108. [3]Ibid., p. 110.

For an export-oriented state, this latter formula would serve to limit the size of the tax base and, thereby, limit revenue collections.

Further, these empirical observations serve as an indicator of the stakes which are involved for individual states. If one assumes that states are interested in utilizing apportionment formulas which will give them the broadest possible base, their choice of specific apportionment formulas will depend to a large extent on whether they are a production or sales-oriented economy. There is in this latter observation the inescapable conclusion that no tax or apportionment formula will be found which would be acceptable to the several states.

Revenue Adequacy

Inasmuch as state government may not engage in deficit spending to finance current expenditures, they are very much concerned with the adequacy of revenue sources in the short and long run. With respect to value-added taxes, the question has been, "Will the tax generate the same amount of revenue as the tax or taxes it will replace in the immediate short term and over the long run?" Judging by the experience in West Virginia and remarks made by other writers, this concern has probably been of overriding importance to legislators.

It is not surprising, therefore, that the bulk of the empirical analysis has pertained to this issue. In general, the analysts have concentrated on the differential impact of the change to a value-added tax and, with the exception of Michigan (which had a value-added tax), no effort was made to assess the productivity of this revenue source over time. Further, because of the obvious complexities involved, none of the studies cited utilize formal analytical models in their calculation of the yield and distributional impact of one tax versus others. The absence of such models, however, gives the reader no indication of the underlying economic assumptions under which we might judge the reasonableness of the estimates provided. Finally, the studies have used different methods for estimating the tax base and different versions of the value-added tax.

Types of Value-Added Taxes Studied. The Papke '59 and Ebel '57 studies of the Michigan experience analyzed the Michigan Business Activities Tax, which was a cross between the gross and income form of the value-added tax. Included in the base of the tax were profits before taxes, payroll, depreciation on fixed assets (other than real estate), and depletion allowances. Thus, for firms with high real estate and low fixed assets, it was an income form of the value-added tax, but for those with large amounts of fixed assets and limited real estate, the tax was a gross value-added form. In addition, the tax took account of ability to pay inasmuch as it permitted firms whose itemized deductions were less than 50 per cent of their gross receipts to take a full 50 per cent deduction. Further, it permitted firms whose payroll exceeded 50 per cent of their gross receipts to deduct either 50 per cent of the excess or 10 per cent of the gross, whichever was smaller. Beyond these provisions, it also provided that the first $12,500 of value-added base be exempted from the provisions of the act, which together with the minimum 50 per cent provided a total minimum exemption of $25,000.[1]

Bonsar's 1966 study of its application to Indiana used a modified form of the value-added tax inasmuch as it included only net profits and

---

[1]Ebel, Michigan Business Activities Tax, pp. 120-21.

payrolls, leaving out rents and interest. Papke's West Virginia report in 1966, Ray's Texas study in 1967, and Ebel's Hawaii study in 1973 came closest to the income form of the tax inasmuch as they attempted to approximate payments to wages, rents, interest, and profits as the base of the tax.

Adequacy Estimates. The only concrete evidence on the revenue productivity of the value-added tax at the state level is, of course, the Michigan experience. As noted earlier, that experience indicated that the tax acted in a contra-cyclical way. When compared with alternative levies, it was less sensitive to the business cycle than a comparable profits or net income type tax.[1] For all of the other studies, either the question was not seriously raised because estimates for only one year were provided or, if raised, reference was made to the Michigan experience.[2]

Equity Treatment of Business Enterprises

All of the state studies attempted to compare their particular version of the value-added tax with other hypothesized taxes or with existing levies. For example, Bonsar compared the value-added tax with the combined gross receipts-net income tax in Indiana, while Ray compared the value-added tax with an alternative hypothetical gross receipts tax and a net income tax, as well as with the set of business taxes in Texas represented by the franchise tax, state ad valorem tax, and an assortment of other business taxes. Papke's 1966 report to the West Virginia

---

[1]Ibid . p 60

[2]Ebel, Evaluation of a Value-Added Tax, p. 56.

Legislature compared the value-added tax alternatively with the existing turnover taxes and a possible corporate income tax levy. Ebel looked at the comparison of a value-added tax with the net income and general excise taxes levied in Hawaii, and a comparison of gross receipts, corporate net income, and value-added taxes with the Michigan value-added tax.

With the exception of Ray's study, which did not assess structural equity, all of the studies found that structural equity--treating firms in similar circumstances similarly--would be improved provided that the value-added tax was extended to both corporate and non-corporate business. The tax would, however, shift the distribution of tax payments more toward the manufacturing sector than any other industry. More specifically, Bonsar found that shifting to a profit and payroll value-added tax would significantly increase manufacturing tax liability if limited to the corporate sector; however, if the value-added tax were extended to the unincorporated sector, the change in manufacturing tax liability would be reduced and would, in his opinion, not constitute a major change.[1] Ebel's 1972 study of the Michigan experience used a different notion of structural equity which conceptually is more consistent with the idea of equal treatment of equals. Instead of simply comparing the change in tax bills among industries, Ebel used the magnitude of variation of industry average tax bills from an all-industry average. In so doing, he found that the degree of variability from an all-industry-average tax bill would be greatest under the gross receipts tax followed by a corporate net income tax, the Business Activities Tax (value-added), total net income tax, and a pure income value-added tax. Thus, in terms

---

[1]Bonsar, Business Taxation in Indiana, p. 140.

of this variability, the Michigan Business Activities Tax was superior to the gross receipts and corporate net income tax, but inferior to a net income tax on corporate and non-corporate business and an income value-added tax. Ebel suggests that either the Michigan Business Activities Tax should have been modified to reflect more closely the concept of income value added or repealed in favor of a net income tax, applicable to all business enterprises.[1]

In his Hawaii study, Ebel finds similarly that the income value-added tax achieves the least variability around the all-industry-average tax bill, but notes that if the inter-industry differentials associated with other types of levies can be shown to reflect economic rents, then the differentials may be justified on the grounds that the state would share in the degree to which economic rents are enjoyed by the industries affected.[2]

Limitations of Data Base

It is evident in all of the state studies that the analysts have had significant problems in developing accurate measures of the value-added base because of the absence of adequate data at the state levels. Consequently, all of the studies utilized an indirect allocation procedure for deriving the base of value added, utilizing existing state data supplemented by estimates by the National Planning Association, Census of Manufacturers, and Treasury Department. Under the circumstances, it was the only course of action possible, given the decision to engage in an empirical analysis.

---

[1]Ebel, Michigan Business Activities Tax, p. 94.

[2]Ebel, Evaluation of a Value-Added Tax, p. 50.

This approach, however, raises serious questions about the accuracy of the estimates obtained. There is reason to question the value-added estimates mentioned, especially with respect to the magnitudes likely to be reported by individual firms. We have attempted to compare Papke's indirect estimates of value added in West Virginia[1] with a direct method of estimating West Virginia value added using a sample of corporate tax returns filed in West Virginia.[2] This comparison showed that, while Papke's indirect estimates for wholesale trade, retail trade, and contract construction were in substantial agreement with the direct estimates, Papke's estimates for other sectors, such as mineral extraction, manufacturing, and service sectors, were significantly higher than those derived by the direct method. In fact in some sectors such as mineral extraction and services, the indirect value-added base when expressed as per cent of gross exceeded 100 per cent.[3]

Summary and Concluding Observations

Though value added has been used for over a century as a conceptual framework for measuring income flows to the factors of production, its use as a base for taxation of business enterprise has been of relatively recent origin, dating back to the 1920's. Following World War II and especially since the late 1960's, there has been an acceleration of interest or adoption by more and more governments at the state, national, and international levels.

Along with this interest at the practitioner level, there exists a large body of professional literature dealing with the economic effects

---

[1]Papke, "State Business Tax Structure," September 12, 1966.

[2]Leyden, "Some Empirical Observations," [3]Ibid., pp. 524-25.

of this type of tax. The number of articles and books is misleading, however, in the sense that very few have attempted to deal with the issues in a formal analytical manner. The type of value-added tax considered and the economic issues discussed differed according to whether the standpoint was international, national, or sub-national. The work at the sub-national level is even more deficient with respect to formal analysis because of the complexities involved when dealing with open economies. In general, although the literature suggests that the value-added tax generates fewer distortions of resource allocation than other less general levies, there is great uncertainty about the pertinence of the underlying assumptions and about the validity of the conclusions.

Finally, if the intent is to explore a broader range of economic effects of a value-added tax at the sub-national level in a theoretically consistent way, the analyst will have to go beyond the existing individual state studies. In Chapter IV, we will explore the use of general and partial equilibrium models as ways of analyzing the economic effects of replacing the existing turnover tax in West Virginia with an income value-added tax.

CHAPTER III

THE WEST VIRGINIA TURNOVER TAX AND THE PROPOSED VALUE-ADDED TAX

The Debate in West Virginia

Since the early thirties, the tax treatment of business firms in West Virginia has been a matter of sporadic debate and concern among legislators, businessmen, and government administrators. In 1932, under the "Tax Limitation Amendment," the state constitution was amended to limit the rates at which property taxes could be collected. Consequently, in 1933 property taxes as a proportion of total state and local revenue declined from 75 to 35 per cent. The outcome of this event was virtually to eliminate property taxes as a source of revenue at the state level and to limit severely the taxing and spending power of local government units. Thus, the state was faced with the necessity of drastically revising its revenue and expenditure structure if it was to continue providing as many public goods and services as it had before the amendment. The legislators moved to increase revenue from non-property tax sources and to assume responsibilities for funding education, welfare, and local roads, which were the responsibility of local governments.[1]

Part of the revenue restructuring was designed to collect the amount of state business property taxes lost as a consequence of the Tax

---

[1]For more details on the Tax Limitation Amendment and the subsequent events see Claude J. Davis et al., West Virginia State and Local Government (Morgantown, W. Va.: West Virginia University, 1963), pp. 170ff.

Limitation Amendment. In 1934, the 1925 turnover tax, which had applied 10 rates to 18 different business activities was altered to apply 14 rates to 20 different classes of business activity. The turnover tax rates were set in a way that would make each class of business activity pay that additional amount lost through the reduction in property tax. Sand and gravel mining received the largest percentage increase, the rate on sales becoming seven times its 1932 rate. The smallest turnover tax rate increase was applied to manufacturing activity at only 1.5 times its 1932 rate.[1] Over subsequent years, the reduction in property taxes paid by business became the basis for the current series of 16 turnover tax rates applied to 30 different classes of business activity.

As the years passed and desired revenue exceeded expected revenue, the legislature began singling out industries for providing additional taxes. This was accomplished by increasing the turnover tax rates on those classes of business activity which should, in the opinion of the legislature, bear the burden of the increased taxes. Thus, from one year to the next, a firm or industry could not be sure that the tax rate for the privilege of doing business in West Virginia would not be doubled or tripled.

This capricious treatment, together with the continued expansion of demand for state government support and the failure to enact a tax package in 1953, led to the establishment in 1954 by the then Governor Marland of "The Governor's Commission on State and Local Finance." The

---

[1]For an appreciation of the amount of lost property tax revenue and the specific rate changes see Fifteenth (FY 1933, 1934) and Sixteenth (FY 1935, 1936) Biennial Report of the West Virginia Tax Commissioner (Charleston, W. Va.: State of West Virginia).

purpose in establishing the commission was

> . . . chiefly that of finding facts . . . with the expressed hopes that out of such basic information West Virginia can build a balanced and equitable system of taxation sufficiently adequate to meet . . . pressing needs . . . .[1]

The governor's commission found that with respect to business taxation, "West Virginia's problem [was] not so much excessive taxing, as it [was the] extreme uneveness of burdens."[2] Since the commission was limited to "finding facts," they did not propose any changes. They did, however, mention a number of possible alternative ways of raising revenue, including a personal income and a corporate net income tax as well as revisions in the rate structure of the turnover tax. None of the alternatives outlined were adopted.

In 1959, the legislature established a study group, the "State Tax Study Commission."[3] It's purpose was similar to the 1954 study group, "To study [the] present tax structure (state, county, and municipal), including requirements, sources, yield, inequities, and impact, having due regard to the effect on the state's economic growth and development."[4] In their first report, they noted that the status of business taxation since the 1954 report had not changed. If anything, "changed economic conditions and statutory changes [since 1933] would appear to have increased [sic] rather than improved the rate structure."[5] Their

---

[1]The Governor's Commission on State and Local Finance, Tax Facts in West Virginia: The State Tax and Revenue Structure (Charleston, W.Va.: State of West Virginia, 1954), n.p. (inside front cover). Italics mine.

[2]Ibid., p. 48.

[3]See State Tax Study Commission, First Report of State Tax Study Commission: West Virginia Taxes: (State and Local) (Charleston, W.Va.: State of West Virginia, 1959), p. 1.

[4]Ibid. [5]Ibid., p. 12.

principal recommendation on the turnover tax was to decrease the number of different rates from 22 to 18, to reduce the inequities under the tax, and to introduce an across-the-board percentage increase for any increases in revenues thought necessary. In addition, they recommended a net income tax on corporations which would be paid in addition to the corporate tax liability under the turnover tax.[1]

This commission met the same fate as the 1954 group. Their findings were not used to change the method of business taxation. One must conclude that the alternatives offered were considered worse than the disease. This attitude is best reflected in the 1954 commission report: "West Virginia cannot raise as much money from any other single base at any conventional rate, as can be raised from gross sales."[2] Thus, no fundamental change in the business tax structure was made for the period 1933 to 1967.

In 1967, following two years of study, the legislature considered an income value-added tax along with a corporate net income tax to replace the turnover tax. This was part of an overall program of recommended "tax reform" which included changes in personal income and retail sales taxation.[3] The proposed value-added tax would have permitted

---

[1]State Tax Study Commission, Final Report of State Tax Study Commission: West Virginia Taxes: (State and Local), (Charleston, W.Va.: State of West Virginia, 1960), pp. 94, 102.

[2]The Governor's Commission on State and Local Finance, Tax Facts in West Virginia: A Summary Statement of the Findings of the Commission (Charleston, W.Va.: State of West Virginia, 1954), p. 5.

[3]This program was based on a series of unpublished reports to the Joint Committee on Government and Finance of the West Virginia Legislature over the period July 10 to September 12, 1966 by James A. Papke, a fiscal consultant from Purdue University. They are as follows:

July 10: "Objectives of a Tax Program for West Virginia"

deductions for inter-firms purchases and depreciation from each firm's gross value of production in West Virginia. In effect, it would have levied the tax on payments to the factors of production, i.e., on wages, rents, interest, and profits, in West Virginia. Controversy arose over the estimates of revenue because they were largely based on national statistics, there being no good primary data available at the state level. Beyond this, questions were also raised of what it would do to or for business in West Virginia. Wholesale movements of industry out of the state and substantial unemployment were predicted.

After considerable debate, the "reform package," including the value-added tax, was voted down by the legislature with the exception of the Corporate Net Income Tax Bill. This tax was passed and signed into law primarily for the purpose of gaining information about the conduct of corporate business activity in West Virginia. It permits the corporations to use their turnover tax liability as credit against their net income tax liability and, consequently, pay only the higher tax. In most instances the turnover tax is the higher. Revenues from this income tax have stabilized at around $5 million per year, compared with the

---

August 8: (A) "The Incidence of State-Local Taxes in West Virginia: Distribution of Tax Payments Among Resident Household Income Groups"

(B) "Revenue Effects of Alternative Tax Structure Adjustments"

August 17: "General Outline of Gross Margins Tax"

August 22: "The Consumer Sales Tax Credit or Rebate"

September 12: "The State Business Tax Structure: A Quantitative Analysis for Policy Deliberation"

approximately $155 million collected in fiscal year 1973[1] under the turnover tax. The 1967 legislature also implemented a turnover tax rate increase on manufacturing activity from 0.40 per cent to 0.80 per cent of gross to provide the additional necessary revenues, and the turnover tax was applied to formerly exempt professionals [(lawyers, physicians, etc.) who were in strong opposition to the value-added bill] at a rate of 1.05 per cent of gross. According to some reports, the manufacturers' increase was a compromise offered to the legislature by the manufacturing interests--"We've come to a point where we lose a leg or a foot and we'd rather lose the foot."[2] This interpretation, however, is subject to some disagreement. Other (anonymous) representatives argued that there never was such an agreement, but that it was rather the price imposed on the manufacturers for their strong opposition to the value-added tax bill.

Regardless of the circumstances, the legislature was consistent in its approach; i.e., it again isolated specific business segments to provide the increased revenue needed. Sentiment against this legislative propensity continued.

> Unquestionably, something is going to have to be done about West Virginia's tax structure,. . . as . . . [the Minority Leader of the Senate] points out, the gross sales tax is littered with a multitude of different rates, and it has been too easy in the past for the legislature to increase one or two categories with a minimum of resistance. But this has served to widen the inequities under the gross sales [turnover] tax law.

---

[1]Howard Carson, ed., West Virginia Blue Book, 1973 (Charleston, W.Va.: West Virginia State Senate, 1974), p. 1073.

[2]Charleston (W.Va.) Gazette, 3 February 1967, p. 9.

[3]Harry Hoffman editorial, "Tax Stability Needed," Charleston (W.Va.) Gazette, 2 May 1969.

In 1970, two "tax reform packages" were introduced for legislative consideration.[1] A Democratic package included increases in personal income tax rates, tax credits for retail sales tax paid, a severance tax on extractive activity (mining) and a modified version of the 1967 income value-added tax to replace the turnover tax. The Republican package included a retail sales tax food exemption, increase in the retail sales tax rate and modification of the rate structure under the turnover tax. If there were controversies in 1967, with a Democratic governor and legislature and with only one set of proposals working against the status quo, the reader can imagine the controversies which existed with a Republican governor and a Democratic legislature and with two opposing packages fighting against the status quo. The upshot was that neither side got what it wanted. The Democratically controlled legislature passed all of the bills offered by its leaders, but the Republican governor vetoed all of them. Only the veto of the personal income tax increase was subsequently overridden by the legislature and became law in 1970.

Although the legislature met in special sessions in the summer of 1970, the legislators did not act on business taxation until the following year. In 1971, the legislature raised the turnover tax rate on coal from 1.35 per cent to 3.40 per cent of gross and established a 10 per cent across-the-board increase on all other turnover tax rates including manufacturing, whose rate went from 0.80 to 0.88 per cent of gross.

---

[1]Following the defeat of the "1967 Reform Package," the Bureau of Business Research at West Virginia University was asked to pick up where Papke left off. A team of economists, including myself, were brought together to accomplish the assignment. This group had the benefit of more comprehensive information on the conduct of corporate business activity as reflected in the data provided under the new Corporate Net Income Tax Law.

The legislature was determined to put a severance tax on coal, but because the coal interests were fearful that a separate severance tax would make them more vulnerable to rate increases, they lobbied successfully for an increase in the turnover tax rate instead.

The discussion of the value-added tax did not include any substantial formal economic analysis of the effects of the tax specifically on West Virginia. What was provided were the estimates of value-added tax revenues and changes in industry tax bills for 1967 based on national statistics when the issue was considered in 1967 and based on state industry data when it was considered in 1970.[1] In both periods no explicit identification was made of the assumptions under which the estimated revenues and initial impacts were generated. Nor was there any information to be had regarding the effects of the tax in other states which might have provided clues to its possible effects in West Virginia. Those studies which were done were largely limited to the use of national statistics supplemented by selected state data.[2]

Though a good deal of the opposition to the value-added tax bill in 1970 was a function of the political differences between the Republican executive and Democratic majority legislature, the issue was joined in terms of several arguments. A review of the arguments made about the turnover tax and the proposed change to a value-added tax may help the reader to see the relevance of this study.

One argument was that tax liability should not be so narrowly defined as to constitute an imposition which has personal overtones. This

---

[1]See respectively the report by Papke, "Policy Deliberation," and Leyden, "Some Empirical Observations," pp. 502-31.

[2]A review of these studies is provided in Chapter II.

standard may be violated in the wording of the tax laws, the interpreting of the tax laws through administrative regulations, or the enforcing of the law.[1] The opponents of the value-added tax argued that personal deals were made with representatives of all business except the so-called labor-intensive firms and the railroads. The House Minority leader remarked that the 1970 version of ". . . the bill is what amounts to a 'sweet-heart contract' between the legislature and taxpayers. The only two groups not kissed, . . . were labor intensive industries and railroads."[2] He observed that in 1970 very few lobbyists appeared in opposition to the measure. This was in contrast to his 1967 experience when "the halls were so filled with lobbyists that they 'came out your ears' and delegates couldn't rest at home because their phones rang every minute or two."[3]

> I've had no complaints from the manufacturers, and that does not set right with me. . . . If there's one thing [I have] learned in the House in 18 years, it is that "you are going to hear long, loud and clear from people covered by a tax bill."[4]

A state labor spokesman, however, argued that

> . . . between the existing business and occupation [turnover] tax and the proposed "adjusted gross receipts" tax . . . we are convinced that VAIT [value-added income tax] is the wiser choice . . . .[5]

---

[1]Shoup, Public Finance, pp. 21-47.

[2]Statement of House Minority Leader George H. Seibert, Jr., Charleston (W.Va.) Gazette, 5 February 1970.

[3]Ibid.

[4]George H. Seibert, Jr., "Tax Measures Handed Moore," Charleston (W.Va.) Daily Mail, 5 February 1970, p. 1.

[5]Statement of the late Miles C. Stanley, President of the State AFL-CIO Council (70,000 membership), "Legislative Tax Plan Endorsed," Charleston (W.Va.) Gazette, 28 January 1970, p. 1.

Although no specific response to the "sweetheart" charge was made by the proponents of the bill, their argument generally stressed that the value-added tax would provide similar treatment to all firms using a common tax base related to business' employment of the factors of production.

A second argument was that a small change in the circumstances of the taxpayer should not be the occasion for a significant change in tax liability. "There must be no gaps, jumps, or, in general, discontinuities in the tax. . . ."[1] The turnover tax was found faulty, in this regard, as firms could integrate vertically or take other steps that would make large differences in their tax bills. In some instances this involved no more than a minor change in activities. For example, a number of firms pay manufacturing rates of 0.88 per cent of gross who in reality engage in the mining of sand and gravel, which is taxed at a rate of 4.34 per cent of gross. Further, informed speculation in the West Virginia State Tax Department suggests that at least 5 per cent of the taxable base under the turnover tax is reported in a class and rate lower than intended under the law. Typical avoidance patterns are found in shifts of tax base from coal to manufacturing and from service to retail. Those who argued for the value-added tax pointed out that the circumstances of production would not result in any difference in the rate of tax they would pay. No arguments to the contrary were made by the opponents of the bill.

Another argument sometimes heard is that taxes ought to be levied according to the benefits received by the individual taxpayer. When applied to West Virginia's situation, the turnover tax, being based on a

---

[1]Shoup, <u>Public Finance</u>, p. 24.

firm's gross receipts, was not perceived to be an adequate measure of its consumption of public goods and services. In contrast, the value-added tax, based on the employment of the factors of production, was perceived as a better proxy of public goods and services consumed, applicable to corporate and non-corporate business alike.[1] Additionally, some argued that,

> It encompasses the ability to capture revenues from interstate and intrastate business generated within the state--not possible under either the business and occupation [turnover] tax or . . . [the] proposed adjusted gross receipts tax. . . .[2]

By implication, this argument reflects a common sentiment that out-of-state owners and consumers are benefitting from the services provided by the state without paying their fair share. The ability to internalize these positive spillovers was obviously an important consideration for those advocating the adoption of the value-added tax. Due and Friedlander correctly observe, however, that despite the general merit of this argument, it requires the acceptance of the assumption that there is a direct relationship between the provision of public goods and services and the employment of the factors of production.[3] Needless to say, other arguments pertained to the effects of the two taxes on business decisions and efficiency. In particular, this part of the debate focused on five factors: employment; automation; plant location; price pyramiding; and geographic tax base.

---

[1]See Papke, "Policy Deliberations," p. 8.

[2]Editorial, "Value-Added Package Deserves State Test," Charleston (W.Va.) Gazette, 11 February 1970, p. 4.

[3]Due and Friedlander, Government Finance, p. 432.

The first three of these phenomena are interrelated inasmuch as they refer to the decisions of business firms over different periods of time. In the short run in which the size of individual firms' physical plant is said to be fixed, firms may alter the number they employ with corresponding changes in output. In the long run when firms are in a position to make decisions about the size, nature, and location of their production facility, they may choose to change the amount of investment per worker, and productivity per worker may show a corresponding change. Firms may also choose to change the location at which they do business, with the gains to one region becoming a corresponding loss to another.

First, the switch to a value-added tax was predicted to influence business decisions in terms of continued employment of labor. It was argued that the

> . . . fatal flaw . . . [with the value-added tax] was that [it] taxed wages. The direct consequence is that companies which employ men to do work will be forced to discharge their workers and to replace them with machinery.[1]
>
> [The value-added tax proposal would] encourage people to convert from being an employer of mankind to automation.[2]
>
> If you want what happened to the coal industry to happen to all industries, then pass this bill.[3]

Another dimension of the opposition's argument was interjected by a leading small businessman who argued that large employers would move

---

[1]Don Marsh, "Value-Added Tax Bill Gets Approval of House," Charleston (W.Va.) Gazette, 1 February 1970. An article describing the opposition's argument to passage of the value-added bill.

[2]Remarks of House Minority Leader George H. Seibert, Jr., quoted in "Delegates Approve Democrats' Taxes," Morgantown (W.Va.) Sunday Dominion-Post, 1 February 1970.

[3]Remarks of House Minority Leader, George H. Seibert, Jr., quoted in Don Marsh, "Value-Added Tax Bill."

their employees elsehwere, but the small businessman lacked the ability to do so:

> It is going to discourage industry from coming in and the ones here will start shifting their employees elsewhere . . . while larger industries complain about paying higher taxes, they can move their employees around the country to other plants for the best economic situation. But small firms like [mine] cannot.[1]

In contrast, the House Finance Chairman contended that "the tax was not large enough to have any influence on corporate decisions to automate or not to automate."[2] This argument was furthered in a state editorial:

> What they overlook--or at least fail to include in their arguments--is that automation already is a trend in industry, and has been for some time. The prime objective of any industry is to earn profits, and the decision to automate will be based on this consideration rather than any tax of two and a half per cent.
>
> Also conveniently passed over . . . was the fact that profits, rents and interest--which would be interest paid on money borrowed to automate--also enter into the determination of the added value tax. Therefore, it is illogical to think the tax would encourage layoff of workers, since any drop in taxes there would be added back, and perhaps even increased, through the profits and interest factors.[3]

Beyond this it was argued that taxes do play a role in plant location, but not through the level of form of the taxes but rather their stability, which is the critical variable in plant location decision. Other factors which play a larger role than taxes are the availability of land, access

---

[1]Remarks of William Bright of Bright, Inc., who employs 300 people in his plant in Summersville, West Virginia. Quoted in "Value-Added Tax Business Killers, Says Businessman," Charleston (W.Va.) Daily Mail, 4 February 1970.

[2]Remarks of House Finance Chairman, Lewis N. McManus cited in Don Marsh, "Value-Added Tax Bill."

[3]Harry Hoffman, "In the Dark and Yelling," Charleston (W.Va.) Gazette, 3 February 1970. See also editorial, "Stability--That's What Matters for Business," Charleston (W.Va.) Gazette, 23 December 1969, p. 4.

to final markets and raw material-suppliers, and the quality and quantity of labor.[1]

Another point to which there was no counter-argument was that the turnover tax could not get at certain revenues generated by business that the value-added tax could.[2] This alleged erratic coverage under the turnover tax arises from three sources: (1) income received by non-residents on business located in West Virginia; (2) the exclusion by law of interstate income of certain business enterprises located in West Virginia such as railroads and other carriers; and (3) the difference in tax base treatment between non-carrier businesses whose product is produced in more than one state and to businesses which are wholly operated in the state. The proponents argued that all three sources would be included in the tax base since the value-added tax is based on an origin principle which looks to the place where value-added income is created rather than where the income is received, as in Source 1 above; where the carrier activity begins and ends in West Virginia as in Source 2, above; and where the business firm produces its product, as in Source 3 above.

Both sides seemed to agree that the existing turnover tax was less stable, predictable, and conducive to the state's economic development:

> Industry knows it must pay taxes, wherever it locates, and by and large it is willing to pay its fair share. But what industry wants most of all in a tax program is stability--a program that will permit it to plan ahead, with reasonable knowledge of what to expect in tax expenses over a period of say 10 years. What is most disturbing to existing industries--and discouraging to

---

[1]Charles E. Hamilton, Executive Director, West Virginia Manufacturers Association, "Tax Stability Backbone of Producers," Charleston (W.Va.) Sunday Gazette-Mail, 25 January 1970, p. 3P.

[2]Editorial, "Value-Added Package."

prospective industries--is to have something new in taxes sprung every year or so.[1]

The proponents of the tax change argued that the value-added tax would provide the greater certainty about a firm's tax bills. This did not mean that they were guaranteeing no rate changes, but that business firms would be able, with appropriate projection techniques, to anticipate the revenue needs of the state and their likely share of whatever increase in revenue might be required of the business community as a whole. Thus, they were guaranteed that future tax rate increases would be shared equally among all businesses, and not applied differently to specific sectors as in the past. This view is reflected in the statement of the West Virginia Senate President, who argued that ". . . the value added tax will provide a more stable tax climate which will help industry since any increase needed to meet state financial obligations would be done on a percentage basis treating all businesses alike."[2] No arguments to the contrary were made by those opposed to the value-added tax measure. There were also arguments about the nature of the two taxes from the state's point of view. In particular there was discussion of the taxes from the standpoint of revenue adequacy, stability of revenue, and administrative efficiency.

Emphasis on adequacy appeared to be the death knell for the value-added tax both in 1967 and 1970 because of uncertainty about the ability of the tax to generate revenue. In 1967 proponents in the legislature looked for the value-added tax to yield $20 million over the projected

---

[1]Editorial, "Stability--That's What Matters."

[2]Statement of Senate President Lloyd Jackson, Point Pleasant (W.Va.) Register, 13 January 1970.

yield of the turnover tax, but tax department estimates reported that it would only increase revenue by $11 million.[1] One observer reports that,

> This meant then, in 1968 those who were charged with the responsibility of finding sources of additional tax revenue would be faced with the same problem, which would mean that the . . . [value-added] tax rate must be increased or additional taxes found from some other source. . . .[2]

In 1970, the rate of the proposed value-added tax based on unofficial estimates was set by the proponents before they received any indication of the "official" projected base. This was a serious error in strategy because the opposition had control over the official estimates. On hindsight the result was predictable; ultraconservative estimates of the base were made,[3] coupled with a new argument that because it was a new tax, it would not yield 100 per cent of the estimate. In fact, it was argued that the value-added tax would only yield 88 per cent of the estimated revenue and that it would take three years of operation before the actual yield could come up to the projected yield.[4] Despite protestations, the proponents were helpless, as "the legislature . . . [had to] be guided by 'official estimates,' since the [West Virginia] Constitution makes the Governor responsible for estimating tax yields in assuring a balanced budget."[5] These events occurred at the close of the

---

[1]Observation of Charles S. Armstead, member of West Virginia House of Delegates, in "Proposed New Tax Wouldn't Do What It Was Supposed To!" Morgantown (W.Va.) Post, 7 June 1967, p. 13.

[2]Ibid.

[3]Editorial by Harry Hoffman, "Time for Greatness," Charleston (W.Va.) Gazette, 10 February 1970, p. 4.

[4]Letter of Charles H. Haden, West Virginia State Tax Commissioner to State Legislature described in "Dem Tax Plan Seen Falling Short of Need," Charleston (W.Va.) Daily Mail, 3 February 1970.

[5]Hoffman, "Time for Greatness."

legislative session, and it appears that the proponents could not effectively counter this very important argument. The questions of the effects of the tax change on revenue stability and administrative efficiency as well as on equity and efficiency become academic as the legislative session concluded without any action taken on "reform" of the business tax structure.

This recurring controversy over alternative taxes to be adopted in West Virginia culminated, as noted above, in the arguments about two fairly specific alternatives--the existing turnover tax and a proposed value-added tax. To provide additional background for the analytical portions of this study, we shall describe in more detail the provisions of the two alternatives that were being considered in 1970.

Turnover Tax Provisions

The West Virginia turnover tax system is covered by two statutes, the Business and Occupation Tax (B & O Tax) and the Annual Tax on Income of Certain Carriers (Carrier Tax).[1] A reading of these statutes reveals that there appear to be three distinct measures of turnover tax base--gross value of production, gross receipts from sales, and value of production (value-added).

Table 5 summarizes the provision of the two statutes and shows both the defined base and the rate applicable to each class of business activity. In particular, Part A.1 shows that the tax base for mineral extraction and completed manufactured products is the gross value of production as measured by the gross proceeds from the sale of such activity,

---

[1]For precise statute language, see the West Virginia Code of 1966, Chapter 11, Article 12A and 13, respectively. Charlottesville, Va.: Michie Co., 1966 and Cumulative Supplements for 1967-1969.

TABLE 5

BASES AND RATES OF THE TURNOVER TAX SYSTEM IN WEST VIRGINIA, 1967

Tax Base	Tax Rate (Per Cent)
A. Gross Value of Production Tax Base	
1. Extraction of Coal and Other Natural Resources	
(a) Coal	1.35
(b) Sand, Gravel and other Mineral Products not quarried or mined; Oil, Blast Furnace	3.95
(c) Natural Gas (1st 5,000 of Gross Production Exempt)	7.85
(d) Limestone or Sandstone quarried or mined, and Timber	2.00
(e) Other Natural Resources	2.60
2. Manufacturing, Compounding or Preparing for Sale	0.40/0.80[a]
B. Value Added in Production of Partial Manufacturing, Compounding, or Preparing for Sale	0.40/0.80[a]
C. Gross Receipts from Sales in West Virginia	
1. Contract Construction	2.00
2. Retail	0.50
3. Wholesale	0.25
4. Amusements	0.65
5. Service Business, Rental, Small Loan and Industrial Loan	1.05
6. Utilities	
(a) Street, Interurban and Electric Railways	1.30
(b) Electric Light and Power Companies--Sales and Demand Changes for Domestic Purposes and Commercial Lighting	5.20
(c) Electric Light and Power Companies--All Other Purposes	3.90
(d) Water Companies	4.00
(e) Natural Gas Companies and Toll Bridges	3.90
(f) Other Public Utilities (Except Carriers)	2.60

TABLE 5--Continued

Tax Base	Tax Rate (Per Cent)
C. Gross Receipts from Sales in West Virginia--continued	
7. Intrastate Carrier Activity	
(a) Motor Vehicle Carriers, Railroad Car Corporations, Express Corporations or Companies	1.50/3.00[a]
(b) Telephone Corporations	2.75/3.40[a]
(c) Telegraph Corporations	5.00/3.00[a]
(d) Pipe Line Corporations	1.50/3.00[a]
(e) Airline Corporations and Operation of Steamboat or Other Watercraft	3.00
(f) Railroad Corporations	0.50/3.00[a]

[a]Effective July 1967 the rate changes for both manufacturing and carriers were as indicated to the right of the slash. These did not impact on revenue until 1968, however.

regardless of the place of sale or delivery. For domestic firms, this poses no particular problem, but for multistate firms, it requires that they separately account for their West Virginia mineral extraction and manufacturing operations so as to be able to identify their sales to other states and nations. Thus, we find a number of individual corporations operating in the state who are in reality part of a larger corporate organization. In effect, gross sales is the tax base for both classes of business activity, but the base is statutorily defined as the gross value of production to avoid becoming vulnerable to the commerce clause prohibitions against the taxation of sales outside the state. Thus, a philosophy of uses-of-income rule is reflected in the base definitions, but its measure is one which suggests a sources-of-income rule. This appears to be an interesting circumvention of the commerce clause.

For manufacturers who partially manufacture their products in West Virginia and elsewhere, the state permits a different treatment (Table 5 Part B). For this class of activity, they are permitted to use one of two formulae in apportioning the total sales derived from such manufacture to West Virginia. They may use payments to labor in West Virginia relative to payments to labor everywhere or the cost of manufacture in West Virginia relative to the cost of manufacture everywhere. The tax base is still gross sales except that it is now apportioned to the state.

For industries classified as commercial, contract construction, utilities or carriers, we show in Part C of Table 5 that they are subject to a tax based on their gross receipts from sales in West Virginia. The sources-of-income rule is clearly evident here, with separate accounting required of all firms. Clearly there is no need for subtle language under these conditions, since domestic sales activity may be subject to tax by individual states. There is need for separate accounting, however, even for domestic carrier firms. Both domestic and multistate firms who are "carriers" must separate their receipts into those which derive from business which begins and ends in West Virginia and those that arise from activity which crosses state lines. A gross receipts tax is levied on the intrastate business receipts while a net income tax is levied on the interstate business, using formula apportionment. In this study, we do not concern ourselves with the "net income" tax provision of the carrier tax except in the estimate of revenue requirements (Chapter VI).

Though we conclude that the turnover tax is a gross sales tax, the tax department goes to great pains to argue that it is not. Witness the following language which is part of their biennial report:

> . . . The tax is measured by the application of rates against values of product, gross proceeds of sales, or gross income according to the classification of the business activity in which the taxpayer is engaged. Despite the commonly applied erroneous name, "Gross Sales Tax," it is not a sales tax. Neither is it a transaction tax in the sense that once it is paid on a particular article or service or activity it need not again be paid. It is not, strictly speaking, an income tax, although in most instances, the gross income is the measure of the tax. Under the production and manufacturing classifications the measure of the tax is the value of the article produced or manufactured as shown by the gross proceeds derived from the sale thereof, provided the proceeds of sale are indicative of the true value of the article. If more than one person engages in a single activity or transaction, as in the case of the contractor and subcontractor, each must pay a tax measured by his entire income regardless of the tax paid by the other.[1]

This language and the seeming differences in base are attributable to the existence of the Federal Interstate Commerce Clause which prohibits the levying of privilege taxes on the basis of gross sales. For our

---

[1]West Virginia State Tax Department Thirty-Second Report, 1967-1968 (Charleston, W.Va.: State of West Virginia, 1968), p. 18.

purposes we will proceed with our description of the West Virginia turnover tax system by classifying it as an *in rem*, multiple stage privilege tax whose base is gross sales, inasmuch as it is levied on the value of sales in 30 different classes of business activity to which 16 different tax rates apply. To the extent a firm engages in more than one of the activities identified in Table 5, it must disaggregate its gross receipts into the relevant classes and pay the appropriate rates applicable to those classes. Thus, the effective rate of tax imposed per dollar of gross sales will vary depending on the relative amount of business conducted under each business activity class and the applicable rate. Individual firms, therefore, may find their tax rates varying from one year to the next without any change in the tax law.

Among the special treatment provisions is one which permits only the natural gas producer to exempt the first $5,000 of gross receipts from taxation. In addition, if the natural gas producer is also a distributor, he may use his tax liability as a producer as a credit against his tax liability as a distributor. This favorable treatment may have been due to the fact that natural gas producers are subject to the largest statutory rate--7.85 per cent of gross sales. What has happened though is that it has encouraged the vertical integration of natural gas production and discouraged any large scale operations.

The law also provides for special treatment of the poultry processing industry by permitting what is ostensibly a manufacturing activity to be classified and taxed as a wholesaling activity. In 1967, this meant that poultry processors were taxed at a rate of 0.25 per cent, while other food manufacturing firms such as beef and pork processors were taxed at the manufacturing rate of 0.40 per cent of gross sales.

Geographically, the language of the statute serves to establish legal differences in base which have no real distinction in fact. This very lack of distinction, however, serves the purpose of treating domestic and multistate business similarly inasmuch as the tax base is measured by gross sales--whether separately accounted for, apportioned by some other characteristic, or specifically allocated to the state.[1] The differentiated tax rate structure, for different but closely related production activities, leads to significant changes in tax liability with little change in real operating characteristics. For example, mining activity (taxed at 1.35 per cent) has been known to be classed as manufacturing (taxed at 0.40 per cent) by the expedient of adding a washing process to the material mined. Similarly, some coal firms subcontract their operation to a service firm and thereby classify their activity as services (taxed at 1.05 per cent) and not mining. In general, the existence of 16 different rates across 30 different classes of business activity encourages firms to seek the lowest tax class liability. Thus, there is a decided lack of continuity in tax treatment as a consequence of the differential rate structure where variations in tax rates among similar classifications of business activity may be 100 per cent or more.

---

[1]The failure to appreciate this lack of distinction has led more than one writer, including the author, to argue that the turnover tax statute gives the multistate manufacturers an advantage over the domestic manufacturer because the latter must pay on gross value while the former pays on net value. See, for example, Vance Q. Alvis, "Turnover Taxation in West Virginia," <u>Sales Taxation</u>, West Virginia University Legislative Fiscal Studies, <u>vol. 1, no. 3</u> (Morgantown, W.Va.: West Virginia University, 1970), pp. 43-44. An estimate of the differential treatment of multistate versus in-state firms is provided in Appendix E.

Value-Added Tax Provisions

There is, of course, no value-added statute existing in West Virginia and, therefore, we may not make direct observations about its administration or enforcement. We do, however, have the advantage of looking at the provisions of a specific bill which was proposed for adoption in 1970.

In the 1970 legislative session, the bill (Committee substitute for House Bill 588) was submitted to and passed by both Houses of the West Virginia Legislature, but was vetoed by the governor.[1] The bill was an attempt to write a tax statute as close to a "pure" income value-added concept as possible. It reflects a "uses of business income" approach to the division of income for multistate business and provides for both formula apportionment and specific allocations.

Briefly, the bill arrives at value added through calculating three magnitudes: (1) Gross Income for Tax Purposes; (2) Entire Value-Added Income; and (3) Taxable Value-Added Income.

Gross Income for Tax Purposes. Gross income for tax purposes is the gross receipts of the taxpayer minus sales of capital assets, capital gains, payment of indebtedness, cash discounts and allowances, refunds, rents received on business property from firms or individuals subject to this tax, interest received except for financial organizations, dividends received, and interest income on obligations or securities of any authority, commission or instrumentality of the U.S. The exclusion of these

[1]The actual bill was written by Charles W. Loeb, an attorney of Charleston, West Virginia in consultation with the author and is based largely on the bill written by Loeb with James Papke in 1967. For the complete text and veto message, see "House Bill 588" and "Executive Message No. 16" in the Journal of the House of Delegates, West Virginia 1970.

forms of income comes about for two major reasons. One is the laws of the United States prohibiting taxation of certain types of income and the second is the definition of value added. In the cases of sales of capital assets and capital gains income, neither one of these constitutes current income and as such is not an element of value added.[1] Cash discounts and allowances are simply a means of getting at net receipts while income received as a consequence of acting as an agent is not properly income of the firm. Rent and interest received are excluded because the decision was made to pick it up as it is paid rather than as received in accordance with the uses of business income principle. Dividends are a part of profits and are picked up as such, following the idea that the base of the income value-added tax is concerned with the uses of business income and not with the realization (sources) of business income.[2] This latter decision closes part of the leakage from the tax base associated with earnings by non-residents. Interest on United States government obligations or its instrumentality are prohibited from taxation by the law. Finally, it should be mentioned that rent, interest, dividends, and royalties received by firms from individuals or firms who are not subject to the value-added article are included in the gross income of the firms and, as will be explained later, subject to either specific allocation or

---

[1]Douglas H. Eldridge raises some doubt over whether the latter is quite appropriate in the case of capital gains on depreciated assets. See his "Equity Administration and Compliance, and Intergovernmental Fiscal Aspects," The Role of Direct and Indirect Taxes in the Federal Revenue System. A conference report of the National Bureau of Economic Research and the Brookings Institution (Princeton, N.J.: Princeton University Press, 1964), p. 184.

[2]U.S., Congress, Excise Tax Compendium, p. 100.

formula apportionment in arriving at the taxable value-added income. Thus, if an individual firm rents non-business property, the receipts therefrom, would be included in gross receipts and the private citizen would have no statutory tax liability. The same is true if a firm received interest from a non-business entity. This, of course, closes another leakage in the value-added bases, i.e., when there is a tax-exempt area to which goods or services flow to or emanate from. Dividends and royalties are not likely to originate from individuals to firms; hence, they have no bearing on this particular matter.

There remains the problem of identifying the tax base leakage which occurs when royalty income is received by firms or individuals for the extraction of minerals, gas or oil, and other leakages such as those arising from payments for patents, copyrights, trademarks or other intangible personal property which are included in the income received by the firm and deducted as an expense when paid. All of these are considered to be business receipts and as such includable as part of the income base according to the provisions of this article. The problem which arises has to do with whether it is likely to be enforceable when the recipient resides in another state and/or is the only source of income from within this state. The conclusion seems inescapable that a leakage is likely to occur, given the language of the bill. On the other hand, if the treatment were reversed, i.e., if royalties received were excluded from gross receipts and royalties paid were included in the value-added income--the situs of the tax liability would shift to the firm paying the royalty and would be made more consistent with the objective behind the uses of business income philosophy, i.e., trying to capture as much of the value-added income generated in the state as possible. Thus, the proposed statute would appear to be inconsistent on this score. Subsequent consideration of this bill should give serious consideration to reversing the situs of royalty tax payments to an origin basis in line with that of other provisions of the bill.

In addition to these provisions there was provided a "specific exemption" which would have permitted taxpayers to exempt portions of their taxable value-added income on a sliding scale. No attempt is made in this study to assess the impact of this provision, nor as will be seen later, is this part of the statute included in our analysis since it is in fact an abberation of the intent of the value-added bill.[1]

Entire Value-Added Income. The second step is that of deriving the entire value-added income of the firm irrespective of its situs. The deduction from gross income for taxpayers which are permitted are as follows:

1. Net Inventory Adjustment
2. Cost of Goods Sold (exclusive of labor costs)
3. Repairs
4. Bad Debts
5. Taxes (excluding income taxes)
6. Interest Paid (financial organization only)
7. Charitable Contributions
8. Casualty and Theft Losses
9. Depreciation
10. Advertising
11. Freight and Postage
12. Utilities
13. Insurance (including Workmen's Compensation)
14. Supplies
15. Travel Expenses
16. Dues
17. Professional Services
18. Royalties Paid
19. Miscellaneous Business Expenses

---

[1]See Leyden, "Some Empirical Observations," pp. 24-26 for a discussion of the revenue effects of this provision.

With the exceptions of items 6 (interest paid) and 18 (royalties paid), the reasons for the deductions are rather obvious having to do with ordinary and necessary business expenses which properly are not a part of the definition of value added. Item 6, interest paid by financial organizations is allowed because of the different status of banks whose product is money. The intent was to determine the net interest earnings of the banks; interest paid being considered as a cost of acquiring funds to loan. Item 18, royalties paid appears to be justified if one accepts the implied assumption that West Virginia is an importer of royalties rather than an exporter. As noted earlier, this would seem to be a weak assumption. The remaining step is that of deriving the taxable value-added income.

Taxable Value-Added Income. For firms whose business activities take place entirely in the state, the entire value-added income is equal to the taxable value-added income. For firms with multistate operations, the allocation and apportionment procedure is established in one or more ways depending on the source of the value-added income:

Rents and Royalties

> Rents received from real property, from non-business entities and royalties received from real property located in the state are wholly allocable to the state. Rents received from tangible non-business property and royalties received from tangible personal property is allocable to the state to the extent of its utilization in the state.

Interest and Dividends

> These are based upon the taxpayer's residence: If the commercial domicile is in the state, then interest and dividends are wholly allocable to the state.

Patents and Copyrights

Patents and copyright royalties are handled in a manner similar to the treatment of rents and royalties.

Other Income

All of the income except that mentioned above and income arising from the transportation and communication sectors is apportioned to the state by a two factor formula--property and compensation, as follows:

$$1/2 \left(\frac{\text{VP West Virginia}}{\text{VP Everywhere}} + \frac{\text{W West Virginia}}{\text{W Everywhere}} \right)$$

Where VP = average value of taxpayer's real and tangible personal property owned or rented in the area noted.

and W = total amount of compensation paid in the area noted.

In the transportation sector, except for railroads and those solely engaged in the transportation of property which are subject to the same two factor formula just described, the allocation and apportionment provisions are as follows:

Nature of transportation	Allocation or Apportionment Formula
(1) Liquid coal or slurry	$\frac{\text{Barrel miles; W. Va.}}{\text{Barrel miles; everywhere}}$
(2) Gas by pipeline	$\frac{\text{Thousand cubic feet miles; W. Va.}}{\text{Thousand cubic feet miles; everywhere}}$

The specific procedure employed for estimating the two tax bases is contained in Appendix D.

CHAPTER IV

TURNOVER VERSUS VALUE-ADDED TAXATION IN WEST VIRGINIA: INCIDENCE AND PRICE CONSIDERATIONS

The ultimate objective of this study is to trace out relevant effects of a proposed income value-added tax in West Virginia, compare these effects with the existing turnover tax, and contribute to the preparation of estimates of, or judgments about, differential excess burdens and other consequences. The relevant effects will include: (1) short-run effects on prices; (2) impacts on distribution (that is, who bears the burden?); (3) impacts on excess burdens, i.e., departures from economic efficiency; and (4) other considerations that may be pertinent from the state's viewpoint.

In this chapter, we will concentrate on the price effects and incidence of the turnover tax and the differential incidence of the value-added tax. In Chapter V, we will look at efficiency and selected excess burden impacts; Chapter VI will deal with those issues which are pertinent from the state viewpoint, i.e., the adequacy, stability, and administrative efficiency of the two taxes.

Before getting into the rationale for the specific models chosen, three background observations seem in order. First, with the implementation of any one tax policy, individual households and firms will adjust to the new circumstances, and the adjustment may have effects on the distribution of income (tax incidence), the efficiency with which resources are utilized in the private sector (excess burden), and the stability and growth of the economy. Second, regardless of where taxes are statutorily imposed, they may affect factors of production and product prices and allocation.

Finally, the effects of a particular tax may vary according to which of three possible assumptions is made about the use to which revenue is put.[1] One assumption, balanced budget incidence, is that the tax is used to finance additional government activity. The effects of the tax as such cannot easily be identified since the analyst must also take account of the effect of the additional expenditures made by the government. The second alternative assumption, absolute incidence, is that nothing is done with the tax revenue. In effect, the tax is seen as a deflationary instrument which withdraws a certain number of dollars from the income stream. Thus, the tax is more appropriately viewed as a compensatory policy instrument for the achievement of stability goals. The third assumption, differential incidence, is that the tax is used to lower or replace an existing tax. Assuming that the new tax produces the same real resource transfer as the lowered or eliminated tax and that the form of the tax does not modify the pattern of government expenditure, tha analyst may be able to look directly to the differential effects of the new tax.

Let us turn to the rationale for the principal analytical models chosen. Our aim will be to use models some of whose analytical

---

[1]Musgrave, Theory of Public Finance, p. 211.

conclusions can be used to make projections of certain effects of the value-added tax.

Alternative Analytical Approaches

Typically, analysts viewing the effects of tax policy have taken one or both of two approaches. The first approach has been that of comparative static partial equilibrium analysis, where the analyst looks at the effects of a tax on the equilibrium level of price and quantity in a particular market, *ceteris paribus*. This may be alternatively expressed as an analysis of the first-order effect of a tax. Implicit in this approach is the idea that second-order effects (reactions in other markets) may be ignored.

Thus, the analyst may analyze the first-order effect of a specific tax policy change by observing how a tax on labor will affect the decision tc work while holding all other things constant (*ceteris paribus*). Then he may hold work-effort constant and look at the first-order effect of the same tax policy on the decision to purchase goods and services, *ceteris paribus*. In some instances, the second-order repercussions may be so slight that they may be ignored.

In other instances, however, the second-order effects may operate in a way which will have effects contrary to, or stronger than, the conclusions derived in the partial equilibrium approach. Under these latter circumstances, the analyst, if he is to understand the effects of the tax, must use a different approach, say that of comparative statics general equilibrium. In this approach, some of the things which were held constant or neglected are permitted to vary; the individual effects that bounce back from other parts of the economy are taken into account and thereby provide a more complete understanding of the effects of a given tax policy. Even in this general equilibrium context, however, not all impacts and repercussions are taken into account. The analyst must abstract from the real world if his models are to be manageable. Beyond this the analyst may abstract from the real world by neglecting or making special assumptions about some variables. This would be the case if he considers their effects relatively unimportant or if he wants to limit his analysis to a particular subset of circumstances.

In what follows, we shall discuss two formal analytical general equilibrium approaches which deal respectively with tax policy in a closed and an open economy. Following this we shall examine a partial equilibrium approach to tax policy in an open economy. At the conclusion of this discussion, we will assess how these approaches may aid in the attempt to analyze the particular tax policy issue under study here.

General Equilibrium Approach

A widely used general equilibrium model has been that developed by Harberger in 1962.[1] The Harberger approach was that of a comparative statics closed economy model which was designed to examine the long-run incidence of the corporate income tax in the United States.

Harberger begins by implicitly assuming a no government closed economy, i.e., there are no trade flows between countries. There are two industries, corporate and non-corporate, each producing a single product. These two industries employ two factors of production--labor and capital. Both industries are assumed to be operating in a

---

[1]Arnold C. Harberger, "The Incidence of the Corporate Income Tax," The Journal of Political Economy 70 (September 1962):215-40.

competitive market structure where there are no barriers to entry or exit and the factors of production are paid the value of the marginal product. Further, each industry's marginal cost is equal to the price of the product. This means that the economy is in short- and long-run equilibrium and has achieved economic efficiency. Harberger further stipulates that each industry's production relationship is one which may be described by a Cobb-Douglas production function which is homogeneous and of the first degree, i.e., each industry is operating under constant returns to scale, the employment of the factors of production is governed by their relative prices, and the payments to the factors just exhaust the total value of product produced.

The supply of the factors of production is fixed in the aggregate, but is permitted to vary between industries as a function of the change in relative prices for labor and capital which may be measured by their elasticity of substitution. This means that if factors become unemployed in one industry as a result of a change in their relative prices, they will be employed in the other industry. A reverse movement of the other factor will also take place so that there will be a realignment of the employment of the factors of production. Thus, the economy is always at full employment. All prices are expressed in terms of a numeraire-labor, whose price is set equal to one, so that only relative price changes are observed. This means that no monetary relationship needs to be specified. This combination of the numeraire assumption with the assumptions of full employment and zero savings activity effectively omits from consideration questions relative to the effect of corporate tax policy on stability and growth.

On the demand side, the initial quantities purchased are such that their initial prices are equal to one so that changes in product prices may be observed in relative rather than absolute terms. With the introduction of government into the model, Harberger uses the concept of balanced budget incidence, but in order to separate the distributional effects of government expenditures from the effects of the corporate income tax, he makes two additional assumptions. First, the pattern of demand by government for both goods will not differ from that of the consumers if both sectors face the same prices. Thus, initial aggregate demand is maintained and there is no budget effect associated with government expenditures. Second, changes in the distribution of income do not affect the composition of demand. Taken together, these two assumptions enable Harberger to analyze changes in demand as a function of changes in the relative prices of the two goods. These latter two assumptions appear to have the effect of making the balanced budget incidence assumption equal to the differential incidence assumption since both implicitly leave the initial allocation of resources unchanged if initial prices prevailed, but permit modification in the allocation of resources with changes in relative prices.

Overall, the assumptions postulated permit an analysis of the effect of the taxes on the relative employment of and prices paid to the factors of production and through these effects, the effect on the distribution of income, i.e., how the burden of the tax is shared between capital and labor.

Through a system of simultaneous equations, Harberger shows that the balanced budget incidence of the tax is a function of the relative initial shares of labor and capital in both industries, the price elasticity of substitution of factors of production between industries, the price elasticity of demand between the two products and the cross-elasticity of demand between the two products. After analyzing 10 different combinations of these variables, he proceeds to apply his model to the United States, using data covering the period 1953-1955. He concludes that

> It is hard to avoid the conclusion that plausible alternative sets of assumptions about the relevant elasticities all yield results in which capital bears very close to 100 per cent of the tax burden. The most plausible assumptions imply that capital bears more than the full burden of the tax.[1]

A second general equilibrium model, which represented an extension of the Harberger model, was developed by McLure in 1969.[2] In this comparative statics model, McLure analyzes the set of broad taxes levied by one state in an open-economy setting, i.e., a defined economy which is part of a larger economy, e.g., one state in the United States or one country in a group of countries as in the European Economic Community. There are two states, the taxing state X and the non-taxing state Y. There are no taxes initially and the economy is in short- and long-run equilibrium. The production of each state is aggregated so that the analysis centers upon a single good x produced by state X and a single good y produced in state Y. The basic market assumption is that both states operate under competitive conditions and that the production of goods x and y is governed by a Cobb-Douglas production function which is

---

[1]Ibid., p. 234.

[2]Charles E. McLure, Jr., "The Inter-regional Incidence of General Regional Taxes," Public Finance 24 (September 1969):457-84.

homogeneous of the first degree. There are two factors of production, capital and labor, and the aggregate supply of the factors is fixed. The output of both states is just exhausted by the payments to the factors of production. The ratio in which the factors are employed in each state is, therefore, a function of their elasticity of substitution which in turn is a function of their relative prices in each state. Labor is assumed to be immobile so that no migration from either state occurs. Capital, on the other hand, is considered mobile, but its owners are not. Instead, McLure assumes that some proportion of the total supply of capital is owned by the residents of state Y.

On the demand side, it is assumed that the government and each of the factors of production considered as a group in both states have the same marginal propensity to spend and the same income compensated elasticity of demand for good x. Thus, all income effects of the tax are held constant and we are left with an analysis of the substitution effect associated with changes in the relative prices paid to the factors of production and paid for the two goods. To avoid any spillover effects through monetary phenomena, all values are expressed in terms of a numeraire--the good y whose price is said to be fixed. All changes in price, therefore, will be expressed in relative terms and will be shown in changes in the price of good x in the taxing state and the price of the factors of production in both states. This permits a direct indication of the effect of a general tax on the terms of trade between the two taxing jurisdictions.

Given the assumptions above, McLure defines incidence in terms of the change in real income of labor and capital in the taxing state and the non-taxing state. This change in real income arises from two sources: first, on the source of income side, from changes in the relative prices paid to the factors of production; and second, on the uses of income side, from changes in the relative price of the two products and the total amount purchased of the product of the taxing state by the residents of the two taxing jurisdictions. McLure then develops a series of simultaneous equations in which he focuses on the exportability of various general taxes through their effects on the sources and uses of income.

McLure shows that a change in real income occurs because of changes in relative factor prices and the change in the relative employment of capital in the two states. Specifically, he shows that there is an inverse relationship between the returns to labor and capital in the non-taxing state. Thus, if a tax lowers the price received by capital, it will have the effect of raising the return to labor in the non-taxing state, because there will be a migration of capital into that state, thus raising the productivity of labor. In the aggregate the residents of state Y will benefit if the amount of capital invested in the state exceeds the share of capital owned by residents of the state Y. Unless the non-taxing state is a net debtor on capital account there can be no benefit from a production or factor tax. Further, before one can establish whether the non-taxing state will benefit from the tax, one must look to the changes in the price paid to labor relative to the tax paid to capital.

McLure also shows that other changes in real income are a function of the extent of tax exporting through changes in the price of the taxing state's output x and the share of total output of state X purchased by the residents of the non-taxing state. McLure then analyzes the effects of specific factor and consumption taxes, given the assumptions noted above. A tax on labor in the taxing state is wholly borne by labor in the state, through a reduction in the price paid to labor just equal to the tax imposed. No effect occurs on the uses of income side. McLure argues that the effects of a tax on production are dependent upon the income compensated elasticity of demand and the elasticity of substitution for the factors of production in the taxing and non-taxing states. If these elasticities are zero, the return to capital will fall, and wages will rise in the non-taxing state and fall in the taxing state. On the uses of income side, the burden of the tax will be distributed according to the initial shares of the taxing states' output purchased by the factors of production in both states. If only the income-compensated elasticity of demand is zero, there is no effect on the sources side and the production tax will be borne in proportion to the initial shares of the taxing state's output purchased by the non-taxing state.

If the elasticity of substitution of the factors of production in either state is zero, there is no effect on the use of income side for there can be no change in the employment of the factors of production. More specifically, if capital may not be substituted for labor in the taxing state and capital is mobile, then the effect of a production tax will cause the entire burden to fall on labor in the taxing state, since capital will not remain unless its price is equal to that in the non-taxing state. If factor proportions are fixed in the non-taxing state, and if demand for the taxing state's output is perfectly elastic, the tax is borne by labor in the taxing state and by capital in both states. Capital will in both instances migrate from the taxing jurisdiction and provide benefits to the non-taxing state's labor. And if the non-taxing state is a net debtor on capital account, it will benefit overall.

McLure also provides a comprehensive analysis of the export potential of consumption taxes, but since our interest is on production (turnover) and factor (value-added) taxes, we will not attempt to review these findings here.

Partial Equilibrium Approach

A third work, and one which comes closest to the specific tax policy change we are concerned with, is that done by Carl Shoup in his treatise on public finance in 1969.[1] In this work, Shoup spends a considerable amount of time discussing the economic implications of the move from a consumption form of value-added to a uniform turnover tax in a closed economy. In addition, he makes a few general remarks on the implications of such a move in an open economy context, again using the consumption form of value-added tax as the alternative. We shall first present Shoup's arguments with respect to the tax change in a closed economy. The reader will note that his arguments, though couched in general equilibrium terms, are less formal and therefore less precise than the Harberger or McLure models presented above. The reader should note that in order to fully explain his analysis, our discussion of Shoup will include his remarks on the burdens and excess burdens of turnover and value-added taxation. Following this, we shall review his arguments on the feasibility of using partial equilibrium analysis for

---

[1]Shoup, Public Finance.

exploring the incidence and economic effects of such a tax change in an open economy context.[1]

Shoup begins by noting that turnover taxation had its origins in the aftermath of World War I as countries tried to gain "large amounts of revenue with tax administrative machines that had been crippled by war, ..."[2] Turnover taxation as such refers to a levy against the production, distribution and sales of goods and services as long as there is a consideration involved and the seller-buyer transaction is not considered as a casual relationship. Because of the difficulty of ascertaining their value, intra-firm transfers are not generally considered in the calculation of the base.

In this analysis of turnover taxation, Shoup notes that the incidence of any tax, including the turnover tax, in a closed economy is a meaningless one and that the traditional partial equilibrium tools are of no use to us. Not only is it a general tax, it is also only one side of the public finance transaction. Useful analytical statements can be made, however, if we look at the tax from a differential incidence perspective in a general equilibrium setting.

From this latter perspective and in a closed-economy, Shoup compares a uniform turnover tax with a consumption value-added tax. Given equal degrees of vertical integration, he notes that

> . . . the turnover tax produces [the] heavier impact on factors who produce and on consumers who purchase goods that are heavily weighted with early-stage value-added, if the degree of vertical

---

[1]The reader should be aware that Shoup's analysis of the change is from a consumption value-added tax to a uniform turnover tax, while this review is presented as if the change were from a turnover tax to a consumption value-added tax.

[2]Ibid., p. 207.

> integration is not much greater for those goods than for goods embodying late-stage value-added.[1]

A simple illustration will serve to demonstrate this phenomenon. In the illustration below, if we assume the existence of two products A and B, each with the same total value added and each subject to the same tax rate of 1 per cent of gross at each exchange, we may observe that the difference between the two products is that good A has most of its value added created in the early stages while good B's value added is created much later.

Point of Sale	Stage of Production	Value-Added	Gross Value Before Tax	Tax at 1 Per Cent
	GOOD A			
1	Raw Material Extraction	$ 60.00	$ 60.00	$ 60.60
2	Manufacturing	20.00	80.60	81.40
3	Wholesale	10.00	91.40	92.31
4	Retail-Service	10.00	102.31	103.33
	Total	$100.00		
	GOOD B			
1	Raw Material Extraction	$ 10.00	$ 10.00	$ 10.10
2	Manufacturing	25.00	35.10	35.45
3.	Wholesale	30.00	65.45	66.10
4	Retail-Service	35.00	101.10	102.21
	Total	$100.00		

A uniform tax of 1 per cent of gross at each point of sale results in a final price of $103.33 for good A and $102.21 for good B. The difference of $1.12 is directly attributable to the early-stage value-added characteristic of good A.

With the change to a consumption value-added tax, there will be a fall in the prices of early-stage goods or a rise in factor rewards or a combination of both. It is difficult to establish _a priori_ the degree

---

[1]Ibid., p. 217.

to which either or both of these phenomenon will occur. Shoup argues that the extent of the effect on either product prices or factor prices depends on the elasticities of demand for the product as well as the elasticities of supply of the factors of production. This problem aside, he argues that the differential incidence on income classes of the tax change are impossible to ascertain because we know nothing about the consumption mix of early- and late-stage value-added goods by income classes. He conjectures that low-income consumers are likely to be early-stage value-added consumers. If that is true, the movement from a turnover to a consumption value-added tax would shift the average burden from low to high income classes.[1]

This may not be true of the tax burden at the margin, however. Under equal yield revenue assumptions, the turnover tax rate will be lower since the base is larger. The low-income consumer, although subject to a lower average rate of turnover tax than under the consumption value-added tax, could be subject to a higher marginal tax under the consumption value-added tax than the turnover tax, especially if he is at the point where his marginal purchases are of the middle- and late-stage value added. The reverse effect would apply to the higher-income consumers.

With respect to excess burden and efficiency, Shoup argues that the turnover tax creates excess burdens in production, work-leisure and consumption choices. From a production point of view, there are three particular ways in which excess burdens may arise. First, it discriminates against non-vertically integrated firms which are subject to the

---

[1]Ibid.

tax as the product moves through the stages of production.[1] With the imposition of the turnover tax, firms are induced to vertically integrate and the effect is to reduce efficiency. Moving to a consumption value-added tax would create no inducement to vertically integrate beyond that expected from causes other than the tax. On the contrary, those firms which were vertically integrated because of the turnover tax would no longer find it to their advantage to continue as vertically integrated entities. The move to a consumption value-added tax would encourage firms to specialize. Second, the turnover tax creates excess burden and reduces efficiency in the treatment of capital intensive methods of production. Shoup notes that "the rate of substitution of future goods for present goods as seen by the producer differs from that faced by the supplier of funds."[2] This is analogous to the case in which a sales tax is imposed on a good or service. In this case the sales tax acts as a wedge pushing apart the marginal rate of substitution in consumption and the marginal rate of transformation in production. Similarly, in the market for capital goods the uniform turnover tax drives a wedge between the prices facing purchasers of capital goods cum tax and the prices received by the producers of capital goods ex tax. Third, Shoup goes on to argue that an additional excess burden occurs because the turnover tax varies the amount of the ". . . divergence between the two rates of substitution erratically, taking only those capital goods or those components of a capital good that are not produced within the using firm."[3] With

---

[1]See Chapter V, p. 199 for an illustrative example of this phenomenon.

[2]Shoup, Public Finance, p. 224. [3]Ibid.

the introduction of a consumption value-added tax, no tax would be imposed since capital purchase would be exempt from the tax. The movement from a turnover to a consumption value-added tax would lead to increased economic growth, inasmuch as the latter tax permits capital purchases to be deducted from current gross value-added. The incentive at the margin to substitute inefficient labor-intensive activity in lieu of capital would no longer be present.

Regarding work-leisure choices and excess burden, one must assume that an excess burden is created by both taxes. In an otherwise efficient economy, the individual can be made better off under either the turnover or value-added tax if he is given the option of paying a flat fee equal to what he might pay under either tax. The substitution effect of the imposition of either the turnover or value-added tax would induce individuals to work less since the price of leisure will have declined. There is, however, an offsetting income effect which would lead to more work. Depending on the relative strength of these two forces, the taxpayer could work more or less.

The movement from a turnover to an equal-yield consumption value-added tax would probably induce low-income households to work less. Shoup's reasoning behind this conjecture is based on a complex series of observations. Early-stage value-added goods are more heavily burdened under the turnover tax and this burden falls largely on consumers. Low-income households consume higher quantities of early-stage value-added goods than their middle- and high-income counterparts.[1]

---

[1]Keep in mind that "early-stage value-added" goods means those items that acquire relatively more of their value added at early stages--e.g., beans and rice in contrast to frozen foods and automobiles.

Thus, low-income households are subject to differentially higher average tax burdens under the turnover tax, but not necessarily higher marginal tax burdens, if their marginal purchases are of middle- and late-stage value added. With the shift to a consumption value-added tax, middle- and late-stage value-added goods would be taxed higher and would, therefore, cause the price of leisure for low-income households to decline since the purchasing power of the marginal dollar earned declines.

Thus, Shoup is arguing that both the substitution and the income effect are unambiguously in the direction of tending to induce the low-income household to work less.[1] This conclusion is in marked contrast to that which may be drawn under the traditional analysis of the work-leisure choice. Shoup notes that in this latter context, a given tax is compared with a no-tax situation and the use of the revenue is ignored. Under these conditions, the question of whether one would work more or less with the adoption of a turnover tax is

> . . . virtually insoluable by a priori reasoning, or rather the answer is that it all depends. Choosing among sets of equally plausible assumptions about rates of change in elasticity of supply of labor as the take-home pay changes under a tax that is presumed not to affect the wage gross of tax, the analyst can reach either a more-work or a less-work conclusion.[2]

There is also an excess burden created in consumption by the turnover tax inasmuch as it causes the relative prices of early-stage value-added goods to rise by more than those of middle- and late-stage goods. This in turn induces increases in the consumption of middle- and late-stage

---

[1]This is not explicitly stated in the text, but was brought to my attention in private correspondence with Professor Shoup.

[2]Shoup, Public Finance, p. 231.

value-added goods. With the move to a consumption value-added tax, the relative price difference between early- and late-stage value-added goods would be removed. As a consequence, the consumption of late-stage value-added goods would decline and early-stage value-added goods would rise, thereby reducing the excess burden in consumption which arose under the turnover tax.

To summarize Shoup's findings, we have seen that in differential incidence terms, the turnover tax causes excess burdens in production and consumption and that the movement to a consumption value-added tax will have the effect of reducing some of these excess burdens. There remain, however, other excess burdens such as those arising from the work-leisure choice. Further, the consumption value-added tax is probably a less regressive tax because the heavier tax on early-stage value-added goods will have been removed. We have also seen that there are other effects about which one can only conjecture because: There is no way of arriving at an answer to a question which depends on facts which may not be known _a priori_ (consumption by income classes of early- and late-stage value-added products); or because by the very nature of the tax change it is not possible to abstract from the use to which the revenue is put (absolute incidence). Under these conditions one is measuring or speculating on the combined effect of the tax and the use to which it is put, and not the tax itself.

Thus, Shoup argues against the use of partial equilibrium analysis in ascertaining the incidence of turnover taxation in a closed economy and uses the concept of differential incidence to explore its effects. He does not, however, maintain this view when he looks to the incidence and economic effects of turnover taxation in an open economy.

> In an open economy, the incidence of a general . . . tax becomes ascertainable to a degree, because the "general" sales tax is no longer truly general. . . . The use made of the general sales tax revenue will be concentrated in the taxing country and so will no doubt influence appreciably the demand and cost schedules of virtually all goods in that country. This fact, . . limits severely what can be said about the incidence of a general sales tax in an open economy without specifying the counterpart measure . . . . [T]he existence of the rest of the world as a tax-free area to which consumers in the taxing country, if not always factors, can resort makes possible the construction of supply and demand schedules for certain goods under assumptions of perfect elasticity of demand for exports and supply of imports. To some extent, then, the "general" sales tax in an open economy can be analyzed in much the same fashion as an excise tax in a closed economy.[1]
>
> . . . [T]his incidence analysis cannot divide the domestic income groups as finely as can partial equilibrium analysis for a small tax in a closed economy. The only distinctions that can be drawn among domestic factors, and consumers, refer to their employment in, or consumption of products of, the export industries, the import-competing industries, and the remaining domestic industries.[2]

With this justification for his analysis, Shoup briefly discusses the incidence of the turnover tax in an open economy under both the destination principle and the origin principle. With respect to turnover taxes on an origin basis (the manner in which they are levied in West Virginia), Shoup argues that given perfect elasticity of demand for exports and supply of imports, the incidence of the turnover tax is divided between all domestic factors and domestic consumer spending on domestic value added. If the elasticity of demand for exports and supply of imports is not perfectly elastic, some of the tax will rest on export consumers and on domestic consumers of import-competing products to the extent that prices rise in both markets.[3]

[1]Ibid., p. 213. [2]Ibid., p. 10. [3]Ibid., pp. 216-217.

Usefulness of Alternative Approaches

In evaluating the usefulness of these alternative approaches, we may observe that Shoup's arguments on the partial equilibrium open-economy approach seem to have general validity, if it can be shown that West Virginia products are such a small part of the total national output that second-order effects of the tax may be ignored. This approach, however, limits the conclusions which may be drawn. Further, even if the Shoup approach is used, we will have to be clearer than he has been about the assumptions underlying the analysis. We will also have to be aware that the structure of the turnover tax in West Virginia is significantly different from the uniform turnover tax posited by Shoup and, therefore, may alter the conclusions drawn.

With respect to the Harberger model, there is no doubt that its applicability to the West Virginia situation is very limited for a number of reasons. First, the model only deals with a closed economy and abstracts from the very environment in which our tax analysis falls. Second, we are dealing in this study with a tax which applies more than one rate to the various industries in West Virginia and to ignore this structural consideration would seriously impair the applicability of the analytical results. Finally, if we bring this structural consideration into the Harberger model, it would require that we know something about the shares of capital and labor within each of the industries, the relevant elasticities of substitution between capital and labor in each of the industries taxed differently, the price elasticities of demand for each of the industry products and the cross-elasticity of demand between all products. Thus, the analytical complexity and empirical data requirements prevent its consideration for our use. The model does provide, however, a clear indication of the complexities of economic analysis even in the simplest of cases and warns us against drawing unwarranted conclusions from other less complete models. Further, although it does not provide us with an explicit model for our analysis, it does give some insight into possible assumptions for dealing with other kinds of analysis.

Similar remarks may be made about the McLure model, although it is more complex and more general than the Harberger model. Further, we know of no econometric model which could operationalize his model as it currently stands. And if we were to impose the requirement that it be specific to the West Virginia turnover tax and the proposed value-added tax, the task would be virtually impossible. McLure's model, however, has considerable merit for, like the Harberger model, it provides further insight into the analytical complexities of dealing with tax issues in an open economy and the need to avoid drawing conclusions which are not supported by the underlying theory and/or capable of being verified by empirical data.

In principle, we conclude that the general equilibrium approach to establishing the economic effects of tax policy is the most appropriate. Further, the Harberger and McLure models are noteworthy in this regard However, the current state of understanding, and our ability to deal with specific taxes in an open economy do not permit their formal approach to be used for the tax change under investigation in West Virginia. We may, however, provide some insight into the economic effects of the tax change if we limit the scope of our inquiry and use the partial equilibrium approach suggested by Shoup. Also, we may be able to develop further insights by extending the analysis with less formal general equilibrium considerations, using some of the assumptions and analytical insights developed by McLure.

Thus, even though the Shoup approach limits the conclusions which may be drawn, it appears to be the most feasible for developing an initial understanding of the incidence and efficiency effects of the turnover tax in West Virginia. In the following section, therefore, we will first analyze the incidence of the turnover tax in West Virginia using Shoup's brief remarks as a point of departure. We shall also be more specific about the assumptions under which the analysis is conducted. Where appropriate, we will note where the conclusions may differ from those developed by Shoup or those which are generally argued in the literature on excise taxation. This analysis will include both short- and long-run considerations. Following the partial equilibrium analysis of incidence, we will explore the general equilibrium implications of the conclusions derived, drawing on the work of Harberger and McLure. This will be followed by a discussion of the differential incidence associated with the replacement of the turnover tax by an income value-added tax. As in the case of the turnover tax, the differential incidence of the value-added tax will be explored in both partial and general equilibrium terms. Following this theoretical discussion, we will develop specific simulation models to estimate some of the effects of the tax change on final prices in export and domestic markets and provide a basis for judging whether changes in the employment of the factors of production are likely to occur.

The assumptions noted below provide a basis for deriving the incidence of the turnover tax in West Virginia under a limited set of circumstances. As these insights are gained, some of the assumptions will be relaxed or modified to establish whether the restrictive assumptions materially affect our considerations.

Theoretical Considerations

Incidence of the West Virginia Turnover Tax

We begin by assuming that West Virginia business activity is composed of three broad sectors, each of which operate exclusively in three markets--export, import competing and domestic. The firms which make up each sector locate their production facilities entirely in West Virginia. This assumption abstracts temporarily from the problem of multistate operations. We further assume that all firms sell directly to consumers, that there are no inventory accumulations, and that there are no firms operating in more than one market. We also assume that competitive conditions prevail such that there is freedom of entry to and exit from each industry, the prices paid by consumers are equal to the average total cost and marginal cost of production, and each firm is operating at its most efficient point. In addition, we assume that there are only two factors of production--labor and capital.

The turnover tax rate levied on each sector is the resultant of the individual rates levied on the different forms of business activity. Within each sector, the tax impact on individual firms will vary considerably, depending on the type of business activity engaged in. For, as we note in Appendix D as a consequence of individual firms paying different rates for each class of business activity, the effective tax rate imposed on individual firms will be a composite one representing a series of individual rates weighted by the dollar value of the class of business activity. This composite rate is assumed to be the same for the sectors operating in the three markets and permits us to abstract from the complicated task of accounting for marginal change in the employment of the factors of production because of differences in taxes between sectors. There are no taxes of this type levied in the surrounding states. (In fact, the turnover tax is levied in only four states and thus the West Virginia turnover tax may be viewed as a tax over and above that which is usually levied on businesses in other states.) Further, the price prevailing in each of the markets before the tax is also a composite index of prices of all goods produced weighted by their respective quantities sold.

With these general assumptions, we will look at the incidence of the turnover tax in two time periods. The first time period is defined as one in which the supplies of the factors of production are fixed and elasticity of demand ranges from zero to infinity. We will call this the market period. In the second period, which permits longer-run adjustment, we will explore eight possible combinations of demand and supply conditions which are likely to be operative in one or more of the three markets. From the demand side, we will distinguish between perfectly elastic demand (as perceived by the industry) and less than perfect price elasticity of demand (as perceived by the industry). This set of assumptions will be referred to as the "longer-run" period. These are not necessarily long-run. In fact, only Cases 2 and 6 conform to a typical long-run period in which the factors of production are completely mobile and production is governed by a Cobb-Douglas function. All of the other cases represent a series of alternative sets of assumptions which may be possible over a longer time than the immediate market period, but not so long as to allow the assumptions of Cases 2 and 6 to prevail.

On the supply side, we will explore the effects of assuming two types of production functions. The first is a Cobb-Douglas production function which is homogenous of the first degree, in which the shares to capital and labor are constant, i.e., constant returns to scale, and generalized diminishing return. The second is a production function in which production is said to be governed by fixed technical coefficients, i.e., the elasticity of substitution between labor and capital is zero. With respect to the supplies of the factors of production, we will assume that capital is mobile and alternatively labor is fixed or mobile.

The combined effect of these demand and supply conditions yields eight possible cases which may be operative in one or more of the markets in the second-time period in which longer-run adjustments may take place (see Table 6). We will proceed on the assumption that while all eight cases may be possible in the export market, only Cases 5-8 are likely in the import-competing and domestic markets. In the general equilibrium analysis which follows the partial equilibrium analysis of incidence, we will assume that the state government and the owners of the factors of production in West Virginia have the same marginal propensity to spend and the same income-compensated elasticity of demand for each of the three composite goods. This will permit us to abstract from the distributional effects on income arising from the spending of the tax proceeds. Transitional impacts on the level of resource usage will be neglected; in effect monetary, fiscal, and other policies to maintain relatively full

TABLE 6

APPLICABILITY OF ALTERNATIVE LONGER-RUN ASSUMPTIONS TO THE EXPORT, IMPORT-COMPETING, AND DOMESTIC MARKETS IN WEST VIRGINIA

Price Elasticity of Demand as Perceived by the Industry		Perfect $\eta_D = -\frac{\Delta Q}{\Delta P} \cdot \frac{P}{Q} = \infty$				Less than Perfect $0 \leq \eta_D < \infty$			
Production Function		Cobb-Douglas $q = AX_1^{\alpha}X_2^{1-\alpha}$ Elasticity of Substitution $\sigma = 1$		Fixed Proportion Elasticity of Substitution $\sigma = 0$		Cobb-Douglas $q = AX_1^{\alpha}X_2^{1-\alpha}$ Elasticity of Substitution $\sigma = 1$		Fixed Proportion Elasticity of Substitution $\sigma = 0$	
Supply of Labor		Fixed	Mobile	Fixed	Mobile	Fixed	Mobile	Fixed	Mobile
Market	Export	X	X	X	X	X	X	X	X
	Import-Competing	N/A	N/A	N/A	N/A	X	X	X	X
	Domestic	N/A	N/A	N/A	N/A	X	X	X	X
Case		1	2	3	4	5	6	7	8

N/A--Not Applicable

employment will be assumed. Finally, we assume that the economy, both in West Virginia and the United States, is in short- and long-run equilibrium prior to the institution of the turnover tax in West Virginia.

Our analysis of the distributional implications of the turnover tax will be limited primarily to looking at the first-order effect of the tax on consumers in West Virginia and consumers of West Virginia products in the rest of the nation, and on factors of production in West Virginia.

We will not attempt to ask: "What is the incidence of the tax with respect to income groups in West Virginia or in the United States?" because the answer is highly dependent on currently unavailable information about the relative consumption of early- and late-stage value-added goods and on knowledge about the overall consumption of West Virginia goods by these income groups. For incidence analysis purposes, we will assume that the amount of resource transfer given up in private is equal to the resource transfer received by the state, i.e., no excess burden. Within the context of the partial equilibrium model, departures from this assumption are not likely to affect the overall pattern of incidence derived.

Although we will make some statements about the incidence and differential incidence of the two taxes for the eight cases, we will not be able to make pertinent estimates for all eight either through direct observation or by simulation (owing in part to the complexity of the data required to do so). We will, however, be able to look at some of the effects of these two taxes under the assumption of fixed technical coefficients of production. Our analysis begins with a discussion of price effects and incidence in the export market, followed by an analysis of the second- and third-order effects of export market changes on other markets. This will be followed by a similar discussion of the import-competing and domestic markets.

Export Market

Export Market--Market Period

With fixed factor supplies, from a partial equilibrium view, if the export sector produces for a market in which it is a relatively small part of the total market such that it is faced by a perfectly elastic demand and with resources which are highly specialized to the firm and the sector, the entire burden of the tax will rest on the factors of production in proportion to the initial shares of labor and capital employed in the sector. If the return to labor and capital is completely flexible downward, there will be no output effect. If, however, the return to labor is rigid in the downward direction, as is likely to be the case in the short run, there would be a reduction in output as export producers adjust production to conform with the after-tax value of the marginal product of labor. If this occurs, some unemployment or underemployment (if hours are reduced, but workers are not laid off) will occur. If we assume full employment, there will be an indirect response by the monetary authorities to bring the economy back to full employment. The impact of this activity on general price levels is not the effect of the tax but the effect of a separate full employment policy goal pursued at the national level.

If economic rents are earned prior to the imposition of the turnover tax and these rents in the aggregate are at least equal to the turnover tax, there will be no response by the monetary authorities nor any reduction in output of the export sector. The only effect of the turnover tax will be to reduce the economic rents received by these specialized factors, assuming the returns to labor and capital are completely flexible downward.

In general, the entire effect of the tax occurs on the sources of income side and no effect will occur on the uses of income side. Assuming fixed factor supplies within the sector, the burden will not be shared equally among the individual firms since the differentiated rate structure will cause capital and labor employed in high-taxed activity (e.g., mineral production, other transportation, communication and public utilities, and contract construction) to bear heavier burdens than those engaged in low-taxed activity (e.g., manufacturing).

The same outcome will not be true if the export sector produces a product which faces less than perfectly elastic demand, such as coal mining. If the price elasticity of demand is zero, the entire burden of the tax will be shifted forward, providing the elasticity of supply for the sector is not zero. In this case the entire incidence of the tax occurs on the uses of income in the non-taxing jurisdiction. Under these conditions, there is no output effect and no effects on the sources of income in West Virginia. If both sector supply and demand elasticities are zero, the outcome is indeterminate. If, however, the price elasticity of demand is greater than zero, but less than infinity, and the elasticity of supply of the sector is zero, we conclude that the entire burden of the tax will occur on the sources of income in West Virginia and the effects will be identical to those posited earlier. If the price elasticity of demand is greater than zero, but less than infinity and the price elasticity of supply is greater than zero, then the incidence of the tax will fall on both the uses of income of export consumers and on the sources of income of factors of production employed in the export sector.

Export Market--Longer-Run

Continuing with our partial equilibrium analysis, we find that in subsequent time periods, there are eight possible cases in which the incidence of the tax may differ depending on the assumptions made with respect to demand, production function, and the mobility of the factors of production.

Case 1--Export. In the first case, we continue with the assumption of perfect elasticity of demand. In addition, we assume capital is mobile, but its owners and labor are not.[1] Further, production is governed by a Cobb-Douglas production function which is homogeneous of the first degree, i.e., elasticity of technical substitution is equal to one. Under these circumstances, the burden will shift entirely to the fixed factor--labor. The price of capital in West Virginia will rise to its pre-tax price as capital migrates to untaxed employment and there will be a corresponding reduction in the price paid to labor. Output will be reduced until the condition of constant shares to capital and labor are re-established. The export sector in West Virginia will become more labor-intensive as the ratio of capital to labor declines.

From a general equilibrium view, these first-order effects under Case 1 will induce second- and third-order effects in other markets. The reduction in factor income in West Virginia will impact on the uses of

---

[1]The assumption that capital is mobile but its owners are not assumes that capital owners are willing to change the location of their investment in response to a change in rate of return, but do not have to physically relocate to take advantage of such opportunities. In this circumstance, the income from capital outside the taxing jurisdiction that is owned by persons inside the taxing state would flow back into the state.

income side in the import-competing and domestic markets causing a shifting backward of the respective demand curves for outputs. Further, the migration of capital to untaxed industries in the United States will, at the margin, lower the prices paid to capital and raise those of labor outside of the state, but not significantly. To the extent that it does and the owners of capital are West Virginians, it will affect the uses of income in West Virginia. If we assume that the patterns of purchases are the same for the government as for the labor and capital whose incomes are reduced, the shifting backward of the demand curve in the import-competing and domestic markets is likely to be matched by a comparable shift forward in the respective demand curves, causing no net third-order effects on the sources of income in the import-competing and domestic sectors. Thus, for Case 1 conditions, we conclude that the incidence of the turnover tax on the export industry will remain on the fixed factor, labor.

Case 2--Export. In Case 2 we retain all of the assumptions as under Case 1 except that the supply of labor in the export sector is assumed to be mobile in the long run. If both labor and capital are mobile in the long run, output will be reduced further until the returns to both factors are equal after tax to the value of their marginal product. In effect, those factors which are less efficiently employed in the export market will exit to the non-taxed industries and the rents enjoyed by the more efficiently employed factors will be reduced. Thus, the burden of the tax will continue to be borne by those employed in the export sector.

From a general equilibrium view, the migration of factors to the non-taxed sectors will, at the margin, lower the price paid to capital and labor in the non-taxing industries and, consequently, lower the prices paid by consumers of competing export goods in the non-taxed industry. This will have the effect of shifting the demand curve for West Virginia exports down, and thus create a further burden on the export sector over and above that of the direct tax burden imposed by the state. This output effect is likely to be quite small, however.

As in Case 1, the reduction of demand due to the impact of the tax on the uses of income by those factors which are continued in employment will be matched by a comparable shift forward of the government demand curves, causing no net impact on the import-competing and domestic sectors beyond that associated with the third-order output effects on export demand noted in the previous paragraph.

In Cases 3 and 4, we retain the assumption of perfect elasticity of demand but assume that the elasticity of substitution of the factors of production is zero. Case 3 assumes that labor is fixed, while Case 4 assumes that it is not.

Case 3--Export. Under Case 3, the incidence of the turnover tax will shift to labor but in order for labor to be fully employed, it will require that the same amount of capital be employed as before. Therefore, the price paid to labor will be lower than under the previous Cobb-Douglas production assumption and there will be no output effects in the export sector. The price paid to capital will again rise to its pre-tax level and the shares of labor and capital payments will change in favor of capital. The burden imposed on labor is equal to the amount required to return capital to its pre-tax level. Similar conclusions about the general equilibrium implications of Case 3 conditions as under

Cases 1 and 2 may be made under the assumption of fixed technical coefficients in the uses of income by the factors of production. Labor will be made worse off by the redistribution of income to capital owners and by the tax revenues paid to state government. This in turn will affect the demand for import-competing and domestic products, but the assumption of equal marginal propensity to spend of state government will have the effect of offsetting this negative impact, providing that the increased share going to capital is spent on import-competing and domestic goods in West Virginia. To the extent it is not, this will have the effect of lowering the demand in these markets and may induce output reductions at the margin. This effect, however, is not likely to affect our conclusion that the primary incidence of the tax will fall on labor in West Virginia.

Case 4--Export. Under Case 4, where we assume that labor is mobile, the imposition of the tax may be viewed by export producers as a shift downward of the demand curve facing them. The extent of output reduction will be a function of the relative elasticity of supply of the factors of production. If both capital and labor have equal elasticities at the margin, the burden will be shared in proportion to their employment. Output will be reduced until the return to the factors after the tax is equal to the value of their marginal product. The incidence of the tax will rest on the remaining, less efficiently employed, factors. If the elasticity of the supply of capital is greater than the elasticity of supply of labor, some additional burden will be borne by labor as occurred under Case 3.

From a general equilibrium view, any reduction in output will cause aggregate state income to decline and thus require that a higher turnover tax rate be imposed on the export sector to extract the same real income. This implies an excess burden on those factors remaining employed, who will experience heavier individual tax burdens.

On the sources of income side, the released resources will migrate outside of the state and be absorbed by industry in the United States. Productive capacity in the remaining states will increase and this could impact on the export demand schedule for West Virginia, at the margin. The strength of this influence is not likely to be so strong that it overwhelms our conclusions with respect to the incidence of the tax in this market. The reduction in output of West Virginia's export industry implies a "geographic" excess burden, the benefits of which will be enjoyed on the use side by consumers of the expanded output of the export-competing non-taxed industries in the United States.

Cases 5 through 8 differ from Cases 1 through 4 in the sense that we are assuming that the export sector perceives the demand for its product as being less than perfectly elastic. Under these conditions, the incidence of the tax will be shared between the consumer and producers of the export goods as a function of the elasticity of demand and supply. The more elastic the demand relative to supply, the more the burden will be borne by the producer and vice-versa. The price will rise and output will be reduced until the price received ex tax by the producer is equal to average total cost and marginal cost at the lower level of output.

Case 5--Export. With respect to Case 5, in which we assume a Cobb-Douglas production function which is homogeneous of the first degree and capital is mobile, but labor is not, the producer's portion of the tax will be borne entirely by labor. Output will be reduced as producers seek to raise prices until the return ex tax is equal to average total cost and marginal cost at the lower level of output. If the supply of capital is perfectly elastic, capital will migrate out of the industry until the return ex tax is equal to the return in non-taxed alternatives. At the lower level of output, the relative share paid to capital will remain the same, but this implies that for labor to be fully employed the price paid to labor declines.

The export sector will become more labor intensive as labor is used more intensively to produce the lowered quantity of output. From a general equilibrium view, the migration of capital out of the state will impact on the sources of income outside the state with the price of labor in the non-taxing jurisdiction rising as more capital is employed. There will be a corresponding decline in the price of capital in the non-taxing jurisdiction as industry becomes more capital intensive. The reduction in income of the labor factor employed in the West Virginia export market will impact on the West Virginia import-competing and domestic markets, but no output effects are likely to arise, given our assumption of equal marginal propensity to spend of the different factor groups and state government. This does not take account of the direct effects of the turnover tax on the import-competing and domestic markets not their indirect effects on the export market, all of which are discussed later.

Case 6--Export. If labor and capital supply in the export market are completely mobile in the long run as in Case 6, the burden of the tax will fall entirely on consumers. Prices will increase and output will be reduced as labor and capital migrate out of the state until the return to both labor and capital is equal to that in the non-taxing jurisdiction. As these resources are released, the supply curve will shift upward and the entire burden of the tax will be borne on the uses side by the consumers of the export industry's product. The extent of output reduction will depend on the price elasticity of demand for exports. The lower the price elasticity of demand for exports, the smaller will be the output reduction and the larger will be the price increase. In any event, the entire burden of the tax on the exporting firms will be borne by the consumers of the export sector and, in this sense, the tax may be fully exported outside the state.

The burden of the tax, however, will not be uniform among the consumer groups because of the differential rate structure under the turnover tax. Consumers of high-taxed exports will bear heavier burdens per dollar of purchase than consumers of low-taxed exports. From a general equilibrium view with both capital and labor migrating into the non-taxing jurisdiction, the return to both labor and capital in the non-taxing jurisdiction will be reduced at the margin, but not appreciably. In addition, if labor and capital migrate to export-competing firms, the decline in output in West Virginia may be offset by an increase in the supply of export-competing goods. If this is matched by a corresponding shift in the demand for export-competing products, there need be no reduction in the prices paid to labor and capital in the non-taxing jurisdiction.

Cases 7 and 8--Export. Cases 7 and 8 are identical to Cases 5 and 6 except that we now assume that the production function is governed by fixed technical coefficients. Under Case 7 we further assume that labor is fixed, but capital is not. If the price elasticity of demand is greater than zero, there will be no output reduction since the same amount of capital will be required to fully employ labor. The burden of the tax will occur solely on labor as its price falls and capital's price rises until the return to capital after tax is equal to that in non-taxed alternatives, i.e., outside the state.

As far as aggregate demand within West Virginia is concerned, the reduction in labor's price and the consequent income effect on the use of income by labor will be matched by a comparable outward shift of demand by state government.

Under Case 8, which assumes that labor is mobile, the incidence of the tax will again depend on the relative elasticity of demand and supply. The adjustment of factor prices for the producer's portion of the tax burden and general equilibrium implications are identical to that of Case 4.

Import-Competing Market

The import-competing sector in West Virginia is characterized by firms which produce for local (West Virginia) consumption but face competition from producers which lie outside of the turnover tax jurisdiction of the state. Let us assume that this sector is faced by an outside industry whose supply is perfectly elastic. Further, we assume that the demand for the product is less than perfectly elastic and the sector in West Virginia is characterized by a Cobb-Douglas production function which is homogeneous of the first degree. There are two factors of production--labor and capital--whose supplies take on the same values as in the export sector.

Import-Competing--Market Period

In the market period, if industry supply is perfectly inelastic, the incidence of the tax will fall entirely on the factors of production employed in the industry as a function of their initial shares of total product value. If wages are inflexible downward and no economic rents are being earned, some output reduction will occur with consequent unemployment effects identical to that described in our analysis of the export sector under Cases 5 through 8. The price of the product to the producer in West Virginia ex tax will have to fall by the full amount of the tax.

Import-Competing--Longer-Run

Cases 5 and 6--Import-Competing. Beyond the market period, Cases 5 through 8 are possible alternative configurations. In Case 5, assuming that capital is completely mobile and labor is not, output will be reduced as capital migrates out of the state, the price of capital will return to its pre-tax level, and the price of labor will decline until the proportional share of income going to the factors is re-established at a lower level of output. From a general equilibrium point of view, this will have the effect of lowering the supply curve of West Virginia import-competing products, and the share of non-taxed imports from outside will increase. No change in prices will occur if we assume that capital migrates to the same industry but outside of the state. If production outside of the state is also governed by a Cobb-Douglas production function of the same type, the price of capital will decline, the price of labor will rise, and output will increase in the non-taxed industry. The non-taxed import industry outside the state will become more capital intensive and the taxed import-competing sector in West Virginia will become more labor intensive. If capital migrates to non-import industries outside the state, the price of import-competing products will rise as total supply is reduced, labor and capital in the non-taxed import industry will receive larger total payments at the margin, not as much capital will migrate, and not as much impact will fall on labor in West Virginia. Assuming that the import-competing sector has some locational advantage, there will be no change in the output of the import-competing sector since the locational advantages would be reflected in the payment of economic rents to the factors. Under these circumstances, the burden would still fall on the factors of production in West Virginia but unless the tax exceeded the economic rents paid, there would be no change in the employment of the factors of production over the long run. The burden of the tax would be borne in proportion to the initial shares of rental payments to the factors of production. If, as in Case 6, both factors of production are mobile in the long run, the burden of the tax will still be on the factors of production who remain employed, but the output effect would be stronger since the elasticity of supply would be greater than in Case 5, <u>ceteris paribus</u>.

<u>Cases 7 and 8--Import-Competing</u>. In Case 7, with fixed technical coefficients and immobile labor, the incidence and general equilibrium implications of the turnover tax will be identical to that described in

Case 3 since the perfectly elastic supply curve serves to limit the alternative opportunities open to producers. No output change is likely, however, given flexible relative wages. In Case 8, with mobile labor, the effect will be identical to Case 4 with output reductions being matched by output increases in the non-taxed industries. The output reduction will mean that state production declines and a higher tax rate will be required than with no output change.

Domestic Market

The remaining industry to be examined consists of those firms which produce wholly in the domestic market and for which there are no competitive firms operating outside of the state, in effect a closed economy on the use of income side, but an open economy on the sources of income side. If we assume a price elasticity of demand greater than zero, there being no untaxed alternative for the domestic consumer, and if we assume fixed supply of the factors of production in the market-period, we can argue in partial equilibrium terms that the burden of the tax will fall on the factors of production in West Virginia. To go beyond this limited conclusion brings us into the realm of uncertain effects and the necessity of moving further toward general equilibrium analysis. Under any other circumstances, our analysis must take account of both the tax and expenditure together. In this case, our conclusions are not about the effects of taxation, but about the effects of taxes and expenditures.

In general equilibrium terms, we may get around this dilemma by assuming that the transfer to the state does not change the relative mix of products produced, if initial prices prevail, and that the marginal propensity to spend by consumers and the government are the same. Under these assumptions, we may ignore the income distribution effect of the revenue expenditure and concentrate on the change in relative prices which may occur with the imposition of the tax. In a subsequent time period, if capital is mobile and labor is not and if production is governed by a Cobb-Douglas production function which is homogeneous of the first degree (Case 5), the incidence of the tax will be shared between the consumer and producer as a function of their relative elasticities. On the sources of income side, total output will decline, but the relative share of income to capital and labor will be the same. In effect, the state will have a reduction in its productive capacity and the producer's portion of the tax will be borne entirely by labor. Similar reasoning applies on the use of income side for consumers of domestic goods. On the use of income side, the decline in price paid to labor will be reflected in a downward shift in labor's demand curve for import-competing and domestic products, consistent with the now lowered level of total income. This will be matched by comparable opposite shifts in the state's demand curve for the same products, leaving no net change in aggregate demand or in the pattern of demand.

Under Case 6, with completely mobile labor and capital, further output declines will occur as producers attempt to pass the tax forward until the return to labor and capital is equal to that received by labor and capital outside the state. The entire burden of the tax will rest on the remaining persons in their capacities as consumers.[1] One might

---

[1]The idea that the burden of the tax will be borne by people in their capacity as consumers is justified on the grounds that the turnover tax is unlike a general sales tax which does not affect relative prices, but reduces the value of the marginal product of all factors, rich or poor by the same percentage. In contrast, turnover taxes (especially when they are levied at the state level) are not the same as general sales

question why some factors would remain to accept lower real income when they would not accept lower nominal income than could be obtained outside the state. The answer is that the demand for West Virginia domestic products is assumed to be less than perfectly elastic because, not being "import competing," it represents the total supply of such goods to West Virginia residents and, therefore, some price increase is possible, e.g., retail sales. If this is not true, then the demand for domestic products would cease to exist and all domestic consumption would be imported from outside. This possibility seems unlikely, however. Beyond the output effect, no additional change will occur on the uses side since the reduction in income on the uses side will be matched by the increase in income of the state government. On the other hand, if we assume that production is governed by fixed technical coefficients (Case 7), and labor is not mobile, the decline in labor's price will be even more drastic and there will be an increase in the share of total income going to capital. To the extent that this is reflected in differences in the demand for products, there will be a modification of the output of domestic goods. To the extent that capital is owned outside the state, this could mean a reduction of overall output, if the owners do not spend the increased share of dollars in West Virginia.

In Case 8, where labor is assumed to be completely mobile, the incidence of the tax is similar to Case 8 in the export- and import-competing analyses except that the income-compensated elasticity of

---

taxes and such taxes (turnover and sales taxes that are not fully equialent to general sales taxes) can be regarded as burdening people according to their spending patterns. See Joseph A. Pechman and Benjamin A. Okner, Who Bears the Tax Burden?, Studies of Government Finance (Washington, D.C.: The Brookings Institution, 1974), p. 31 and Musgrave, Theory of Public Finance, p. 348ff.

demand is likely to be lower and therefore more of the burden will be imposed on the consumers of West Virginia's domestic products. Some reduction in output is likely to occur due to the migration of capital and labor to the non-tax jurisdiction. The reduction of income on the use of income side, though, will be offset by the positive income effect of the revenue expenditures by state government.

Differential Incidence of the Income Value-Added Tax

We turn now to the differential incidence of an income value-added tax. We shall retain the same assumptions as under the turnover tax except that we are replacing an existing turnover tax with an equal yield income value-added tax and rate which provides the same real resource transfer as under the turnover tax. Both short- and long-run adjustments to the turnover tax are assumed to have been worked through. In general, the incidence of the income value-added tax is similar to that under the turnover tax in the sense that the change in tax will lead to the same general impact on the source and use of income but the burden will not be shared in precisely the same way because of the change in tax liability as the tax base changes from one of gross product or sales values to one of value added.

To understand how tax liabilities may change, a brief digression is in order. With the replacement of the turnover tax by a value-added tax we can show that for any firm or industry the percentage change in tax bill is measured by the following linear equation:

(4-1 $$\%\Delta Ti = -100 + \frac{V_r}{V_t}(V_i)(100)$$

where $\%\Delta Ti$ = percentage change in tax liability for a firm or industry

and -100 = Y intercept representing the removal of the turnover tax

and V_r = equal yield income value-added tax rate

and V_t = turnover-tax rate

and V_i = value-added ratio of a firm or industry =

$$\frac{\text{Income Value-Added Tax Base}_i}{\text{Turnover Tax Base}_i}$$

If the value-added ratio for a firm or industry is equal to the state-wide value-added ratio, there will be no change in tax bills and, hence, no change in incidence. If, however, a firm or industry's value-added ratio is higher than the average for the state, it will experience an increased tax liability. Conversely, if a firm or industry has a lower value-added ratio than the state-wide average it will experience a reduction in its tax bill. This statement will be true if all firms and industries pay a uniform rate under the turnover tax. In West Virginia, however, the differentiated rate structure imposes non-uniform tax liabilities and, therefore, some adjustment must be made to the equation above, namely

(4-2) $$\%\Delta Ti = -100 + \frac{V_r}{V_t}V'_i(100)$$

where V' is an adjusted value-added ratio which takes account of the relative proportion that the turnover tax liability for a firm or industry is to the average turnover tax liability for all firms.

thus,

$$V'_i = \frac{\text{Income Value-Added Tax Base}_i}{\text{Turnover Tax Base}_i} \div \frac{\text{Turnover Tax}_i/\text{Turnover Tax Base}_i}{\sum_{i=1}^{\eta}\text{Turnover Tax} \Big/ \sum_{i=1}^{\eta}\text{Turnover Tax Base}}$$

In the latter equation, equation 4-1 is weighted inversely by the extent to which an individual firm or industry pays more or less than the average turnover tax for all industries relative to the respective turnover tax bases. In the case where the firm or industry paid exactly equal amounts of turnover taxes relative to the turnover tax base, equation 4-2 reduces to equation 4-1.

Thus, firms or industries which might intuitively be viewed as high value added may in fact experience a reduction in tax liability if they paid considerably more turnover taxes than the average firm. The questions of which firms or industries would have positive or negative changes in tax bills, therefore, is an empirical one which we shall take up in Chapter VI. (Also, the actual tax bases depend on what adjustments the factors of production and the firms make. Thus, while the formula would always apply, the resulting tax liabilities would differ for the short run and long run according to what adjustments occurred.) For purposes of our theoretical differential incidence discussion, firms and industries which experience positive changes in tax liabilities will be identified as "high value-added" firms or industries while those who experience reductions in tax liability will be designated "low value-added" firms or industries. In this context, the reader should keep in mind that the "value-added" designation is an adjusted one which takes account of the previous turnover tax liability. Within each broad sector, there will be a redistribution of tax liability from firms and industries which have low-adjusted ratios of value added to gross to firms and industries which have high-adjusted ratios of value added to gross.

We are now in a position to discuss the differential incidence of the income value-added tax in each of the three markets. Before doing so, however, we need to make two assumptions. First, we assume that the value-added rate set is such that the revenue collected is equal to that under the turnover tax. Second, the aggregate value-added tax liabilities for each of the three broad sectors is equal to that paid under the turnover tax. The latter assumption is made in order to simplify the analysis, but is believed to be a reasonable assumption: If one considers that there are many firms and industries which operate in each broad sector and that these firms run the gamut of the production process from high to low value added, it seems reasonable to argue that overall sector tax liability may not change appreciably with the shift to an income value-added tax. Obviously, if the export sector is dominated by high value-added firms and the import-competing and domestic sectors are dominated by low value-added firms, more of the tax burden would shift to the export sector and our assumption would be violated. In the aggregate, if for each sector the overall tax liability does not change under the value-added tax, the "new" incidence will be the same as that under the turnover tax. However, the disaggregated burden on the source and uses of income will not be shared in the same way. Within each sector there will be a redistribution of tax liability from firms which have low-adjusted ratios of value added to gross to firms which have high-adjusted ratios of value added to gross. Though we will not go through the entire litany of the two time periods, as we did in the case of the turnover tax analysis, we will provide a brief synopsis for each of the three broad sectors.

Export Market. In the market period, we noted earlier that if the export sector produces for a market of which it has a relatively small part, such that it is faced by a perfectly elastic demand curve, and produces with resources which are highly specialized and fixed in the short run, the differential burden of the tax will rest on the factors of production in the industry. The entire effect of the tax change occurs on the sources of income side and no effect occurs on the uses side. The net change (positive or negative) in tax payment experienced by the firm will be shared by capital and labor in proportion to the amounts employed when the tax change is imposed. No change in output will occur, however. If the market period price elasticity of demand is less than infinite and the short-run supply is perfectly inelastic, the entire differential burden will be borne by the factors of production employed in the industry with gains to the factors of production employed in low value-added firms and losses to those employed in high value-added firms. If the price elasticity of demand is less than infinity and the elasticity of supply is less than perfectly inelastic, the gains and losses will be borne by both consumer and producer. On the uses side, there will be no change in the aggregate burden, but individual consumers may be made better or worse off depending on the relative portion of the budget spent on high and low value-added products.

In a subsequent time period, with the same demand conditions prevailing and assuming that capital is completely mobile but its owners and labor are not, and production is governed by a Cobb-Douglas production function which is homogeneous of the first degree (Case 1), the change in tax burden will shift to the fixed factor--labor. In the case of high value-added firms, there may be a reverse movement of capital from high to low value-added firms. With capital migration to the low value-added firms there will be an increase in output, the low value-added firm will become more capital intensive and the return to labor will rise as the influx of capital makes it more productive. The high value-added firm will become less capital intensive and the return to labor will fall as the outflow of capital reduces its productivity. On balance there should be no appreciable change in aggregate output over and above that occasioned by the imposition of the turnover tax, if the marginal productivity of labor and capital in both high and low value-added firms is the same. If labor is not mobile, the reduction in labor income in the high value-added firms will impact on the use of income side in the import-competing and domestic markets, causing a further shifting backward of the respective demand curves. This movement, however, will be offset by the shifting outward of the demand curve which is occasioned by the increase in income received by labor in the low value-added firms in the industry, assuming equal marginal propensities to spend.

Under Case 2, with mobile labor and all other conditions the same, we conjecture that at the margin, output will probably rise more than in Case 1 in the low value-added firms and fall more in the high value-added firms with both labor and capital migrating out of the high value-added firms and into the low value-added firms. The other general implications are the same as under Case 1.

If production is governed by fixed technical coefficients, and assuming that capital is perfectly mobile and labor is not (Case 3), the positive change in tax bills for high value-added firms will fall on labor with the corresponding gains enjoyed by labor employed in the low value-added firms. There will be no output change under these circumstances but burdens on labor in high value-added firms will increase. It should be noted that these are relative changes in burdens. In our earlier analysis of the incidence of the turnover tax, we noted that tax burdens within the industry would not be uniform. The higher the average effective turnover tax rates imposed, the higher the relative burdens on labor under the turnover tax and vice-versa for lower than average effective turnover tax rates. With the change to a value-added tax, these differential burdens on labor under the turnover tax are likely to be more nearly equal, but not always. If a firm paid higher than average turnover taxes and had a value added to gross ratio which is higher than average, the burden would increase. On the other hand, if a firm paid higher than average effective turnover tax rates but had a lower than average value-added ratio, they would have their tax bill reduced and, consequently, lower the burden. The reverse is true for firms which paid lower than average effective turnover tax rates.

If both capital and labor are mobile in the long run, there will be an increase in output in the low value-added firms and decreases in output of high value-added firms as both capital and labor migrate from high to low value-added firms.

The differential incidence of the value-added tax when the demand is less than perfectly elastic with respect to price (Cases 5-8) is similar to that of Cases 1 through 4, except that some portion of the change in tax burden will fall on consumers of the output of low and high value-added export firms. We have already noted these differential incidence implications in our earlier remarks. The producer's portion of the differential incidence will be as we have identified for Cases 1 through 4.

If the marginal propensity to spend is equal among consumer groups for West Virginia exports, no change in aggregate demand should occur since the loss in income occasioned by price increases of high value-added firms should be offset by price declines of low value-added firms. There may, however, be a shift in the consumption of high and low value-added export goods with the change in relative prices of the two types of export goods.

Import-Competing Market. With the imposition of the income value-added tax, the differential incidence in the market period (with fixed factors of production) will be completely borne by labor and capital in proportion to their contributions to the value added of the firm. This follows from our assumption of perfect elasticity of supply of imports from outside suppliers which acts in the same way as perfect elasticity of demand in the export sector. As in the export sector, this change in tax may be positive or negative.

In a subsequent time period, as in Case 5, there will be a net migration of capital from high to low value-added firms until the marginal returns to capital are again equal. As under the turnover tax, the differential burden of the value-added tax will be borne by labor in high value-added firms with gains going to labor employed in low value-added firms. If labor is mobile (Case 6) there will be a migration of labor from the high value-added firm to the low value-added firm until the burden of the tax is shared equally in proportion to the share of value added contributed by labor. Under Case 6 conditions, both labor and capital will bear the burden of the tax in proportion to their contribution to value added. The more elastic are the supplies of the factors of production, the stronger the shift in output will be from high to low value-added firms. If, as in Case 7, production is governed by fixed proportions and labor is fixed, the differential incidence is identical to that of Case 3 for the export sector while with variable labor and fixed proportions, the differential incidence is the same as Case 4 of the export sector.

If we assume equal marginal propensities to spend among the factors of production employed in the high and low value-added firms, there need be no change in aggregate demand since the decline in demand by factors employed in high value-added firms will be matched by increases in demand of those employed in low value-added firms. At the margin, the mix of high and low value-added products produced will shift and low value-added goods which were produced and sold through imports will now become import-competing and some high value-added goods formerly produced in the state may now become imports.

Needless to say, there could be either a net increase or decrease in total tax burden, depending on the actual elasticities of response and the changes in excess burden; therefore, the increases in aggregate demand and income need not precisely offset each other. Also the tax bills levied on the three broad sectors may not be the same, initially or subsequently, as they had been with the turnover tax. This equality was assumed here to simplify certain parts of the analysis, but in the end one's conclusions must be imprecise.

Domestic Market. The differential incidence of the income value-added tax within the domestic sector is similar to Cases 5 through 8 of the export sector. At the margin, we can expect that output will increase in low value-added firms and decline in high value-added firms. Unless the price elasticity of demand or the elasticity of supply of the domestic sector is zero, the differential burden will be experienced by both consumers and producers as a function of their relative elasticities. On the uses side, some parts of the burden will shift from consumers of the products of low value-added firms to consumers of the products of high value-added firms.[1] Whether this means a change in the relative position of individual consumers depends on the consumer's mix of products purchased from high and low value-added firms. On the sources side, the producers' burden will shift from labor and capital employed in low value-added firms to those employed in high value-added firms. Under conditions of fixed labor supply, mobile capital, and a Cobb-Douglas producton function homogeneous of the first degree (Case 5), the burden of the tax which formerly rested on labor as a function of the effective turnover tax rate imposed on individual firms will now be redistributed, with reductions in burden for labor employed in low value-added firms and increases in burden for labor employed in high value-added firms. Some portions of the domestic sector, however, which previously paid lower than average turnover tax rates and which have low value added (e.g., retail and wholesale) may experience increases in tax bills with the change to a value-added tax.

If both labor and capital are mobile (Case 6), larger changes in output (positive and negative) will probably occur as a consequence of the movement of labor and capital from high value-added firms to low value-added firms.

Under conditions of fixed technical coefficients with fixed labor and mobile capital (Case 7), no additional changes in output will occur as a result of the tax shift, but at the margin some portion of the burden will shift from labor in low value-added firms to labor in high value-

[1]See p. 128 above for the defined distinction between high and low value-added firms.

added firms. With completely mobile labor and capital and fixed technical coefficients (Case 8), the entire burden of the tax will occur on the uses of income side as labor and capital migrate from high to low value-added firms. The net effect of the tax change on output and on the uses of income may on balance be neutral, given equal marginal propensities to spend for the different consumer groups if the mix of high and low value-added goods is approximately equal for all consumers. From the source of income view, given equal marginal productivities, the same reasoning applies. Finally, the relative price of export- and import-competing goods will change and because of these changes, some domestic product prices will fall and still others will rise with additional impact on the factors of production employed. These second- and third-order effects should not change the differential incidence patterns in any systematic way, however.

Summary

In summary, the analysis leads one to expect that the incidence of the turnover tax and the differential incidence of the income value-added tax depend on the time period of analysis and the assumptions made with respect to demand, production function, supply of the factors of production, and the markets for which West Virginia firms produce.

The market period incidence of the turnover tax will fall on the fixed factors of production in West Virginia under conditions of perfect elasticity of demand for exports and supply of import products. If the demand for exports and supply of import products are perfectly inelastic, the entire incidence of the tax will fall on the consumers of West Virginia's exports and import-competing products.

To the extent that the elasticity of demand for export and supply of import products is greater than zero, but less than infinity, the incidence of the tax will fall on both the consumers of, and the factors of production employed in, the West Virginia export and import-competing sectors, unless the supply of exports and import-competing products is perfectly inelastic. If the latter circumstances are true, the turnover tax incidence will fall on the factors of production in West Virginia.

If we assume that the supplies of the factors are fixed and production is governed by fixed technical coefficients, no output change will occur, nor will there be any resource migration. Because factor supplies are not really fixed, some output declines could occur in the short run as well as some reduction in the employment of the factors of production. Assuming a passive monetary-fiscal policy at the federal level, the unemployment will signal an appropriate monetary response and overall prices will rise to accommodate sufficient additional shifting of the burden to the consumer until full employment is re-established. But we will not take up the various possibilities that arise when one considers the dynamics of unemployment or inflation. We may also expect no output declines if there are locational advantages to producing in West Virginia which are reflected in economic rents paid to the factors of production and these rents in each of the firms do not exceed the taxes levied under the turnover tax, assuming, of course, that the returns of these factors are flexible downward. The locational advantages would then yield the fixed factor supplies assumed part of the time above.

Any changes in final demand prices, employment of the factors of production, or output, will not be uniform within the sectors, however, because of the differentiated rate structure of the turnover tax. Those factors and consumers whose activity and consumption is taxed at above average rates will experience higher tax burdens while factors and consumers whose activities are taxed at below average rates will experience lower tax burdens. But further adjustments will depend on cross-elasticities and repercussions, unless assumed away.

In addition to the assumption with respect to demand, the longer-run incidence of the turnover tax will also depend on the form of the production function and the elasticity of supply of labor and capital. In particular we identified eight possible configurations or cases in which the incidence of the tax may be assessed. If the supply of capital is perfectly elastic and the supply of labor is fixed, the entire burden of the producer's portion of the tax will shift to labor. Further, output will decline if the operative production function is of a Cobb-Douglas type, but if the production function is of the fixed proportion type, no output effects will occur. In the latter circumstances, the return to labor will be less than under the Cobb-Douglas form. If both capital and labor are mobile in the long run, then both output and employment of the factors of production will decline in West Virginia and increase in the non-taxed areas.

From a general equilibrium view, other changes will take place. On the use of income side the change in relative prices as between the export, import-competing, and domestic markets will cause some realignment of consumption as will changes in the relative prices between West Virginia exports and competing non-taxed goods. No income effects on the uses side are likely, given our assumption of equal marginal propensities to spend by the different income recipients. On the sources of income side, changes in the price received by the factors of production in West Virginia will result in shifts in the demand for import-competing and domestic goods, but ignoring excess burdens, no change in aggregate demand will occur given our assumption of equal marginal propensities to spend. If excess burdens are present, we can expect output declines, higher tax rates to maintain the same real level of expenditures by state government, and some repercussions on aggregate demand.

The differential incidence of the income value-added tax involves burdens on the same general sources and uses of income but a shifting of burden away from factors employed by and consumers of low value-added firms to those connected with high value-added firms. This does not mean, however, that all of the burden is shifted. Some burden still remains on the producers with low value-added and the consumer of their output. Patterns of consumption will follow the changes in relative prices in the product markets, and changes in the employment of the factors of production will follow the changes in the relative prices paid to them.

Empirical Considerations

With respect to the incidence of the turnover tax and the differential incidence of the value-added tax, we have indicated the directional influence of possible effects on prices in consumer and factor markets with corresponding possible changes in demand, employment of the factors of production, and output. Some general equilibrium considerations have been introduced with the aid of selected sets of alternative assumptions. Propositions about these directional influences have not been tested, nor has any indication been given about the magnitude of these effects. At this point, we wish to explore empirically the price and factor employment effects associated with the shift from a turnover to a value-added tax by simulating the economy under one of the alternative sets of assumptions made in our theoretical analysis. Having done so, we will then discuss the longer-run implications of the empirical data.

For the simulation, we will use the data obtained with a stratified sample of tax returns of corporations doing buisness in West Virginia durirg the period 1967-1969[1] combined with the information obtained about the structure of the West Virginia economy in 1965 through an input-output study developed by Miernyk and Shellhammer.[2] These informational inputs are used for input-output calculations. Input-output explicitly recognizes the structural interdependence of an economy and permits one to trace through the effects of specific changes in a multimarket equilitrium system using linear programming techniques. Insofar as it takes account of the structural interdependence of the economy, input-output includes second- and third-order effects which go beyond the effects described by partial equilibrium analysis. The assumptions required, however, severely limit the conclusions which may be drawn. The input-output estimates, though crude at best, are probes that have not been attempted before. They may give some basis for assessing the effects of the tax change under consideration. We will use this input-output method to estimate some of the implications of certain cases above (i.e., sets of assumptions)--particularly implications about prices in consumer markets.

The form of input-output analysis which we will use is identified as an open, static model. It is open in the sense that some elements of

---

[1]Only the 1967 sample data will be used in this aspect of the study.

[2]William H. Miernyk, Kenneth L. Shellhammer et al., Simulating Regional Economic Development (Lexington, Mass.: D.C. Heath and Co., 1970).

the general equilibrium model are treated as exogeneous to the system. No attempt is made to introduce dynamic elements into the system. In the following, we will attempt to show the extent to which the assumptions underying this form of input-output analysis are consistent with the assumptions of the preceding theoretical discussion.

In general, input-output analysis requires that instead of looking at the firm and its relation to the consumer, the analyst looks to the nature of economic transactions among and within major industries as well as between major industries and the consumer. This does not violate our earlier assumption that the firm sells directly to the consumer, since we, in effect, aggregated all firms in each of the broad sectors and treated them as one firm for the theoretical analysis. Beyond this consideration, there are three additional critical assumptions required for input-output analysis which we need to examine for consistency with our theoretical assumptions.

First, the output of each industry is viewed as being composed of sales to other industries (intermediate goods) and sales to consumers (final goods). The technique requires rejection of the idea that final goods may be viewed as having moved through specific stages of production in a one-way manner. The coal industry, for example, sells coal to steel mills, electric utilities, and other energy users, but it also needs as inputs--steel in the form of equipment, electric energy to run the equipment, and goods from other industries in order to produce the coal. Thus, there are significant circular flows within the productive process and in some industries very little of the output may be sold to consumers as such. This is particularly true of the coal and oil industries. Given this kind of structural interdependence, we must modify our assumption made earlier that the industry sells directly to consumers and replace it with one which argues that though the industry may be shown to sell directly to the consumer, it also may sell to other industries--intermediate products--whose prices may have a bearing on the prices of other products in other markets. Likewise, changes in the prices of intermediate goods purchased from other industries by the same industry will influence the prices of goods it sells to final demand as well as the prices of intermediate goods it sells to the industries from which it purchases intermediate goods.

In terms of the subject of our discussion, the changes in tax which are imposed on individual firms and industries will not, therefore, be reflected directly in changes in price because some firms which experience reductions in their tax bill may pass their savings on to other firms which have experienced increases in the tax bills and vice-versa. Therefore, whether prices of final goods rise or fall depends on both the initial change in taxes and a complex flow of positive and negative changes in the prices of intermediate goods through the inter-industry flows among producers. Eventually these changes will be reflected in the price of the goods produced for consumption, or in the prices of factors of production, depending on the assumptions made with respect to the demand and supply elasticities. This is consistent with the earlier analysis. For instance, we said previously that the value-added tax might be shifted forward to consumers in part and back to factors of production in part; this means that part might end up, after a chain of transactions, on consumers and that part might end up on factors producing various ingredients in the final good.

If this is a correct assessment of the nature of the production process and its relationship to consumer markets, one cannot draw conclusions about the incidence or differential incidence of a tax solely as a function of the proportion of early- and late stage value-added goods consumption by specific income groups as Shoup does in his arguments. Instead, one must look empirically to the change in the consumption mix of the products of high and low value-added firms by consumers of West Virginia's products if we wish to assess the relative welfare position of different income groups. Needless to say, this would be a formidable empirical task.[1]

The second major assumption of input-output analysis is that the technical coefficients of production are fixed in that the inputs required to produce a given commodity are known and unvarying. This is consistent with the constant returns to scale and with our assumption of a production function governed by fixed proportions. It should be noted, however, that in addition to the primary factors of production, labor and capital, we include as inputs to the producing sector purchases of intermediate goods from other industries which are a fixed proportion of each industry's output.

Though prices of the inputs may change, and, therefore, prices in final demand markets, the conditions of production will not if the West Virginia economy is to produce the same mix of final products. This proposition is the third major assumption of the open, static input-output model, i.e., final demand is considered exogenous to the system. The exogenous character of demand is contrary to some of our assumptions about the elasticity of demand. We will, however, employ the input-output model together with the sample corporate data in three simulations of conditions which are consistent with <u>some</u> of our sets of theoretical

---

[1]See p. 128 above for the defined difference between high and low value-added firms.

assumptions. We move now to a discussion of the underlying assumptions, methods, and results of these three alternative simulations.

Simulation Model A

Assumptions and Methods. Before examining the differential incidence of the income value-added tax, we need to specify the assumed long-run incidence conditions from which the change is being made. Inasmuch as the West Virginia turnover tax has been in existence for some forty years, we assume that the conditions of Case 8 apply in the long run to the turnover tax, i.e., the factors of production are completely mobile, fixed proportions in production exist over the relevant range of output, and the long-run elasticity of demand is less than infinity. Under these circumstances, we concluded, in our theoretical discussion, that the long-run incidence of the turnover tax was borne by the consumers of West Virginia products. We assume further that all short- and long-run adjustments in demand, output, and employment of the factors of production have been worked out. The input-output estimated value of sales to final demand by each sector in 1967 is, therefore, assumed to be inclusive of the turnover taxes levied.

With the change to an income value-added tax, we make some extreme assumptions to see some of the possible outcomes. We assume that the price elasticity of demand is equal to zero in the three broad sectors, and that all changes in prices of intermediate goods will be passed on to become changes in the prices of final goods. The process of change in prices is different from our theoretical model, however. Whereas, in our theoretical model we assumed that all firms sold directly to the consumer, we are now assuming that changes in prices will flow to the consumer through a principal industry in a direct way, and in an indirect way, through the changes in prices associated with the flow of intermediate goods in the production process. We further assume that the short-run production function is the fixed proportion type and that purchases of intermediate goods from other industries are a fixed proportion of the total output of each industry. This set of assumptions comes closest to approximating our theoretical assumptions for analyzing possible effects with inelastic demand and fixed proportions in production.[1] Though these assumptions are extreme, they do provide a basis for developing some clues to the effects of such a tax change, a task that has not been attempted before.

To measure the change in prices in final markets, we will first estimate the amount of direct and indirect turnover taxes paid per dollar of delivery to final demand by each industry, and then simulate the amount of direct and indirect value-added taxes per dollar of delivery to final demand. From these two figures, we will be able to construct a simulated index of price changes and note the change in relative prices of final goods for each of the industries as well as note the change in overall prices in the export market and the combined import-competing and domestic markets. Given the nature of our data, it is not possible empirically to separate these latter two markets. Nor is it possible in the export market to separate sales to consumers from sales of intermediate products to other industries outside of the state. This means that our projection of the effects of the tax change will not be as precise as in a theoretical discussion. In the export market, it will mean that price

---

[1]See p. 109.

changes accompanying the sale of intermediate goods will be diffused to sales of other goods in other markets, about which we have no knowledge. Thus, the direct effect on consumers of West Virginia export goods will be overstated, since "Final Demand" from the West Virginia model perspective is composed of sales to consumers and sales to intermediate industries in the United States. In effect, West Virginia's exports will be handled as though they were all final goods.

If the relative prices of final goods change, short-run and especially long-run considerations would suggest that the mix of final demand goods will change and, hence, may alter the use and quantity of inputs used. Our simulation model, however, does not permit us to develop quantitative estimates of these effects.[1] We will, however, engage in a speculative discussion of the further repercussions and long-run implications of the simulation data after concluding our analysis of the immediate effects.

As we noted earlier, the simulation depends on two principal sources of data: (1) the input-output study for deriving the base year of our study; and (2) our own stratified sample of federal and state

---

[1]One may, by using a closed input-output model, overcome some of the limitations identified by incorporating final demand as an endogenous variable and by identifying the labor and capital coefficients to establish the effects of changes in the price of intermediate goods on factor usage, factor prices, and final goods prices. This would require, however, the acquisition of more time, data, and funds than are currently available. It would, however, represent the next step in a continuation of a study of this sort. See Robert Dorfman, Paul A. Samuelson, and Robert M. Solow, Linear Programming and Economic Analysis (New York: McGraw-Hill Book Co., 1958), pp. 245-48 and Chapter 11 for a discussion of how this might be accomplished. The Dorfman, Samuelson, Solow text in its entirety is a comprehensive discussion of the types and uses of input-output analysis.

corporate tax returns for the period 1967-1969 for deriving the initial value-added base, tax rate, and tax changes.[1]

We begin by using the 1965 transaction table of the input-output study whicn shows the dollar value of sales to and purchases from each industry as well as sales to final demand.[2] This table, which identifies 48 processing industries, was collapsed into 24 processing industries to conform with the industry classification adopted for this study. Table 7 identifies the input-output industries which were merged into the 24 industries of this study. The 48 processing industries are identified in Table 8. In addition, industry import purchases, sales to the export and domestic private sectors were picked up. From this information a 24 X 26 matrix was derived, representing the 24 processing industries plus the two exogenous sectors of final export demand and final private domestic demand (import-competing and domestic). Through a series of algebraic steps, the details of which are provided in Appendix B, this 1965 modified transactions table together with the information provided by our corporate sample was used to derive 1967 estimates of the following magnitudes: (1) gross output by industry; (2) value of sales by each industry to export and domestic markets; and (3) 1967 turnover taxes paid by industry. The assumption used to generate these estimates was that the gross output of the 24 industries in 1967 was proportionally the same as in 1965. During this process of calibrating the 1965 study to fit the year 1967, three problems arose. First, as Table 9 shows,

---

[1]The specific details of the algebraic input-output model and the associated methods used to derive the simulation data are contained in Appendix B. Appendix A contains the detail on the sampling procedure, results, and representativeness of the sample data.

[2]Miernyk, Simulating Regional Economic Development, pp. 239-45.

TABLE 7

MODIFICATION OF THE 1965 INPUT-OUTPUT INDUSTRY MIX TO CONFORM WITH INDUSTRY GROUPS USED IN STUDY

Industry Group In This Study	Industry Description	1965 Input-Output Industries That Were Combined
1	Coal Mining	2, 3
2	Crude Petroleum & Natural Gas	4
3	Building	6
4	Highway & Street Construction	7
5	Special Trade Contractors	8
6	Food & Kindred Products	9, 10, 11, 12
7	Textile Mill, Apparel & Other Textiles	13
8	Chemicals & Allied Products	17
9	Glass & Glass Products	19
10	Stone & Clay Products	20
11	Primary Metals	21
12	Fabricated Metals	22
13	Machinery, Including Electrical	23, 24
14	Transportation Equipment	25
15	All Other Manufacturing	1, 5, 14, 15, 16 18, 26, 27
16	Rail & Related Services	42
17	Motor Freight & Related Services	43
18	All Other Transportation	44
19	Communication & Public Utilities	45, 46, 47, 48
20	Wholesale Trade	29
21	Retail Trade	28, 30, 31, 32
22	Finance	33, 34, 35, 37
23	Real Estate	36
24	Services	38, 39, 40, 41

TABLE 8

1965 INPUT-OUTPUT: 48--INDUSTRY IDENTIFICATION

Industry	Industry Description
1	Agriculture
2	Coal Mining (Underground)
3	Coal Mining (Strip and Auger)
4	Petroleum and Natural Gas
5	All Other Mining
6	General Contractors (Building)
7	General Contractors (Nonbuilding)
8	Special Trades Contractors
9	Food and Kindred Products (n.e.c.)
10	Food and Kindred Products (Dairies)
11	Food and Kindred Products (Bakeries)
12	Food and Kindred Products (Beverages)
13	Apparel and Accessories
14	Logging and Sawmills
15	Furniture and Other Wood Fabrication
16	Printing and Publishing
17	Chemicals
18	Petroleum
19	Glass
20	Stone and Clay Products
21	Primary Metal Products
22	Fabricated Metal Products
23	Machinery (Except Electrical)
24	Electrical Machinery and Apparatus
25	Transportation Equipment
26	Instruments and Related Products
27	All Other Manufacturing
28	Eating and Drinking Establishments
29	Wholesale Trade
30	Retail Food Stores
31	Retail Gasoline Service Stations
32	All Other Retail
33	Banking
34	Other Finance
35	Insurance Agents and Brokers
36	Real Estate
37	All Other FIRE
38	Hotels and Other Lodging Places
39	Medical and Legal Services
40	Educational Services
41	All Other Services
42	Railroads
43	Trucking and Warehousing
44	All Other Transportation
45	Communications
46	Electric Companies and Systems
47	Gas Companies and Systems
48	Water and Sanitary Services

TABLE 9

COMPARISON OF WEST VIRGINIA GROSS
AS ESTIMATED BY THE TAX DEPARTMENT
AND THE INPUT-OUTPUT METHOD
1967 ($000)

Industry Identification	Estimated Gross by Tax Department[a]	Estimated Gross for Input-Output Calculations
Coal Mining	843,247	796,048
Crude Petroleum & Natural Gas	71,448	61,921
Building	163,506	182,122
Highway & Street Construction	219,636	183,943
Special Trade Contractors	100,318	149,340
Food & Kindred Products	98,836	219,457
Textile Mill, Apparel & Other Textiles	105,142	24,586
Chemicals & Allied Products	1,090,294	1,354,077
Glass & Glass Products	226,764	282,289
Stone & Clay Products	133,473	139,323
Primary Metals	892,224	996,208
Fabricated Metals	148,686	126,574
Machinery, Including Electrical	33,972	118,379
Transportation Equipment	42,982	186,675
All Other Manufacturing	171,610	580,969
Rail & Related Services	243,820	224,010
Motor Freight & Related Services	28,252	195,781
All Other Transportation	22,731	53,726
Communication & Public Utilities	435,722	715,739
Wholesale Trade	1,282,033	325,088
Retail Trade	1,918,182	702,081
Finance	25,651	502,657
Real Estate	203,380	63,743
Services	571,031	921,538
Total	9,108,104	9,108,104

[a]Unpublished data furnished by the West Virginia State Tax Department.

the effect of our assumption of constant output proportions did not conform well with the distribution of 1967 gross as identified by the West Virginia Tax Department. There are two technical reasons why a closer identity was not established. First, the tax department reports gross activity not by firm identity, but by the declaration of gross in each taxable class under the turnover tax. By contrast, gross identified for input-output purposes is assigned to specific industries net of the cost of goods sold. The cost of goods sold was allocated to the industries from which they were purchased. Thus, goods purchased for resale by wholesalers and retailers were assigned to the manufacturing industries from which they were purchased and only the markup was assigned to the wholesale and retail industries. Similarly, utility purchases of electricity, water, and sewage were assigned to the appropriate utility industry, just as transportation costs for all industries were assigned to the appropriate transportation industry. This practice is essential for input-output purposes for otherwise one would have virtually all sales to final demand being bunched up in the retail and services industries.[1] There is no satisfying solution to this problem of reconciling reported gross by industry for tax purposes with that defined for input-output purposes; one must simply recognize its existence.

A second related issue which arose was our concern that the input-output estimates of gross, value added, and turnover and value-added tax revenue be consistent with the corresponding estimates based on our corporate sample which are used in other parts of this study. It became apparent that the estimates provided by these two methods would

---

[1]For an elaboration on this point, see the recent discussion in the Survey of Current Business, February 1974, p. 56.

not coincide. The reason, as we have noted in the preceding paragraph, is due to the difference in the definition of gross for tax purposes and that for input-output purposes.

If the magnitude of gross by industry sector differs, as between the two methods, then the estimate of value added, and turnover and value-added taxes will also differ since they are in part based on gross. Since the results of the two methods cannot be reconciled, some comparison of the estimates under the two points of view needs to be provided.

A third issue which arose concerns the differentiated rate structure and its effect on relative prices. In order to show how much relative prices are distorted under the turnover tax and the income value-added tax, a standard in which relative prices are not distorted was needed. These considerations led us to develop three different value-added versions to trace the price effects of the tax change in relative prices.

Version 1. In this version we use the traditional definition of value added (i.e., gross value added rather than income value added)[1] and derive an appropriate rate (to yield the designated revenue) based on the input-output model. Then we trace the initial price effects (assuming no adjustments) on the final demand sectors. Here the interpretation of the data would conform strictly with that of the input-output concept but would have the disadvantage of using a base which included value added everywhere, i.e., the gross value-added form. By using this version as a base line, however, we will be able to trace the distortion in relative prices under the turnover tax and the income value-added tax.

---

[1]Gross value added is defined as total income minus intermediate purchases, not including capital purchases or depreciation allowances. Income value added is defined as total income minus intermediate purchases, not including capital purchases but including an allowance for depreciation.

<u>Version 2</u>. This version represents an attempt on our part to bring the input-output model as close to conformity as possible with the proposed value-added tax statute. It derives value added in input-output terms and subtracts imports and depreciation and eliminates from the value-added tax base those industries which are exempted by the proposed statute. At the same time, it permits changes in the price of intermediate goods to be reflected in the value of goods produced by these industries. As will be noted later, this version comes closest to, though the estimated base is larger than, the value-added tax base estimated through the use of our stratified sample of corporate tax returns. Our speculation is that the reason for the remaining difference has to do with the shifting of bases in the input-output model from low value-added industries into that of high value-added industries, thus implying a lower value-added tax rate than would actually be the case.

<u>Version 3</u>. In this version we treat the value-added tax revenue data by industry as an exogenous input to the model and establish the relevant price effects on the two final demand sectors. The interpretation of the data rests upon industry identities and income value-added levels as defined for statutory revenue purposes and as simulated by the use of our corporate sample for 1967.

A final point to be made is that in all three versions the turnover tax collections by industry were treated as an exogenous variable because of the complications created by the differentiated rate structure. If turnover tax collections had been identified separately in the 1965 input-output study, it would have been possible to generate input-output estimated turnover tax collections by input-output industry for 1967.

This means, therefore, that the input-output industry's turnover tax coefficients identified later in the text are somewhat distorted, i.e., overstated for the wholesale trade, retail trade, and services industries and understated for the manufacturing and communication and public utility industries. The same caveat would be true for the interpretation of the value-added tax coefficients in Version 3.

Simulation Results. The principal measure used to trace through the percentage change in prices in this model is a tax coefficient which has a direct and an indirect component. The direct component is the change in the amount of direct taxes paid per dollar of delivery to final demand by each of the industries. The indirect component is the change in the amount of indirect taxes paid per dollar of delivery to final demand by each of the industries. These arise from changes in prices of inputs reflecting taxes on intermediate goods purchased by each of the processing industries. The sum of these two coefficients gives us the total change in amount of taxes per dollar of delivery to final demand. By comparing the estimated taxes paid per dollar of delivery to final demand under Version 1 with the estimated taxes paid under the turnover tax and the taxes paid under Versions 2 and 3 of the value-added tax, we can get clues to the extent of the relative distortions in prices paid by consumers in the two final demand markets. We will also be able to estimate the extent to which the relative price differences under the turnover tax may be reduced with the shift to an income value-added tax. Table 10 shows the estimated direct and indirect taxes paid per dollar of delivery to final demand under the assumption that all of the tax has been passed forward. Column 1 shows the tax coefficients for the

TABLE 10

TAX COEFFICIENT BY INDUSTRY SHOWING THE AMOUNT OF DIRECT AND INDIRECT TAXES PAID BY ALL INDUSTRIES PER DOLLAR OF DELIVERY TO FINAL DEMAND BY EACH INDUSTRY UNDER THE TURNOVER TAX AND THE INCOME VALUE-ADDED TAX WEST VIRGINIA, 1967

Simulation Model A
(Burden on Consumers)

Industry Identification	Turnover Tax	Value-Added Version		
		1	2	3
	1	2	3	4
Coal Mining	.0157	.0113	.0128	.0098
Crude Petroleum & Natural Gas	.0572	.0113	.0130	.0094
Building	.0275	.0113	.0152	.0144
Highway & Street Construction	.0283	.0113	.0136	.0150
Special Trade Contractors	.0158	.0113	.0164	.0095
Food & Kindred Products	.0055	.0113	.0098	.0056
Textile Mill, Apparel & Other Textiles	.0330	.0113	.0200	.0356
Chemicals & Allied Products	.0095	.0113	.0101	.0116
Glass & Glass Products	.0080	.0113	.0152	.0090
Stone & Clay Products	.0098	.0113	.0133	.0088
Primary Metals	.0079	.0113	.0066	.0126
Fabricated Metals	.0105	.0113	.0100	.0126
Machinery, Including Electrical	.0035	.0113	.0049	.0047
Transportation Equipment	.0032	.0113	.0100	.0042
All Other Manufacturing	.0046	.0113	.0095	.0044
Rail & Related Services	.0108	.0113	.0139	.0152
Motor Freight & Related Services	.0042	.0113	.0149	.0037
All Other Transportation	.0134	.0113	.0106	.0080
Communication & Public Utilities	.0252	.0113	.0084	.0111
Wholesale Trade	.0103	.0113	.0197	.0218
Retail Trade	.0158	.0113	.0167	.0203
Finance	.0015	.0113	.0175	.0019
Real Estate	.0304	.0113	.0186	.0276
Services	.0075	.0113	.0066	.0101
Average taxes paid per dollar of delivery to final demand	.0150	.0113	.0128	.0120
Standard Deviation	.0129	.0113	.0042	.0079

turnover tax and the tax coefficients for the value-added tax under each of the versions (Cols. 2, 3, 4). The coefficients show the total of direct and indirect taxes paid by all industries per dollar of delivery to final demand by the industries identified in the stub of the table. Thus, for the turnover tax, for every dollar delivered to final demand by the coal industry, it is estimated to have generated turnover taxes of 1.57¢. This is to be contrasted with the value-added coefficients 1.13¢ (Version 1), 1.28¢ (Version 2), and 0.98¢ (Version 3).

To estimate whether the change to a value-added tax would reduce the relative differences in taxes borne for delivery to final demand, the ratios were summed and averaged, and the standard deviation was calculated, the results being exhibited at the bottom of Table 10 in Columns 1-4. Under Version 1, our estimates showed no distortions in relative prices inasmuch as the amount of direct and indirect taxes paid per dollar of delivery to final demand was 1.13¢ for all industries. The uniformity of the Version 1 coefficients is of particular interest.[1] They suggest that neutralizing relative price differences due to the turnover tax and generating the same amount of revenue would require a gross value-added tax which would generate a uniform 1.13¢ per dollar of delivery to final demand.

The turnover tax by contrast distorts relative prices inasmuch as the standard deviation of direct and indirect turnover taxes paid per dollar of delivery to final demand was estimated to be 1.29¢. The

---

[1]Parenthetically, this version provides some evidence for the proposition advanced by some that the value-added tax is neutral with respect to final demand. Neutrality, however, requires that nothing be exempted and no credit be given the capital purchases. This is contrary to the traditional argument which states that neutrality is achieved with the consumption value-added tax. See the discussion by Ture, "Economics of the Value-Added Tax," for an example of the traditional argument.

comparable standard deviation with the move to an income value-added tax was estimated to be 0.42¢ (Version 2) and 0.79¢ (Version 3). Thus, under Model A, our simulation suggests that the distortion in relative prices among industry consumer groups would be reduced by 2/3 (Version 2) or 1/3 (Version 3) with the shift to an income value-added tax.

The relative price differences remaining under the income value-added tax are a result of specific leakages in the base attributable to variations in import purchases patterns, depreciation schedules, and the statutory provisions which exempt the following industries: agriculture, insurance, state and local education, medical, and government-operated public utilities. The reader should keep in mind, of course, that these calculations rest on a particular and extreme set of assumptions.

We may also use these tax coefficients to estimate the effect of the tax change on final prices. Since we have assumed that final demand may not change with changes in prices of final goods, we may take any changes in the value of final goods as an expression of their change in price. To express the changes in index terms, we set all prices in the final market equal to one under the turnover tax. Then we add algebraically the change in tax coefficients for each of the industries to this initial price to yield a price index value, i.e.,

$$\text{Price Index}_i = (1 + \Delta TC_i)(100)$$

where i is the ith industry and ΔTC_i is the change in tax coefficients for the ith industry.

For example, the change in tax coefficient for the coal industry under Version 1 is equal to -0.0044 (.0113 - .0157). Adding this value to the initial value of 1 and multiplying by 100 yields an index of 99.56 or a reduction of less than 1/2 of 1 per cent. Table 11 shows, for each

TABLE 11

NEW PRICE INDICES FOR INDUSTRY DEMAND SECTORS
AFTER THE SHIFT FROM A TURNOVER TAX
TO A VALUE-ADDED TAX IN WEST VIRGINIA
1967

Simulation Model A
(Burden on Consumers)

Industry Identification	Value-Added Tax Version 1	Version 2	Version 3
	1	2	3
Coal Mining	99.55	99.70	99.40
Crude Petroleum & Natural Gas	95.41	95.58	95.22
Building	98.38	98.77	98.69
Highway & Street Construction	98.30	98.53	98.68
Special Trade Contractors	99.55	100.06	99.38
Food & Kindred Products	100.58	100.43	100.01
Textile Mill, Apparel & Other Textiles	97.83	98.70	100.26
Chemicals & Allied Products	100.18	100.07	100.21
Glass & Glass Products	100.33	100.72	100.10
Stone & Clay Products	100.15	100.35	99.02
Primary Metals	100.37	99.86	100.47
Fabricated Metals	100.08	99.55	100.22
Machinery, Including Electrical	100.78	100.15	100.12
Transportation Equipment	100.81	100.68	100.10
All Other Manufacturing	100.67	100.49	99.98
Rail & Related Services	100.05	100.31	100.44
Motor Freight & Related Services	100.70	101.07	99.55
All Other Transportation	99.79	99.72	99.46
Communication & Public Utilities	98.60	98.32	98.58
Wholesale Trade	100.09	100.93	101.14
Retail Trade	99.55	100.09	100.45
Finance	100.98	101.60	100.05
Real Estate	98.08	98.81	99.71
Services	100.39	99.92	100.27

of the producing industries, the combined direct and indirect effects on final prices. If all of the tax change is passed forward, the prices in each industry's consumer markets would change as indicated. The reader should note that we are here identifying each industry's change in price for goods sold to the export and the combined import-competing and domestic markets, under the stated assumptions.

Looking at the high value-added industries under Version 2 (value-added taxes determined endogenously) only two industry consumer groups will experience price increases of more than 1 per cent: finance, 1.6 per cent and motor freight, 1.07 per cent. All other high value-added industry consumer groups will experience price increases from 7/100 of 1 per cent (chemicals) to 3/4 of 1 per cent (glass and glass products). For high value-added industries under Version 3 (taxes determined exogenously) only the wholesale trade industry's consumers will experience an increase in price exceeding 1 per cent. All other high value-added industry's consumers will experience increases in price ranging from 1/100 of 1 per cent (food) to 1/2 of 1 per cent (primary metals).

For the low value-added industries (Version 2) decreases of more than 1 per cent in prices will be enjoyed by consumers of crude petroleum and natural gas (-4.42 per cent), building construction (-1.23 per cent), highway and street construction (-1.47 per cent), textile mills (-1.30 per cent), communication and public utilities (-1.68 per cent), and real estate (-1.19 per cent). All other low value-added consumers will enjoy price reductions varying from 8/100 of 1 per cent (services) to 1/2 of 1 per cent (fabricated metals).

Table 12 summarizes the results and shows that 13 industries may be classified as high value added with 11 of the 13 industry groups

TABLE 12

PERCENTAGE CHANGE IN PRICE FOR HIGH AND LOW VALUE-ADDED INDUSTRIES, WEST VIRGINIA, 1967

Simulation Model A--Versions 2 and 3
(Burden on Consumers)

Industry Identification	Version 2				Version 3			
	High Value-Added Positive Change		Low Value-Added Negative Change		High Value-Added Positive Change		Low Value-Added Negative Change	
	>1	<1	>1	<1	>1	<1	>1	<1
Coal Mining				X				X
Crude Petroleum & Natural Gas			X				X	
Building			X				X	
Highway & Street Construction			X				X	
Special Trade Contractors		X						X
Food & Kindred Products		X				X		
Textile Mill, Apparel & Other Textiles			X			X		
Chemicals & Allied Products		X				X		
Glass & Glass Products		X				X		
Stone & Clay Products		X						X
Primary Metals				X		X		
Fabricated Metals				X		X		
Machinery, Including Electrical		X				X		
Transportation Equipment		X				X		
All Other Manufacturing		X						X
Rail & Related Services		X				X		
Motor Freight & Related Services	X							X
All Other Transportation				X				X
Communication & Public Utilities			X				X	
Wholesale Trade		X			X			
Retail Trade		X				X		
Finance	X					X		
Real Estate			X					X
Services				X		X		
Totals	2	11	6	5	1	12	4	7

experiencing price increases of less than 1 per cent and the remaining 2 experiencing price increases of greater than 1 per cent. Eleven industries are classified as low value added with 6 of the 11 industry consumer groups experiencing price declines of greater than 1 per cent and the remaining 5 consumer groups experiencing price declines of less than 1 per cent.

The remaining empirical task is to simulate the overall effects on prices in the export market and the combined markets of import-competing and domestic. To do this each of the 24 industry's price index is weighted by the relative proportion of each industry's value of aggregate final demand, measured before the change to the income value-added tax. Table 13 presents the results for each of the versions in each of the markets.

The overall price level of exports will decline slightly by approximately 6/100 of 1 per cent under Version 2 or by 1/100 of 1 per cent under Version 3. In the domestic market, overall prices will fall by 1/100 of 1 per cent (Version 3) or increase by 8/100 of 1 per cent (Version 2). In relative terms, overall export goods will become slightly cheaper (.14 per cent) when compared with domestic goods under Version 2, but no different under Version 3. These results are consistent with our theoretical assumption (p. 129) that tax liabilities would not change appreciably in each of the broad sectors with the shift to a value-added tax. One may judge that the relative competitive position of the state vis-a-vis the "non-taxed" areas will not be greatly changed in the market period.

By comparing the Version 2 and 3 indexes with that of Version 1, we may observe that neutrality among final prices would require an

TABLE 13

COMPARISON OF NEW PRICE INDICES BY FINAL DEMAND SECTOR
ACCOMPANYING THE SHIFT FROM A TURNOVER TAX
TO A VALUE-ADDED TAX IN WEST VIRGINIA
1967

Simulation Model A
(Burden on Consumers)

Final Demand Sector	Version 1	Value-Added Tax Version 2	Version 3
	1	2	3
Export Market	100.03	99.94	99.99
Domestic and Import-Competing Markets	99.96	100.08	99.99

increase in overall prices of 3/100 of 1 per cent in the export market and a decline in overall prices of 4/100 of 1 per cent in the domestic markets. Any quest for neutrality, however, is academic since the tax form required for such a levy would have to tax import purchases of consumers as well as firms, with no allowances for capital expenditures or the exemption of specific industries, i.e., a gross value-added tax--Version 1.[1] Such tax action would require rejection of currently accepted "truths" that public and private non-profit activities be exempt from taxation, that some form of allowances for capital purchases are deemed necessary to encourage capital expansion, and that one should not discriminate as between imports and intra-state intermediate purchases.

A final question to be asked is "What are the magnitudes of feedback effects not taken into account in this simulation?" Since the estimated effects are less than 1 per cent for the high value-added industries, the feedback effects are likely to be less than 1 per cent and may, for all practical purposes, be ignored. This also applies to the low value-added industries which have estimated price declines of less than 1 per cent. The only exceptions possible in the export market under Version 3 are in the crude petroleum and natural gas, communication and public utilities, building, highway and street construction industries where declines in price exceed 1 per cent and in the wholesale trade industry where prices increased by more than 1 per cent. These simulation results are crude at best and are indicative of possible effects under a limited set of assumptions. In our concluding observations at the end of this chapter, we will attempt to say what, if anything, all three simulations show.

---

[1]See footnote 1, p. 156 above for the context in which neutrality is defined.

Simulation Model B

Assumptions and Method. The principal difference between Models B and A is that we are now assuming that the elasticity of demand for exports and the supply elasticities of imports is infinite. Our intent is to demonstrate by contrast what the effects of extreme assumptions are on the uses of income (Simulation Model A) and on the sources of income (Simulation Model B). By this procedure we may get a feel for the limits by which either the source or uses of income may be affected. In our final simulation (Model C), we will look to some intermediate set of assumptions that will include initial effects on both the sources and uses of income.

Aside from our demand assumption, we assume that the supply of the factors of production are fixed and are used in fixed proportions, that the conditions of Case 8 apply to the long-run incidence of the turnover tax, and that all adjustments in demand, output, and employment to the turnover tax have been worked through. (Indeed, in any particular situation, if the supply of factors is fixed, they would bear the burden of the tax, as long as the price elasticity of demand exceeds zero). Under these conditions the imposition of the value-added tax creates no change in the short-run prices of intermediate goods and, therefore, no change in the price of final goods. There will, however, be changes in the payments to the factors of production in the different industries. Under this set of assumptions, we can estimate the magnitude of change in the return to the factors of production, both collectively and individually.

We can best measure these changes in the prices paid to the factors of production by using our stratified sample of corporate tax returns with which we have previously estimated industry turnover taxes and value added by industry and simulated the value-added taxes. The change in tax for high and low value-added industries will be expressed as a percentage of total value added and as a percentage of estimated wages and payments to capital (rents, interest, and profits) for each of the producing industries. This will provide us with estimates of the magnitude of changes in payments to the factors of production in the high and low value-added industries (with the assumptions specified).

From a long-run point of view, we know that changes in the price paid to the factors of production may alter the combination of inputs used which in turn will lead to changes in the technical coefficients of production, changes in output levels of different industries, and changes in the level of demand. The simulation data collected does not permit adjustments of this sort and, therefore, the question of the long-run implications of the changes in this case will be speculative.

Simulation Results. Given the assumptions above, which deny the possibility of output changes or changes in the prices paid by consumers, the change in tax bills for each industry is the amount the return to the factors of production will have to be reduced. Expressing the change in tax bills as a percentage of the payments to the factors of production (income value added), the necessary percentage reduction will be obtained. We argued in our theoretical analysis that the differential burden of the tax will be borne in proportion to the contribution to value added of the factors of production. The percentage figure derived, therefore, applies to the return to both factors. Table 14 provides our results for this assumed incidence of the value-added tax. Column 2 identifies the value-

TABLE 14

DIFFERENTIAL INCIDENCE OF THE INCOME VALUE-ADDED TAX
WEST VIRGINIA, 1967

Simulation Model B
(Burden on Factors of Production)

Industry Identification	Value Added ($000)	Turnover Tax ($000)	Value-Added Tax ($000)	Per Cent Change in Payments to the Factors of Production (Col. 3 - 4/2)
1	2	3	4	5
Coal Mining	257,604	11,123	6,749	+ 1.70
Crude Petroleum	17,721	3,328	464	+16.16
Building	54,651	3,308	1,432	+ 3.43
Highway & Street Construction	79,324	4,444	2,078	+ 2.98
Special Trade Contractors	40,206	2,030	1,053	+ 2.43
Food & Kindred Products	30,172	743	791	- 0.16
Textile Mill, Apparel & Other Textiles	33,250	790	871	- 0.24
Chemicals & Allied Products	443,148	8,121	11,610	- 0.79
Glass & Glass Products	80,594	1,696	2,112	- 0.52
Stone & Clay Products	36,528	1,029	957	+ 0.20
Primary Metals	442,418	6,635	11,591	- 1.12
Fabricated Metals	51,873	1,114	1,359	- 0.47
Machinery, Including Electrical	14,510	260	380	- 0.83
Transportation Equipment	18,364	327	481	- 0.84
All Other Manufacturing	55,317	1,300	1,449	- 0.27
Rail & Related Services	119,189	2,100	3,123	- 0.86
Motor Freight & Related Services	14,839	577	389	+ 1.27
All Other Transportation	12,771	504	335	+ 1.32
Communication & Public Utilities	252,148	14,300	6,606	+ 3.05
Wholesale Trade	252,778	2,757	6,623	- 1.53
Retail Trade	489,558	9,536	12,826	- 0.67
Finance	18,113	249	475	- 1.25
Real Estate	59,256	1,580	1,500	+ 0.14
Services	288,668	4,737	7,563	- 0.98

added estimates for 1967 for each of the 24 industries. Column 3 shows the estimated amount of turnover taxes levied in 1967, while Column 4 shows the estimated amount of taxes that would have been levied in 1967 under an income value-added tax (Version 3) under the specified assumption. Column 5 shows the effect of the tax change (Col. 3 - Col. 4) as a percentage of value added (Col. 3 - Col. 4/Col. 2) for each of the industries. Overall gains in the return to the factors of production in low value-added industries exceeding 1 per cent are as follows: crude petroleum, 16.16 per cent; contract construction, 2.43 to 3.43 per cent; communication and public utilities, 3.05 per cent; coal mining, 1.70 per cent; motor freight, 1.27 per cent; other transportation, 1.32 per cent. Only two industries have gains of less than 1 per cent: stone and clay products, 0.20 per cent; and real estate, 0.14 per cent. Of the 14 industries classified as high value added, only three may experience reductions exceeding 1 per cent: primary metals, -1.12 per cent; wholesale trade, -1.53 per cent; and finance, -1.25 per cent. The remaining high value-added industries may experience reductions of as much as -0.98 per cent (services) to as little as -0.16 per cent (food). Overall the change in tax burden will be away from coal mining, contract construction, other transportation (except rail), and communication and public utilities and towards other manufacturing (except stone and clay products), rail, wholesale and retail trade, finance, and services.

The impact on the uses of income in West Virginia will follow the change in the return to the factors of production. In the aggregate, assuming equal marginal propensities to spend in the import-competing and domestic markets among the factors of production there would be no change in aggregate demand in West Virginia. In absolute terms, some factors will be made worse off and some better off. If we assume in the very short run the price to labor is fixed, yet assume no unemployment, then the differential short-run burden of the tax will fall entirely on capital, but with fixed proportions there may be negative changes in output in the short run as producers adjust production to conform with the after-tax value of the marginal product of labor. The differential incidence of the tax will still remain on capital but some unemployment or under-employment will occur. The specific output response would depend on knowledge abcut the marginal productivity of labor in each of the industries and the change in overall prices in consumer markets. In real world conditions, some portion of the burden might be shifted forward in the short run to consumers of West Virginia products and output adjustments might be moderated. In part though, we conclude that output would follow the sign of the change in the payments to capital. The larger the magnitude of negative change, the greater would be the negative output effect, _ceteris paribus_. For our estimates, no change in outputs are possible since labor and capital are used in fixed proportion and their supply is said to be fixed in the short run.

To show how the differential incidence effects payments to capital under the assumption that wages are fixed in the downward direction, we divide the overall percentage change in the return to the factors of production by the percentage of value added represented by capital. This is shown in Table 15. Column 2 shows the relative proportion of value added represented by payments to capital as measured by rents, interest, and other payments. Column 3 shows the overall change in the payments to the factors of production while Column 4 shows the effect of dividing these two ratios. Dramatic changes are shown by this exercise. The

TABLE 15

DIFFERENTIAL INCIDENCE OF THE INCOME VALUE-ADDED TAX
WEST VIRGINIA, 1967

Simulation Model B
(Burden on Capital)

Industry Identification	Capital / Value Added	Overall Change in Payments to Value Added (Per Cent)	Change in Payments to Capital (Per Cent)
1	2	3	4
Coal Mining	.18950	+ 1.70	+ 8.97
Crude Petroleum	.35051	+16.16	+46.10
Building	.05555	+ 3.43	+61.75
Highway & Street Construction	.18194	+ 2.98	+16.38
Special Trade Contractors	.22738	+ 2.43	+10.69
Food & Kindred Products	.43343	- 0.16	- 0.37
Textile Mill, Apparel & Other Textiles	.24827	- 0.24	- 0.97
Chemicals & Allied Products	.30285	- 0.79	- 2.61
Glass & Glass Products	.20409	- 0.52	- 2.55
Stone & Clay Products	.16313	+ 0.20	+ 1.23
Primary Metals	.28303	- 1.12	- 3.96
Fabricated Metals	.20708	- 0.47	- 2.27
Machinery, Including Electrical	.22957	- 0.83	- 3.62
Transportation Equipment	.13180	- 0.84	- 6.37
All Other Manufacturing	.33387	- 0.27	- 0.81
Rail & Related Services	.31359	- 0.86	- 2.74
Motor Freight & Related Services	.07704	+ 1.27	+16.49
All Other Transportation	.13366	+ 1.32	+ 9.88
Communication & Public Utilities	.57678	+ 3.05	+ 5.29
Wholesale Trade	.39040	- 1.53	- 3.92
Retail Trade	.31014	- 0.67	- 2.16
Finance	.13081	- 1.25	- 9.56
Real Estate	.25134	+ 0.14	+ 0.56
Services	.40983	- 0.98	- 2.39

largest increases would go to building (61.75 per cent) followed by crude petroleum (46.10 per cent), motor freight (16.49 per cent), highway and street construction (16.38 per cent), special trade contractors (10.69 per cent), other transportation (9.88 per cent), coal mining (8.97 per cent), communication and public utilities (5.29 per cent), and stone and clay products (1.23 per cent).

The high value-added industries by contrast have less dramatic declines in the payments to capital.[1] The largest decline is in the finance industry (-9.56 per cent) followed by transportation equipment (-6.37 per cent), primary metals (-3.96 per cent), wholesale trade (-3.92 per cent), machinery (-3.62 per cent), rail (-2.74 per cent), chemicals (-2.61 per cent), glass and glass products (-2.55 per cent), services (-2.39 per cent), fabricated metals (-2.27 per cent), retail trade (-2.16 per cent), food, textile mill, and all other manufacturing (less than 1 per cent).

If we recognize that state and local business taxes are legitimate deductions for business enterprises, the changes in the return to capital are overstated by the operative marginal tax. In the case of corporations which represent the bulk of dollar volume of business in West Virginia, the rate by which these rates should be adjusted is 48 per cent while for unincorporated businesses, the rate is the marginal personal income tax rate. If federal tax offset adjustments are made, we may in general note that the change will still be dramatic, but the number of industries in which the change is less than 1 per cent will increase. The impact on the use of income in West Virginia from the change in the payments to the factors of production is likely to be negligible if we assume equal marginal propensities to spend among the

[1]The reader is reminded that high value-added industries refers to industries which would experience increases in tax liability (see p. 128 above for a detailed discussion of this definition).

factor owners. Some further output declines could occur in the short run if the owners of capital in the low value-added industries receiving increases in payments are non-residents, while the high value-added owners of capital are residents. There is no evidence available which would permit us to make a judgment as to the likelihood of this occurring.

Given the extreme assumptions of this particular simulation, its outcome is relatively improbable. We will continue with our assessment of the simulation results, however, to show their sensitivity to changes in assumptions.

As noted in our theoretical analysis, Case 3 with fixed labor and mobile capital would put the entire differential incidence of the income value-added tax on the fixed factor, labor, and there would be no change in output, given our fixed proportion assumption in the uses of the factors of production. Table 16 shows the effect and is derived in the same way as Column 4 of Table 15 except that we now use the proportion of value added represented by the payments to labor. Dividing this latter proportion into the overall change in the payments to the factors of production as shown in Table 14 and repeated in Column 3, we can see the estimated differential incidence on labor with the changed assumption. The payments to capital will return to their pre-income value-added tax level.

Among the low value-added industries, the return to labor will increase by 24.88 per cent in the crude petroleum industry and 7.21 per cent in the communication and public utilities industry. Other less dramatic gains, accrue to building (3-4 per cent); coal mining, motor freight, and other transportation (1-3 per cent); and stone and clay products and real estate (less than 1 per cent). Among the high value-added

TABLE 16

DIFFERENTIAL INCIDENCE OF THE INCOME VALUE-ADDED TAX
WEST VIRGINIA, 1967

Simulation Model B
(Burden on Labor)

Industry Identification	Labor / Value Added	Overall Change in Payments to Value Added (Per Cent)	Change in Payments to Labor (Per Cent)
1	2	3	4
Coal Mining	.81050	+ 1.70	+ 2.10
Crude Petroleum	.64949	+16.16	+24.88
Building	.94445	+ 3.43	+ 3.63
Highway & Street Construction	.81806	+ 2.98	+ 3.64
Special Trade Contractors	.77262	+ 2.43	+ 3.14
Food & Kindred Products	.56657	- 0.16	- 0.28
Textile Mill, Apparel & Other Textiles	.75173	- 0.24	- 0.32
Chemicals & Allied Products	.69715	- 0.79	- 1.13
Glass & Glass Products	.79591	- 0.52	- 0.65
Stone & Clay Products	.83687	+ 0.20	+ 0.24
Primary Metals	.71697	- 1.12	- 1.56
Fabricated Metals	.79292	- 0.47	- 0.59
Machinery, Including Electrical	.77043	- 0.83	- 1.08
Transportation Equipment	.86820	- 0.84	- 0.97
All Other Manufacturing	.66613	- 0.27	- 0.41
Rail & Related Services	.68641	- 0.86	- 1.25
Motor Freight & Related Services	.92296	+ 1.27	+ 1.38
All Other Transportation	.86634	+ 1.32	+ 1.52
Communication & Public Utilities	.42322	+ 3.05	+ 7.21
Wholesale Trade	.60960	- 1.53	- 2.51
Retail Trade	.68986	- 0.67	- 0.97
Finance	.86919	- 1.25	- 1.44
Real Estate	.74866	+ 0.14	+ 0.19
Services	.59017	- 0.98	- 1.66

industries, the largest declines of between 1 and 3 per cent occur in the manufacturing industries of chemicals, primary metals, and machinery; rail; wholesale trade; and finance, and services. Labor employed in food, textile mill, glass, fabricated metals, transportation equipment, other manufacturing, and retail trade, all experience losses of less than 1 per cent in income. On the uses of income side, assuming equal marginal propensities to spend, these changes in the payments to the factors of production are not likely to affect the aggregate demand in the import-competing and domestic markets since there will be offsetting changes in the uses of income by the different labor groups in the high and low value-added industries.

Under Case 4, with mobile labor and capital and fixed proportions in production, the effect will be to encourage output and employment changes at the margin, away from the high value-added industries and into the low value-added industries. The most noticeable positive changes in employment and output are likely to occur in the coal mining, crude petroleum, building,and communication and public utilities industries.

On the negative side, the bulk of the reductions are less than 1 per cent with none being more than 2 per cent. These changes are not likely to be observable, given the changes in wages and salaries and consumer prices which have occurred since 1967. If the magnitude of negative changes are not sufficiently large to affect individual decisions with respect to employment or producers' decisions with respect to output, there could be on balance a net inflow of capital and labor into the state raising aggregate output and employment levels. We move now to our final simulation model in which we attempt to assume an intermediate position between that of Models A and B.

Simulation Model C

Assumptions and Methods. Our third simulation takes an intermediate position in contrast to the opposite extremes assumed in Models A and B. Here we assume that some portion of the change in tax will be reflected in the prices of intermediate goods and will, therefore, be passed on in the form of price changes for final goods. The remaining portion of the tax change not reflected in changes in the prices of intermediate products will be borne by the factors of production. The purpose of the projections is simply to get an idea of the sensitivity of the results to an intermediate assumption.

The assumptions have some similarity to those in Cases 7 and 8 except for the implicit assumption that the price elasticity of demand for exports and supply of import-competing products varies between zero and infinity. Also the elasticity of supply of exports, import-competing, and domestic products is assumed to vary between something greater than zero but less than infinity. Our shifting assumptions for each industry permit the elasticity of demand and supply to vary over the entire range of limits specified, providing their combined effect permits the kind of shifting adjustment specified. Here we combined the input-output model for the price effects with the corporate sample simulation for the factor return effects. This requires, therefore, that Version 3 of the input-output model be used since the value-added taxes are determined exogenously through the corporate sample.

Again, we will look mainly at the effects on final prices and on changes in the return to the factors of production and then comment briefly on some of the further repercussions that might occur. We continue with our assumptions of Models A and B that production is governed by fixed technical coefficients and that the supply of the factors of production are fixed. Our assumptions about shifting are: If an industry is export-oriented, it will pass all of the changes forward if it is judged to be highly concentrated; otherwise only 50 per cent of the tax will be passed forward. If the industry produces primarily for domestic demand and is judged to be highly competitive, but not faced with external competition, then all of the tax change will be passed forward; otherwise only 50 per cent will be passed forward. Finally, if an industry is balanced between the export and domestic markets and is judged to be concentrated, it will pass all of the tax forward; otherwise only 50 per cent of the tax will be passed forward.

Our basis for so classifying industries in West Virginia is based, in part, on the data contained in Table 17 which shows estimated sales to the export and domestic markets and the percentage to each market. If an industry sells 60 per cent or more of its product to exports, it is judged an export-oriented industry. If an industry sells more than 40 per cent, but less than 60 per cent, it is judged as operating in both markets. Finally, if an industry sells 40 per cent or less to exports, it is judged as a domestic industry. On the basis of this classification, export-oriented industries identified in Column 1 are: coal mining; crude petroleum; all of the manufacturing industries except food, machinery, and transportation; transportation, except all other; and communication and public utilities. The domestic-oriented industries are: contract construction; food; wholesale and retail trade; finance; real estate; and services. Those industries judged to be operating in both markets are: the manufacturing industries of machinery and transportation equipment; and other transportation (buses, taxis and airlines). Combining all

TABLE 17

INPUT-OUTPUT ESTIMATED VALUE OF SHIPMENTS TO FINAL DEMAND, WEST VIRGINIA, 1967

(Money Amounts in Millions of Dollars)

Market Orientation	Industry Identification	Export ($)	Export (Per Cent)	Domestic ($)	Domestic (Per Cent)
1	2	3	4	5	6
Export	Coal Mining	680	98.79	8	1.21
Export	Crude Petroleum	1	100.00	0	0.00
Domestic	Building	10	6.52	143	93.48
Domestic	Highway & Street Construction	14	9.06	143	90.94
Domestic	Special Trade Contractors	6	9.55	56	90.45
Domestic	Food & Kindred Products	40	20.88	150	79.12
Export	Textile Mill, Apparel & Other Textiles	18	75.25	6	24.65
Export	Chemical & Allied Products	1,114	98.28	20	1.72
Export	Glass & Glass Products	263	97.44	9	2.56
Export	Stone & Clay Products	85	85.40	14	14.60
Export	Primary Metals	942	99.14	8	0.86
Export	Fabricated Metals	83	92.81	6	7.19
Export & Domestic	Machinery, Including Electrical	52	46.27	60	53.73
	Transportation Equipment	104	56.36	81	43.64
Export	All Other Manufacturing	208	64.35	115	35.65
Export	Rail & Related Services	145	85.99	24	14.01
Export	Motor Freight & Related Services	84	63.53	48	36.47
Export & Domestic	All Other Transportation	11	44.35	13	55.65
Export	Communication & Public Utilities	336	66.68	168	33.32
Domestic	Wholesale Trade	76	33.98	148	66.02
Domestic	Retail Trade	93	14.20	565	85.80
Domestic	Finance	28	7.60	339	92.40
Domestic	Real Estate	5	15.45	28	84.55
Domestic	Services	66	8.77	691	91.23
Export	Total*	4,464	61.09	2,843	38.91

*Details may not add to totals because of rounding.

industries together, it is clear that the state is largely export-oriented with 61 per cent of its sales to export markets and 39 per cent to domestic markets.

Beyond this market classification scheme for establishing a specific shifting assumption, we also used a subjective evaluation for deciding whether an industry was concentrated, or not faced with external competition. This evaluation and the market classifications are contained in Columns 2 and 3 of Table 18. Column 4 shows the shifting assumptions used for each industry. Needless to say, these are crude and speculative judgments and assumptions, and, to repeat, the only purpose of the exercise is to get some rough idea about the way varying the assumptions might affect prices and factor payments.

Simulation Results. Table 19 (Col. 2) shows the effect of these assumptions on prices in final markets. To show the extent to which the price index differs from that of complete forward shifting for all industries, Column 3 represents the results of Model A for Version 3, while Column 4 shows the net change in final prices with Model C. In only two industries is there a reverse of the sign of the price index. Transportation equipment manufacturing goes from a price increase under Model A to a price decline under Model C. The difference is 1.07 per cent. Motor freight goes from a price decrease to no change with a net difference of 1/2 of 1 per cent. In all other industries the difference between Models A and C is less than 1 per cent with the bulk of these (18 industries) less than 1/10 of 1 per cent. Four industries have changes between 1/10 and 7/10 of 1 per cent. The implication of this is that the effects on prices is rather insensitive to these shifting assumptions. Part of the reason, of course, is due to the

TABLE 18

INDUSTRY SHIFTING ASSUMPTIONS
WEST VIRGINIA, 1967

Simulation Model C
(Burden Shared by Consumers and Factors)

Industry Identification	Market Orientation	Concentrated or Not Faced with External Competition	Forward Shifting Assumption (Per Cent)
1	2	3	4
Coal Mining	Export	X	100
Crude Petroleum	Export	X	100
Building	Domestic		50
Highway & Street Construction	Domestic		50
Special Trade Contractors	Domestic		50
Food & Kindred Products	Domestic		50
Textile Mill, Apparel & Other Textiles	Export		50
Chemicals & Allied Products	Export	X	100
Glass & Glass Products	Export		50
Stone & Clay Products	Export	X	100
Primary Metals	Export	X	100
Fabricated Metals	Export		50
Machinery, Including Electrical	Export & Domestic		50
Transportation Equipment	Export & Domestic	X	100
All Other Manufacturing	Export		75*
Rail & Related Services	Export	X	100
Motor Freight & Related Services	Export		50
All Other Transportation	Export & Domestic	X	100
Communication & Public Utilities	Export	X	100
Wholesale Trade	Domestic	X	100
Retail Trade	Domestic	X	100
Finance	Domestic	X	100
Real Estate	Domestic	X	100
Services	Domestic	X	100

*50 per cent concentrated and 50 per cent unconcentrated.

TABLE 19

COMPARISON OF NEW PRICE INDICES FOR INDUSTRY SECTORS AFTER THE SHIFT FROM A TURNOVER TAX TO A VALUE-ADDED TAX IN WEST VIRGINIA 1967

Model C vs Model A

Industry Identification	New Price Index For Model C (Burden on Consumers and Factors)	New Price Index For Model A (Burden on Consumers)	Net Difference (Col. 2 - 3)
1	2	3	4
Coal Mining	99.40	99.40	0.00
Crude Petroleum	95.22	95.22	0.00
Building	99.33	98.69	+0.64
Highway & Street Construction	99.35	98.68	+0.67
Special Trade Contractors	99.71	99.38	+0.33
Food & Kindred Products	100.00	100.01	-0.01
Textile Mill, Apparel & Other Textiles	100.11	100.26	-0.15
Chemicals & Allied Products	100.22	100.21	-0.01
Glass & Glass Products	100.03	100.10	-0.07
Stone & Clay Products	99.01	99.02	-0.01
Primary Metals	100.47	100.47	0.00
Fabricated Metals	100.13	100.22	-0.09
Machinery, Including Electrical	100.07	100.12	-0.05
Transportation Equipment	99.03	100.10	-1.07
All Other Manufacturing	99.98	99.98	0.00
Rail & Related Services	100.45	100.44	+0.01
Motor Freight & Related Services	100.00	99.55	+0.45
All Other Transportation	99.46	99.46	0.00
Communication & Public Utilities	98.59	98.58	+0.01
Wholesale Trade	101.14	101.14	0.00
Retail Trade	100.46	100.45	+0.01
Finance	100.05	100.05	0.00
Real Estate	99.77	99.71	+0.06
Services	100.28	100.27	+0.01

fact that we have assumed 100 per cent forward shifting in 14 of the 24 industries.

Table 20 shows the estimated effect, under Model C, of the shift to a value-added tax on overall prices in the West Virginia export and domestic markets and is contrasted with our Model A results from Table 13 The data show that, under Model C assumptions, the export prices will decline by 3/100 of 1 per cent and domestic prices will increase by 5/100 of 1 per cent. This represents a difference in overall relative prices of 8/100 of 1 per cent in favor of exports. The Model C estimates suggest that the price effect on the use of income of consumers of West Virginia products are not likely to be significantly different from those suggested under Model A, or under different shifting assumptions.

The impact on the factors of production associated with that portion of the change in tax not passed forward is shown in Table 21 under the alternative assumptions of flexible and inflexible wages used in Model B. Column 2 identifies the shifting assumption for each industry while Columns 3 and 4 show the effect on the payments to the factors of production under the alternate assumption indicated. No output change will occur if we assume that returns to both capital and labor are flexible, i.e., factor supplies are fixed. Income gains will accure to factors employed in contract construction and motor freight, with matching income losses of less than 1/2 of 1 per cent experienced by the manufacturing industries of food, textile mill, glass and glass products, fabricated metals, and other manufacturing. Assuming equal marginal propensities to spend between those whose incomes have increased and those whose incomes have fallen, there should be few additional effects on the uses of income in the import-competing and domestic sectors.

TABLE 20

COMPARISON OF NEW PRICE INDICES BY FINAL DEMAND SECTOR
ACCOMPANYING THE SHIFT FROM A TURNOVER TAX
TO A VALUE-ADDED TAX IN WEST VIRGINIA
1967

Model C vs Model A

Final Demand Sector	Simulation Model C (Burden Shared by Consumers and Factors)	Simulation Model A (Burden on Consumers)
Export Market	99.96	99.99
Domestic and Import-Competing Markets	100.04	99.99

TABLE 21

PRODUCER'S PORTION OF THE DIFFERENTIAL INCIDENCE
OF THE INCOME VALUE-ADDED TAX
WEST VIRGINIA, 1967

Simulation Model C
(Burden Shared by Consumers and Factors)

Industry Identification	Shifting Assumption	Flexible Wage Assumption: Change in Payment to Factors of Production (Per Cent)	Fixed Wage Assumption: Change in Payment to Capital (Per Cent)
1	2	3	4
Coal Mining	100	0.00	0.00
Crude Petroleum	100	0.00	0.00
Building	50	+1.72	+30.88
Highway & Street Construction	50	+1.49	+ 8.19
Special Trade Contractors	50	+1.22	+ 5.35
Food & Kindred Products	50	-0.08	- 0.19
Textile Mill, Apparel & Other Textiles	50	-0.12	- 0.49
Chemicals & Allied Products	100	0.00	0.00
Glass & Glass Products	50	-0.26	- 1.28
Stone & Clay Products	100	0.00	0.00
Primary Metals	100	0.00	0.00
Fabricated Metals	50	-0.24	- 1.14
Machinery, Including Electrical	50	-0.42	- 1.81
Transportation Equipment	100	0.00	0.00
All Other Manufacturing	75	-0.07	- 0.20
Rail & Related Services	100	0.00	0.00
Motor Freight & Related Services	50	+0.63	+ 8.25
All Other Transportation	100	0.00	0.00
Communication & Public Utilities	100	0.00	0.00
Wholesale Trade	100	0.00	0.00
Retail Trade	100	0.00	0.00
Finance	100	0.00	0.00
Real Estate	100	0.00	0.00
Services	100	0.00	0.00

Alternatively, if we assume that wages may not change, the entire differential burden of the income value-added tax will fall on capital, the specific magnitude of which is shown in Column 4. Dramatic increases in the return to capital are shown for contract construction (5-30 per cent) and motor freight (8.25 per cent). Reductions in the return to capital occurs in six manufacturing industries, three of which have losses of less than 1/2 of 1 per cent--food, textile mill, and other manufacturing--and three with losses of no more than 2 per cent--glass and glass products, fabricated metals, and machinery. We assume no output change, but in reality, output declines and unemployment could occur.

In the longer run, the differential incidence of the producers' portion of the tax will shift entirely to the fixed factor, labor, under Case 3 conditions. No output change will occur because of the fixed factor proportions and the assumption that full employment is maintained. The simulated magnitude of this effect is shown in Table 22. The change in the return to labor on the positive side for the contract construction industry is between 1.57 and 1.82 per cent while for motor freight, it is only 0.69 per cent. On the negative side, the reduction in income to labor ranges from 0.14 per cent for labor employed in food manufacturing to 0.54 per cent for labor employed in machinery manufacturing. Assuming equal marginal propensities to spend among the labor groups, there should be few additional effects on the uses of income in West Virginia in the import-competing and domestic markets. The payments to capital will return to their pre-value-added income tax change level.

Under Case 4 with both capital and labor mobile, the immediate impact of change in payments to the factors of production together with the long-run shifts in demand in response to the change in relative prices

TABLE 22

LABOR'S PORTION OF THE DIFFERENTIAL INCIDENCE
OF THE INCOME VALUE-ADDED TAX
WEST VIRGINIA, 1967

Simulation Model C
(Burden Shared)

Industry Identification	Shifting Assumption	Mobile Capital Assumptions: Change in Payments to Labor (Per Cent)
1	2	3
Coal Mining	100	0.00
Crude Petroleum	100	0.00
Building	50	+1.82
Highway & Street Construction	50	+1.82
Special Trade Contractors	50	+1.57
Food & Kindred Products	50	-0.14
Textile Mill, Apparel & Other Textiles	50	-0.16
Chemicals & Allied Products	100	0.00
Glass & Glass Products	50	-0.33
Stone & Clay Products	100	0.00
Primary Metals	100	0.00
Fabricated Metals	50	-0.30
Machinery, Including Electrical	50	-0.54
Transportation Equipment	100	0.00
All Other Manufacturing	75	-0.21
Rail & Related Services	100	0.00
Motor Freight & Related Services	50	+0.69
All Other Transportation	100	0.00
Communication & Public Utilities	100	0.00
Wholesale Trade	100	0.00
Retail Trade	100	0.00
Finance	100	0.00
Real Estate	100	0.00
Services	100	0.00

will induce output and employment changes away from the high value-added industries and toward the low value-added industries. The differential burden will continue to be borne on both the sources and uses of income, *ceteris paribus*. The *ceteris paribus* assumption, however, is subject to some question. As we noted in Model B, other offsetting effects are likely to be so large as to mask any measurable change in output and employment in the high value-added industries.

Concluding Observations

On the basis of the data presented, we may speculate that the value-added tax will make consumers of certain West Virginia exports better off in the consumption of energy and energy-related products and that some shifts toward the consumption of these products will occur. This will lead to an expansion of output of the crude petroleum industry in West Virginia and increases in the employment of the factors of production.

Some in-migration of resources is likely to occur if the price increases in the other industries are not sufficiently large to induce households in West Virginia to change their consumption habits and thereby affect output in the import-competing and domestic markets. With respect to the manufacturing industries, which are mainly export-oriented, we speculate that the shifts in relative prices between West Virginia's export goods and competing non-taxed goods are not sufficiently large to induce measurable additional effects on the consumption of West Virginia's manufactured exports.

The estimates provided by our simulations are of course highly dubious and, therefore, only limited conclusions can be drawn. In fact, we are reluctant to speculate beyond the bounds of the models themselves, since other assumptions and other models might lead to different conclusions. This is the first time, however, that anyone has tried to explore for even crude clues to the effects of a regional value-added tax.

CHAPTER V

TURNOVER VERSUS VALUE-ADDED TAXATION IN WEST VIRGINIA: EFFICIENCY AND EXCESS BURDEN CONSIDERATIONS

In Chapter IV, we neglected issues concerning inefficiencies and excess burdens and looked primarily at who would bear the burdens. In this chapter, we wish to consider the effect of the two taxes on efficiency and excess burden in the private sector.

Theoretical Considerations

Assuming there are no externalities in production or consumption, there are three necessary conditions which must be satisfied in the competitive model for efficiency to be achieved. First, the marginal rate of substitution between any pair of commodities must be the same for all consumers. Second, the marginal technical rate of substitution between any two inputs must be the same for all producers. Third, the marginal rate of substitution in consumption must be equal to the marginal rate of technical substitution for any two commodities.

If these conditions of marginal equality are not met, efficiency is said to be impaired, since it can be shown that welfare may be improved by the payment of an equivalent lump-sum tax, which by definition does not alter relative prices in consumption or production.

On the uses of income (consumption) side, interference with efficiency may occur in several ways. First, a tax which is levied on some products but not on others may distort consumption choices away from the taxed product and toward the non-taxed products, assuming that the price elasticity of demand for the products is not zero. Second, a tax which is levied on current consumption which does not also tax future consumption artifically encourages future consumption and discourages current consumption. Finally, a tax which lowers the marginal income of factors, unless their supply is perfectly fixed, will tend to lower the supply of those factors and encourage the consumption of leisure (though there will also be an income effect on these choices).

Also on the sources of income side, taxes may in addition interfere with efficiency in a number of different ways. For our purposes, we will be concerned with five specific phenomena. First, a tax which changes the relative prices of the factors of production may, unless the elasticity of substitution is zero, alter the combinations in which the factors are employed and, thus, interfere with the attainment of efficiency. Second, a tax which is applied to some industries and not to others may tend to encourage uneconomic production in the non-taxed industries and discourage production in the taxed industries. Third, a tax which is imposed on industry in a sub-region of a larger geographic area may tend to encourage uneconomic production in the non-taxed region and discourage production in the taxed region. A combined variant of this type occurs when taxes are levied on a sub-set of different industries at different rates in a geographic region. Under these latter circumstances, efficiency is impaired not only with respect to the non-taxed industry but also among the taxed industries. Fourth, a tax may interfere with efficiency if it has the effect of encouraging firms to vertically integrate so as to avoid the number of times a product is taxed as it moves through the stages of production. Finally, taxation on the sources of income side may interfere with the attainment of efficiency if it taxes capital purchases but not internally generated capital. Under these conditions, the changes in the marginal rate of technical substitution between these two sources of capital would serve to discourage capital purchases and encourage internally generated capital. If this occurs in a sub-region, it also encourages capital imports from outside the region if those purchases are not taxed.

To the extent that these patterns of taxation distort relative prices in consumption or production and a substitution effect is observed, inefficiencies and welfare losses may arise. This is so since there is not only a loss in real income due to the resource transfer as measured by the taxes levied, but also an excess burden associated with the substitution effect in response to the change in relative prices. Welfare, therefore, might be improved by the imposition of an equivalent tax which has only an income effect equal to the resource transfer to the state. The only possibility is a hypothetical head tax which has no substitution effect. Such a tax is regarded as impracticable for collecting large amounts of revenue and, therefore, all taxes may impose welfare losses (excess burdens). No firm conclusion can be drawn, however, if inefficiencies already exist. In this latter case, some taxes may act to move the economy to a more efficient position and thereby reduce excess burdens. Similarly, if a tax which induces excess burden already exists, its replacement by another tax may act to reduce or enlarge the existing level of excess burden. In this view, the change in excess burden has some similarity to "differential incidence" and may be termed "differential excess burden."

In our discussion, we will be concerned with the conditions under which the turnover tax may interfere with the attainment of efficiency and whether under these same conditions the substitution of an income value-added tax will reduce the degree of excess burden. Our concern in this regard will be primarily with the excess burdens in West Virginia and we will largely ignore those which might occur in the rest of the country.

Following this theoretical analysis, we will then attempt to develop estimates of the magnitude of certain components of the excess burden under each of the two taxes. We should note at the outset, however, that theory cannot yield precise implications except with the aid of heroic assumptions and few of the efficiency and excess burden effects lend themselves to empirical estimation either because insufficient data are available or because the tax-induced behavior may not be separable from alterations in behavior due to other causes.

To explore the possible existence and magnitude of excess burdens, we need to have definite sets of assumptions in mind. We will limit our theoretical and empirical analyses to certain cases described in the preceding chapter, i.e., Cases 3, 4, 7, and 8 in which, among other conditions, we assumed that the production function was governed by fixed proportions and in which the price elasticity of demand was either perfectly elastic (Cases 3, 4) or less than perfectly elastic (Cases 7, 8). Again, these are extreme and perhaps unrealistic assumptions, but our aim is to make at least a start (hitherto unmade) in developing clues to these effects.

Efficiency and Excess Burden Under the Turnover Tax

Let us begin by assuming that the economy in West Virginia and elsewhere is otherwise efficient before the imposition of the turnover tax and that there are no externalities in production or consumption in the private market. We further assume that a turnover tax is levied in the state of West Virginia which is similar to the one levied in 1967. In addition, we assume that owners of the factors of production employed in West Virginia, and the state government and consumers of West Virginia products have the same marginal propensity to spend and the same income-compensated elasticity of demand for each of the composite goods produced in West Virginia--export, import-competing, and domestic. Finally, we assume that production is governed by fixed proportions of factors in West Virginia and that initially the supplies of the factors of production, labor and capital, are fixed.

Export and Import-Competing Sectors. We argued in Chapter IV that if the price elasticity of demand for exports and of the supply of import-competing products was infinite, the burden of the turnover tax would rest on the factors of production employed in these broad sectors in West Virginia. We also noted that within each of the broad sectors, the magnitude of burden would differ among firms as a function of the type of production activity.

Given these incidence patterns, there can be no interference with the attainment of efficiency on the uses of income side with respect to change in the relative price of alternative goods or in the relative price of present versus future consumption. There is a change in the relative price of work versus leisure, but because the supply of the quantity of the factors supplied to the export and import-competing sectors is fixed, the substitution effect is zero.

On the sources of income side, the existence of fixed factor supplies and flexibility in the prices paid to the factors of production, implies that no inefficiency is possible. The prices of capital and labor will decline to reflect the change in their after-tax value of their marginal products but because of their inelastic supply and an elasticity of substitution equal to zero, employment mix and output levels will not change. Similarly, changes in the methods of capital acquisition, degrees of vertical integration or geographic location of production facilities by firms are not possible with our assumptions that the factors of production are fixed. These assumptions might be fairly reasonable in the market period.

In a subsequent time period, if Case 3 conditions apply to the export sector (Case 7, import-competing), the entire burden of the tax shifts to the fixed factor, labor, and therefore, no excess burdens may arise since only the income effect is operative. If Case 4 conditions apply to the export sector (Case 8 in the import-competing)--i.e., all of our previous assumptions apply except that both labor and capital are mobile--efficiency is impaired and excess burdens do occur. Under these conditions, excess burdens may occur on the sources of income side as a function of the elasticity of supply of the factors. As both factors migrate, output will be reduced and the burden of the tax will be borne by the less efficiently employed factors in proportion to their contribution to value added.

With fixed proportions in production and a ratio of capital to labor which exceeds one, the burden (incidence, not excess burden) of the tax will be disproportionately borne by labor, since for identical elasticities of supply of both capital and labor, the supply of capital will diminish more rapidly than that of labor and to insure the full employment of labor, the return to capital will diminish less rapidly. This may be shown by referring to Part A of Figure 1 in which we have assumed a capital to labor ratio of 2, identical elasticity of supply for the two factors of production, fixed proportions in production, and perfectly elastic demand for output. From the received theory of derived demand, the output supply curve (S_0) is the vertical sum of the input supply curve of labor (S_L) and capital (S_K).[1] Equilibrium before taxes is at D and output price OC. The return to the factors of production is the sum of the payments to labor of OB per unit of labor and OA per unit of capital. With an ad valorem tax equal to VC/OC, output declines from OG to OH and the total tax burden (VCNM) is shared by labor (TBLK) and capital (RAJI) in the ratio of 2:1. Not coincidentally, this is the same ratio of capital to labor and leads to the conclusion that with identical elasticities of demand and fixed factor proportions, the share of burden of the tax on labor will be borne in the reverse ratio of capital to labor. If the supply elasticity of capital is greater than that of labor, the burden on labor will be even greater as shown in Part B of Figure 1, where we have

---

[1]Note that the slope of the capital supply curve is 1/2 that of the labor supply curve. This is necessitated by the scalar difference between the two supply curves. For a complete explanation of this method for illustrating the relationship between input supply curves and output see Milton Friedman, Price Theory: A Provisional Text, rev. (Chicago: Aldine Publishing Company, 1966), pp. 149ff as well as that of Daniel Wisecarver, "The Social Costs of Input-Market Distortions," The American Economic Review 64 (June 1974):361ff.

FIGURE 1

DIFFERENCES IN TURNOVER TAX BURDEN AND OUTPUT EFFECTS IN EXPORT AND IMPORT-COMPETING INDUSTRIES

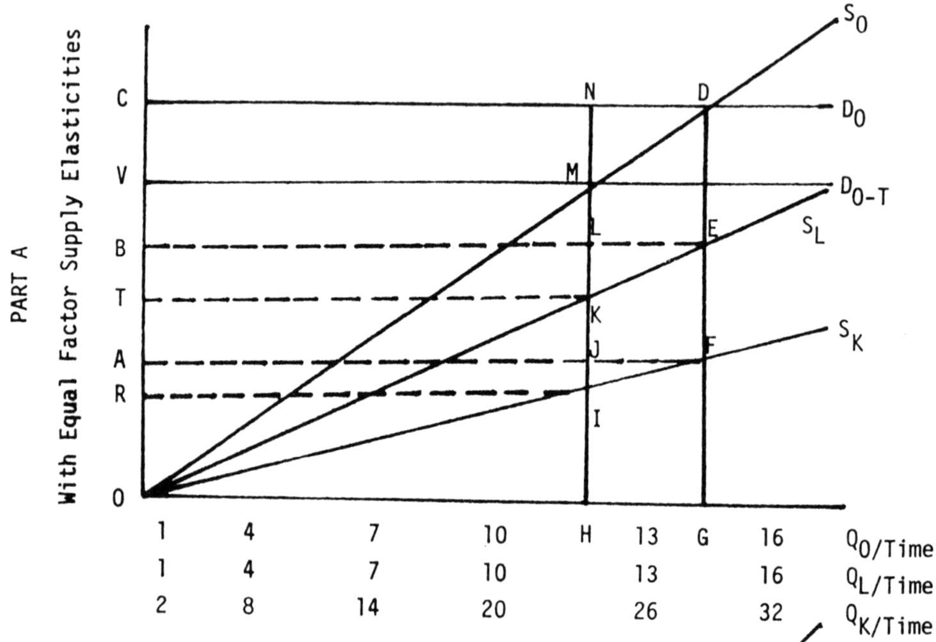

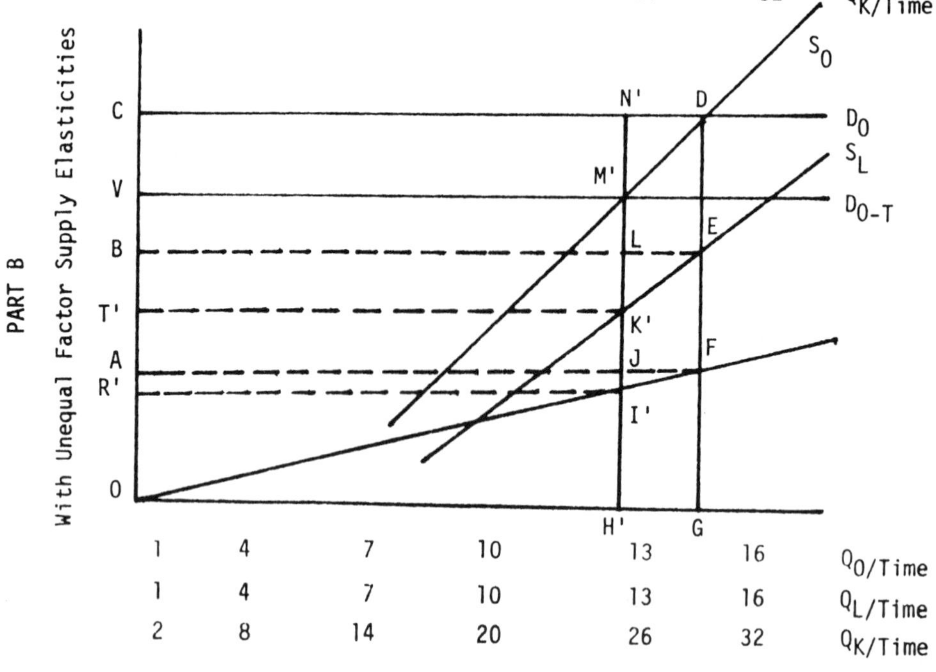

all the assumptions underlying Part A except that we have lowered the elasticity of supply of labor. Total tax burden (VCN'M') is now T'BLK' on labor and R'AJI' on capital in the ratio of 3:1. Thus, output changes will be governed by that factor which has the lower supply elasticity: The greater the divergence between capital and labor supply elasticities, the less will be the output effect (excess burden) and the greater will be the share of burden incurred by the factor with the lower elasticity of supply--if we neglect other sources of inefficiency, such as those described below.

To the extent that factors migrate, excess burdens are created outside of West Virginia if production is accomplished under increasing costs in the industries to which they migrate. If, however, production is accomplished under constant costs, no excess burden will occur.

These excess burdens associated with output changes in each of the broad sectors do not, however, describe the total excess burden since within each of the sectors there is an excess burden created which is due to the differentiated rate structure. In other words, our arguments for the existence of an excess burden in production in each of the broad sectors are those likely to be present if within each of the sectors a uniform turnover tax was levied. With a differentiated rate structure, the excess burden in production is larger and causes output reductions to be larger for low value-added firms and smaller for high value-added firms.

Excess burden, may be larger, at least in one respect, in the long run since the reduction in the payments to the factors of production in West Virginia cause prices of leisure to be reduced and individuals may choose to consume more leisure. The extent to which this excess burden materializes will be a function of the elasticity of supply of labor defined to include the substitution effect only.

Export and Domestic Sectors. Let us now turn to consider the ways in which excess burdens may arise with the turnover tax under the conditions associated with Cases 7 and 8 for the export and the domestic sectors. The principal change from the set of assumptions above is that we are assuming the demand to be less than perfectly elastic. We need not take account of the import-competing sector since we have already noted that Cases 7 and 8 for the import-competing sector are identical to that of Cases 3 and 4 for the export sector. Our assumption of perfect elasticity of supply for the import-competing sector serves to deny the possibility of the import-competing sector passing any tax forward, despite the nature of the aggregate demand schedule for import and import-competing products.

For Cases 7 and 8, the turnover tax will fall on the factors of production if, as assumed, their quantities are fixed (as they might be in the market period). No excess burden on the use of income side is possible. Similarly, if labor is fixed but capital is mobile (Case 7), the entire burden of the tax will shift to the fixed factor, labor, and again no excess burden may occur.

If, however, the conditions of Case 8 apply, efficiency is impaired and excess burdens do occur on both the uses and sources of income. We noted in Chapter IV that the burden of the tax will be borne by both consumers and producers in proportion to the relative elasticities of demand and supply. Some portion of the burden of the turnover tax, therefore, may be shifted forward to export and domestic consumers. The more inelastic the sector supply curve relative to demand the greater will be the burden on the producers, and the less elastic the curves the lower the excess burden.

On the uses of income side, efficiency is impaired in three ways. First, relative prices between exports and non-taxed export-competing products will be altered and consumers will be encouraged to alter their consumption in favor of the export-competing products. The extent to which this will occur is a function of the cross-elasticity of demand for the non-taxed good in response to a change in the price of the taxed export product. Similarly, efficiency is impaired in the domestic market because domestic consumers will find that, as prices of domestic products rise, the relative price between domestic and import-competing products alters and, consequently, shifts consumption in favor of import-competing products. If West Virginia's exports and domestic products are a small portion of the total export-competing and import-competing markets, the extent of realized excess burden in West Virginia may be approximated as a function of the elasticity of demand and supply for export and domestic products.

Second, as output is adjusted in a subsequent time period to conform with the after-tax marginal productivity of the factors of production, there will be a reduction in the returns to the less efficiently employed factors of production which will alter the relative price of leisure. This in turn would cause factor owners to work less than they would under neutral taxation, the extent being a function of the elasticity of supply defined to include the substitution effects only.[1] Finally, to the extent that prices do increase in the export and domestic market, it will alter the relative price of present versus future consumption in favor of the latter in both markets.

On the producer's side, the migration of labor and capital will create excess burdens in production as producers alter outputs to reflect the changed value of the marginal products of labor and capital. The excess burden will follow the same patterns identified earlier under Case 4, where we noted that the magnitude depended on the capital-labor ratio, and the relative elasticity of supply of both capital and labor.

Because of the differentiated rate structure under the turnover tax, the relative excess burden will not be uniform among producers within each of the sectors, however. _Ceteris paribus_, high turnover-taxed consumers and producers will experience larger excess burdens than lower turnover-taxed consumers and producers. Thus, the inducement to shift to non-taxed consumption and production will be stronger for the high turnover-taxed consumers and producers.

Export, Import-Competing, and Domestic Sectors. Beyond these excess burdens, there are other possible inefficiencies. The turnover tax law: (1) encourages vertical integration to reduce the number of tax levy points to which the firms would otherwise be subject; (2) favors spatial de-integration; and (3) discourages domestic purchases of capital.

The vertical integration phenomenon is typically explained by an example similar to that of Table 23 where we observe a product which may

---

[1]Since eventually we will be comparing the turnover tax with an income value-added tax, we are ignoring the income effect which is assumed to be the same under both taxes.

TABLE 23

COMPARISON OF THE EFFECT OF A UNIFORM TURNOVER TAX ON AN INTEGRATED FIRM AND A COMPARABLE SET OF NON-INTEGRATED FIRMS[a]

			Integrated Firm (A)		Non-Integrated Firms (B-F)			
					Complete Forward Shifting		Complete Backward Shifting	
Stage of Production	Value Added	Pre-Tax Cumulative Value Added (Gross Output)	Cumulative Value Added	Tax Revenue	Cumulative Value Added (Includes Tax)	Tax Revenue	Cumulative Value Added (Excludes Tax)	Tax Revenue
1	2	3	4	5	6	7	8	9
Extraction	$ 40.00	$ 40.00	$ 40.00	-0-	$ 40.80 (B)	$0.80	$ 40.00	$0.80
Manufacturing	30.00	70.00	70.00	-0-	72.22 (C)	2.22	70.00	1.40
Wholesale	20.00	90.00	90.00	-0-	94.05 (D)	4.05	90.00	1.80
Retail	10.00	100.00	100.00	-0-	106.13 (E)	6.13	100.00	2.00
Service	10.00	110.00	112.20	$2.20	118.45 (F)	8.45	110.00	2.20
Totals	$110.00	$410.00	$112.20	$2.20	$118.45	$8.45	$110.00	$8.20
Effective Rate (Per Cent)	$\frac{\text{Taxes Paid}}{\text{Gross}}$			2.00		7.68		7.45

[a]Assume a statutory tax rate of 2 per cent.

be produced by a vertically integrated firm (A) (Col. 4) or by a series of individual firms (B, C, D, E, F). In the example, we assume that no advantage obtains from vertically integrating except for the tax saving. (The general point is that the turnover tax leads firms to <u>more</u> vertical integration than would otherwise be economic.) Further, it is assumed that here the turnover tax rate is uniform. Columns 5 and 7 show the relative effect on final prices when the tax is passed on and becomes a part of the tax base. This would correspond to our Cases 7 and 8 where the price elasticity of demand was equal to zero or where the price elasticity of supply was perfectly elastic. For the integrated firm (A), since there are no intermediate market transactions, the product in question generates $2.20 in tax revenue (Col. 5). The price of the product also increases by the same amount if the tax is passed forward. For the set of unintegrated firms, Column 7 shows that with a market exchange at each stage, the product generates $8.45 in tax revenue (Col. 7) if the tax is passed forward or $8.20 (Col. 9) if it is not. Correspondingly, the price of the product will rise $8.45 if the tax is passed forward or remains the same if it is not.

This pyramiding effect, therefore, has two components. The first is the effect of the inclusion in the tax base of the value of production from previous stages, which we shall term "value-added pyramiding." The second component arises when the tax is passed forward and becomes part of the tax bases of subsequent stages of production. This phenomenon, which we shall term "tax pyramiding" can only arise when the turnover tax levied is passed forward to subsequent stages of production.

In our example, the tax pyramiding is equal to $0.25 and is the difference between the totals in Columns 7 and 9. Value-added pyramiding is equal to $6 and is the difference between Columns 5 and 9.

The initial gains to the firm which integrates begin to erode if other firms proceed with vertical integration and are wiped out by externalities if vertical integration throughout the economy becomes complete. Consider that we begin with an economy which is non-integrated and is composed of the five firms B-F and that $2.20 in revenue is required. Further, let us assume that the taxing authorities correctly judge that the tax is not passed forward and that the tax bases are equal to the sum of the individual firm's gross--($410)(Col. 3). If these circumstances prevail, the effective turnover tax rate required would be equal to 0.0054 ($2.20/410.00). Firms might then act to integrate vertically but as this vertical integration took place, the state would find its revenue falling short of need and would act to increase the effective turnover tax rate. If vertical integration was complete, the effective rate would rise to 2 per cent and the same total tax levy would apply to the integrated firm A as was imposed on firms B-F. There would still be a potential for excess burdens, however, since the tax-induced integration would be uneconomic, and individual firms would not make themselves worse off if they "de-integrated."

Even if vertical integration is not complete, the shrinkage of the tax base will cause the turnover tax rate to rise and some additional taxes would be levied on the integrated firm. The burden of the tax, therefore, would not shift to the unintegrated firms by as much as is generally suggested in the literature. In general, however, in an environment in which a uniform turnover tax is levied, the inducement to vertically integrate will be present for all firms, independent of the markets which they serve. To the extent that vertical integration occurs, an excess burden may arise on the uses and/or sources of income, depending on the relative elasticities of supply and demand, assuming that neither takes the value of zero.

For Cases 3 and 7 of the export sector and Case 7 for the domestic and import-competing sectors, no excess burden is possible, since we have already argued that the burden of the tax will fall on the fixed factor, labor. More of the burden of the tax will, however, shift to labor employed in firms which do not integrate.

If Case 4 for the export and Case 8 for the import-competing sectors apply, the tax-induced uneconomic vertical integration induces higher operating costs. If vertical integration is complete, output levels will be reduced further than we had previously assumed. If vertical integration is not complete, the integrated sector will expand output and the non-integrated sector will restrict output "inappropriately" bringing the corresponding excess burdens. Aggregate output will be less than in the absence of the inefficient vertical integration. It is not clear whether output will be less than under vertical integration since the gains in output for the partially integrated sector may offset some of the declines in output of the non-integrated sector.

These observations are dependent on the existence of a uniform turnover tax. In West Virginia, however, as we indicated in Chapter III and are repeating in Table 24, for every class of business activity engaged in by firms in the state, the total value and volume of that activity must be reported and a corresponding tax paid whether or not the

TABLE 24

CLASSES OF BUSINESS ACTIVITY AND RATES
BUSINESS AND OCCUPATION TAX AND
TAX ON INTRA-STATE GROSS INCOME
OF CERTAIN CARRIERS
WEST VIRGINIA, 1967

Classes of Business Activity Subject to Tax	Tax Rate Imposed Per $100 of Tax Base
1. Coal	$1.35
2. Sand, Gravel, or Other Mineral Products Not Quarried or Mined	3.95
3. Oil	3.95
4. Natural Gas	7.85*
5. Limestone or Sandstone--Quarried or Mined	2.00
6. Timber	2.00
7. Other Natural Resource Products	2.60
8. Manufactured, Compounded or Prepared for Sale Products	0.40/0.80**
9. Retailers	0.50
10. Wholesalers	0.25
11. Public Service or Utility	1.30
12. Electric Light and Power Companies (Sales and Demand Charges, Domestic Purposes, and Commercial Lighting)	5.20
13. Water Companies	4.00
14. Electric Light and Power Companies (All Other Sales and Demand Charges for All Other Purposes)	3.90
15. Natural Gas Companies, Toll Bridges	3.90
16. All Other Public Service or Utility Business	2.60
17. Contracting	2.60

TABLE 24--Continued

Classes of Business Activity Subject to Tax	Tax Rate Imposed Per $100 of Tax Base
18. Amusement	0.65
19. Service or Calling and All Other Business	1.05
20. Rentals, Royalties, Fees, or Otherwise	1.05
21. Small Loans and Industrial Loans	1.05
22A. Buses	3.00
22B. Buses (Urban or suburban)	2.00
23. Taxis	3.00
24. Truckers and Transfer Companies	3.00
25. Other Motor Vehicle Carriers, Railroad Car Corporations, Express Corporations, or Companies	3.00
26. Telephone Corporations	3.40
27. Telegraph Corporations	3.00
28. Pipe-Line Corporations	3.00
29. Persons or Corporations Operating a Steamboat, Steamship or Airline	3.00
30. Railroad Corporations	3.00

*Natural Gas has a $5,000 gross income exclusion in computing its tax base. All other industries are exempt from liability for the first $50 of tax liability.

**The higher rate applied in the last half of 1967.

firm is vertically integrated. The tax identifies thirty different stages or classes of production and establishes sixteen unique tax rates. One implication of this rate structure and the language of the law is that there is less tendency toward vertical integration from extraction to manufacturing to wholesale or retail than there is for integration <u>within</u> one of these stages of production.

An example of the latter is where all stages of the manufacturing process tend to occur within one firm operating within the state. If a firm is integrated beyond those manufacturing processes, e.g., has a captive mine and uses coal in the manufacturing process, it must report the value of the coal used and pay a tax on this value at the appropriate tax rate. Then the firm must value its total manufacturing output and pay the tax on that total value. Finally, if the manufacturer also sells his goods wholesale and/or retail through the trade sector, either the wholesale or retail value is taxed, but not both. An exception to this sequence of taxation is provided in the case of those natural gas producers who sell their output at retail or wholesale. They are permitted to deduct the tax paid on the value of the gas at the wellhead (provided the wholesaler or retailer was also the gas producer) from their tax liability under the wholesale or retail class. Vertical integration by such gas producers is encouraged just as integration by those who are engaged in wholesale-retail integrated operations is encouraged. Thus some types of vertical integration are encouraged while others are discouraged (or to look at the other side of the coin, the corresponding forms of specialization are discouraged and encouraged) under one and the same tax statute because of the special privileges granted to specific industries. Moreover, natural gas producers do not have to pay on the first

$5,000 of the gross value of their production, a fact which may help to explain why there are so many small producers organized in interlocking partnerships or joint ventures.

A second element of the West Virginia turnover tax not present in a uniform turnover tax is the differentiated rate structure which encourages differential incentives to integrate vertically. This has the effect of penalizing one form of business activity relative to another and creates unneutral impacts through distorted price differentials for products where the tax is shifted forward and distorts resource allocation among industries whether or not the tax is shifted forward. For example, this structure encourages production activity subject to low tax rates at the expense of production subject to relatively high tax rates.

Although only conjecture about its significance is possible at present, it is interesting to note that the West Virginia turnover tax base (reported gross) is greatest at the lower rates, while the least reported gross is on the higher rates. In Figure 2, the vertical axis shows the total declared gross under each of the categories identified in Table 24, while the horizontal axis measures the rate paid per $100 of gross value. Since there are a range of rates which will either increase or decrease the tax bill, the individual firm is encouraged to either vertically integrate, to declare his operation to be of a nature which corresponds to a lower tax category, or not enter into the production of high-taxed activity. That such a phenomenon may be occuring is reflected in the negative slope of the observations. As rates increase the amount of declared gross declines. The reader is free to speculate whether this is due to: (1) "natural law;" (2) distortion of the organization of business enterprises in such a way so as to insure reporting at a more favorable

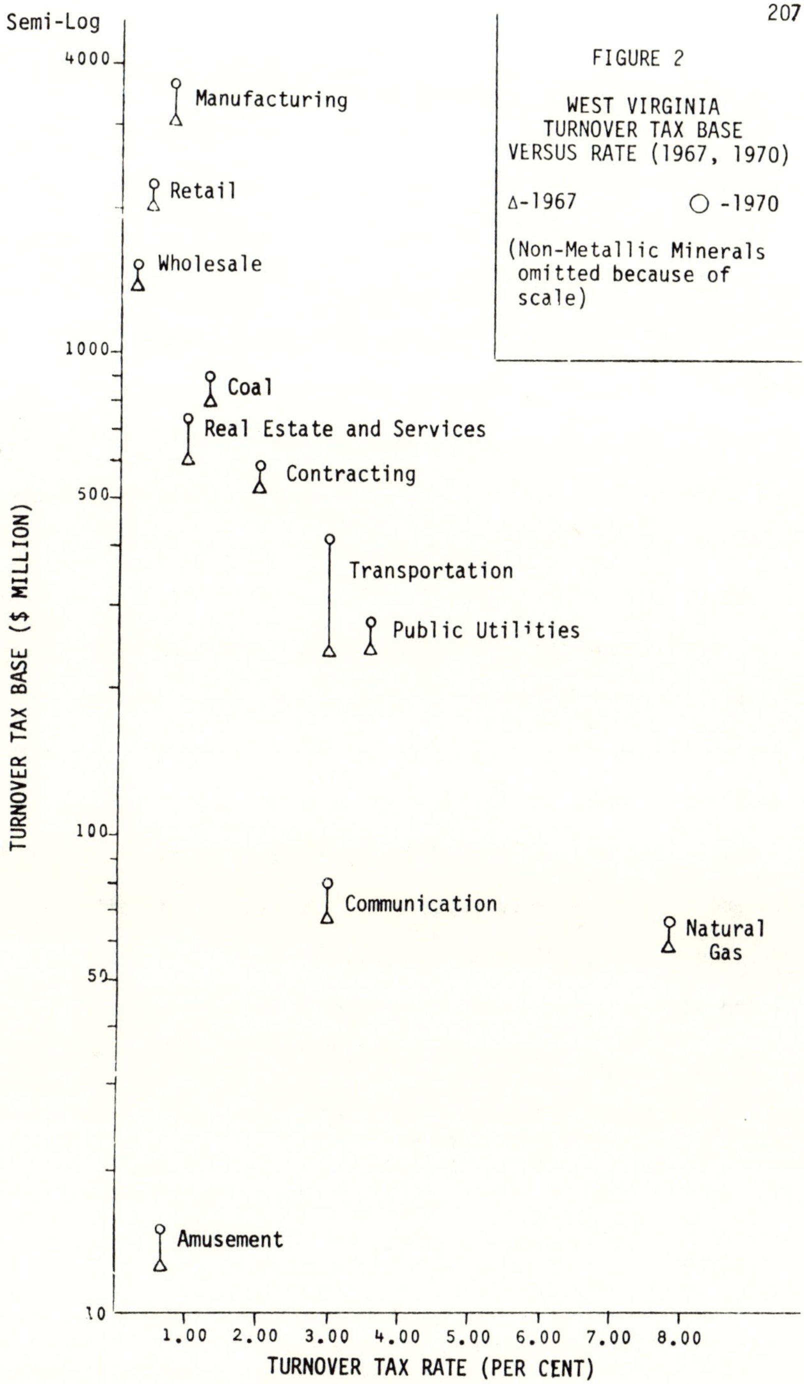

FIGURE 2

WEST VIRGINIA
TURNOVER TAX BASE
VERSUS RATE (1967, 1970)

Δ-1967 ○ -1970

(Non-Metallic Minerals omitted because of scale)

rate structure; (3) misreporting of taxable value since the audit staff is not large enough to do an effective job of enforcement;[1] or (4) the lack of incentive to locate firms which are subject to high turnover tax rates in West Virginia.[2]

This differentiated rate structure raises interesting second-best questions. The potential excess burdens identified earlier, associated with "uneconomic" vertical integration would appear to be reduced to the extent that the "uneconomic" stimulus to vertical integration is withheld. Yet the law has the effect of raising prices and/or reducing factor employment rewards in both the non-vertically and vertically integrated goods sectors, even though the price pyramiding which occurs differs for the taxed industries. (To repeat, the less vertically integrated the firm, the larger number of tax levy points which exist and the larger the degree of tax pyramiding which may occur.) Thus, when this pyramiding is coupled with the differentiated rate structure, the distortion in relative prices and factor rewards becomes quite complex. It is difficult to say *a priori* which set of distortions would be greater. The excess burdens under the uniform turnover tax are probably exceeded by those created by

---

[1]Recent oral testimony by the West Virginia Tax Commissioner Richard L. Dailey indicates that the current ratio of additional taxes collected to audit expenditures is 16 to 1. 1975-76 Budget Hearings, House Finance Committee, West Virginia Legislature, February 28, 1975.

[2]According to some observers, the ratio of the value of construction activity (taxes at relatively high rates) in the state to the level of income is significantly below the corresponding U.S. ratio. In addition a number of what might be considered domestic or local products or services are imported from firms located just beyond the border of the state. See Robert J. Saunders, *The Spatial Concentration of Industry in Appalachia: An Analysis of Potential for Import Substitution* (Washington, D.C.: Appalachian Regional Commission, 1969).

the multiple-rate turnover tax in West Virginia, though the combined effect of interrelated distortions is hard to estimate. There is no question that the higher rates levied on early value-added industires enhances the tax pyramiding effects.[1]

A second potential for excess burden for all three markets in West Virginia is the existence of firms which operate in more than one state partially producing their products in West Virginia and elsewhere. The turnover tax law permits these firms to pay on the gross product in the state as apportioned by either one of two formulae--they can (1) calculate the cost of labor in West Virginia as a percentage of total labor costs everywhere and apply this percentage to the corporation's gross income or (2) calculate the cost of operations in West Virginia as a percentage of total cost of operations everywhere, and apply this percentage to the corporation's gross income.

This generates a special case of the vertical integration phenomenon which operates in the reverse direction by encouraging spatial de-integration. By engaging in operation both in and out of the state, the firm can avoid payment on gross activity in the state. Thus, *ceteris paribus*, a firm that operated wholly within the state and bought its materials in the state would have to pay the tax on its entire gross while a firm which purchased the raw material outside the state and then shipped it to be fabricated in the state would only have to pay on the amount of activity generated in the state as measured by the apportionment formula. It may be partly due to the turnover tax that some 46 per cent of business in West Virginia is conducted by corporations which are considered multistate firms and that 54 per cent of gross industry output in 1965 was represented by purchase or transfer from out-of-state.[2] In

---

[1]See p. 200 above.

[2]Miernyk, *Simulating Regional Economic Development*.

effect, the turnover tax uses a value-added apportionment formula for assigning gross business activity of multistate firms to the state (albeit, using a single factor) while using a gross apportionment formula (100 per cent) for those who operate solely within the state.

Special externalities that wipe out gains to individual firms from this formula will occur as firms adjust their multistate activities, much as the gains from vertical integration are eroded as all firms integrate. Thus, as firms modify the extent to which they engage in multistate operations, the effective rate required to obtain the same real resource transfer will rise and multistate and domestic firms will be subject to higher tax rates. If geographic de-integration is complete, the taxes paid by multistate firms will be the same as if none had attempted to integrate their operations geographically.[1] Yet of course any one firm would be worse off if it did not disperse its operations.

In general this means that there is a greater tax on processed items (such as frozen foods, processed foods, or completed assemblies) than on less highly processed items, such as ordinary tools or do-it-yourself kits, thus shifting consumption and resources from the former toward the latter (unless there is complete vertical integration). The effect of this would be to find firms importing partially finished goods into the state to be finished and shipped out to market or goods partially finished and then moved out of state for completion.

Finally, the West Virginia turnover tax may discriminate against the domestic production and sale of capital goods in West Virginia since

---

[1]See the discussion in Appendix E in which we found no statistical evidence that the multistate firm was differentially treated and suggests that, in fact, spatial de-integration may have been completed.

the importation of capital goods is not taxed. This will discriminate further against the use of capital in West Virginia, for the tax favors production of capital goods in the non-taxed region that might otherwise be cheaper to produce in West Virginia, causing the substitution of labor for capital at the margin or causing the internal production of their own capital by the taxed firms. Our assumption of fixed proportions denies the former but not the latter possibility. In either event, an excess burden is created by the distortion in relative price of capital as between externally and internally produced capital in West Virginia. This means, therefore, that gross state product will be less than would otherwise be the case (i.e., under a non-capital discriminatory tax) because of this inefficiency (or because of migration of firms away from the West Virginia taxing jurisdiction).

At this juncture it seems safe to say that in terms of efficiency and excess burden, the turnover tax has a number of shortcomings. We now turn to the task of judging whether its replacement by a value-added tax can be considered an improvement.

Efficiency and Differential Excess Burden Under the Income Value-Added Tax

With the shift to an income value-added tax, we assumed that the level of taxes levied on the three broad "sectors" would be the same as under the turnover tax. The differential incidence of the tax, therefore, remains the same in this broad aggregate sense. Within each of the broad sectors, however, the initial burden of the tax and the initial impact on prices will be distributed differently.

To examine some possibilities regarding the differential excess burden with the shift to a value-added tax, we need to specify alternative sets of assumptions. We will focus attention on the conditions of Cases 4 and 8. In particular, we assume that both factors of production are mobile, fixed proportions exist over the relevant range of output, and that the elasticity of demand is either infinite (Case 4) or less than infinite (Case 8). We also assume that the adjustments in demand, output, and employment of the factors of production have been worked out. Under these circumstances the burden of the turnover tax falls entirely on the consumers of West Virginia products if the elasticity of supply is infinite (Case 8), or entirely on the factors of production in West Virginia if the elasticity of demand is infinite (Case 4). The same assumptions will apply for differential incidence of the value-added tax in the export, import-competing, and domestic sectors.

Export and Import-Competing Sectors. For the turnover tax, we noted that no excess burdens could be present so long as fixed factor supplies were assumed, but that over a longer time period in which the conditions of Case 4 for the export sector (Case 8--import-competing) were assumed, excess burdens in production could arise in two ways. First, as a consequence of the decline in output in response to reductions in the return to the factors of production, even if the turnover tax burden were uniformly levied; and second, as a consequence of the output reductions due to the fact that the turnover tax is not uniformly levied.[1] With the change to a value-added tax and with fixed factor supplies there would be no output change and, therefore, no change in those excess burdens

[1]See discussion on pp. 202ff.

created under the turnover tax. In a subsequent period of time in which we assume the factors of production are once again mobile (Case 4--export, Case 8--import competing) and the elasticity of demand infinite, the excess burden in production caused by the differentiated rate structure would be removed. There would still remain an excess burden in production as a consequence of the uniform levy on value added, assuming that the level of taxation on the two broad sectors does not change appreciably.

The work-leisure choice is just as likely to be affected by the value-added tax as the turnover tax, but the magnitude of the substitution effect (leisure for labor or employment of other inputs; occupational choice by inputs) might be less under the value-added tax, which would not initially produce such large shifts in relative rewards. With pyramiding and differential rate structure both reduced and with the income effect to reckon with also, however, it is difficult to say what would really happen to the supplies of inputs and the excess burden.

Export and Domestic Sectors. Under the turnover tax, we theorized that if Case 8 conditions applied (i.e., fixed proportions in production, mobile factor supplies, and less than perfect elasticity of demand) inefficiencies could arise in both the use and sources of income in proportion to the relative elasticities of demand and supply. Replacing the turnover tax with a value-added tax would, with fixed factor supplies, leave these pre-existing excess burdens the same. In a longer time period, with both labor and capital mobile, and the price elasticity of demand less than infinity, there will be a shift of the burden from the consumers and producers of low value-added products to consumers and producers of high value-added products.

With the prices of products and factors changing in this fashion, inefficiencies in the use of both outputs and inputs may occur depending on the elasticities of supply and demand in each of the two sectors. If the price elasticity of supply is infinite, the burden will rest entirely on consumers with the prices of low value-added export and domestic products falling relative to those of high value-added export and domestic products. The relative price of high and low value-added goods will change in both the export and domestic markets. Excess burdens due to such price distortions should be reduced with the shift from the turnover tax, since the uniform value-added levy reduces the relative price differences between high and low value-added goods within each of the markets.

Whether excess burdens are reduced by the shift to the value-added tax with respect to the choice between current and future consumption depends on what happens to the relative prices of current and future goods in each of the markets and whether the effect is uniform for all consumers. The tax change could induce, at the margin, a shift in favor of current consumption. In general, however, no *a priori* conclusion can be drawn about a question which depends not only on what happens with respect to prices in the export and domestic markets, but also on the particular monetary-fiscal policies being pursued at the national level and the consumption mix of high and low value-added goods by consumers of West Virginia products. We may judge, however, that the tax change itself will not induce significant price differences in the aggregate, given our assumptions, and that this excess burden will remain the same.

Within each of the broad sectors, the relative prices between high value-added export and domestic products and non-taxed export-competing and import products will widen with corresponding changes in excess burdens. Consumption will shift toward export-competing and import products and away from high value-added export and domestic products, depending on the cross-elasticity of demand for these product groups. Conversely, the relative price spread between low value-added exports and domestic products and non-taxed export-competing and import products will narrow the corresponding shifts toward the consumption of low value-added export and domestic products and away from export-competing and imports, as a function of the cross-elasticity of demand for these competing product groups.

Whether excess burdens are increased or decreased depends on the relative cross-elasticities of demand for export-competing and import products in response to the change in the price of high and low value-added goods. The changes in price would be a function of the changes in output in the high and low value-added industries which are accompanied by appropriate shifts of labor and capital. Factors which remain employed in the high value-added industries will receive lower take-home pay both as a consequence of the reduced demand for those inputs and also as a consequence of the change in the relative choice of work versus leisure. The converse will be true for the low value-added industries. Output increases will be accompanied by increases in the return to the factors of production and there seems likely to be a reduction in the wage distortions, employer responses, and excess burdens. The excess burdens associated with the work-leisure choice will depend on the various input responses to the changes in income and in the relative cost of leisure. Again, whether excess burdens rise or fall in the aggregate is an empirical question which depends on the appropriate cross-elasticities of demand.

If the price elasticity of supply is less than perfect, the differential incidence of the tax will fall on both the use and source of income, and the differential excess burden for high and low value-added goods will be related to the relative elasticities of supply and demand.

Export, Import-Competing, and Domestic Sectors. We noted in our discussion of the turnover tax that there were three other types of excess burdens independent of the markets the three sectors served. They were the inefficiencies associated with tax-induced vertical-integration, spatial de-integration, and capital acquisitions.

In the long run, with respect to the excess burden from vertical integration and the accompanying "value-added" and "tax"pyramiding, the shift to an income value-added tax will serve to eliminate this induced response to the turnover tax. Value added as the base of taxation will be taxed only once. If the tax is passed forward, the purchasing firm will be able to deduct from its tax base the value of products purchased inclusive of the tax. Firms will now find it to their advantage to de-integrate their operation to the extent that this is efficient.

In the case of firms which operate in more than one state relative to those firms which operate only in West Virginia, the imposition of the value-added tax would mean that both types of firms would be treated identically. Thus, there would no longer be a tax-induced encouragement for spatial de-integration and a potential for discriminatory tax treatment between domestic firms and multistate businesses. (If spatial de-integration is complete, however, the external effects mean that the tax liabilities will be the same as they would have been if no firm had dispersed its activities.)[1]

The incentive to produce capital goods within the firm will be reduced, since the tax is levied on the income paid to the factors of production, independent of how they are utilized. Thus, capital goods will not again be taxed as they contribute to value added in future years. If capital goods are purchased from other firms within West Virginia, the tax would be levied on producers of the capital goods. There would, however, be a deferral of its deduction since only depreciation charges may be deducted by the purchaser. Thus, a residual potential excess burden exists with respect to the employment mix of labor and capital in West Virginia as a function of the potential interest earnings on the deferred depreciation. This excess burden is not possible, however, given our assumption of fixed proportions in the production process.

To the extent that capital production is not taxed outside of West Virginia, there remains an excess burden in the production and sale of capital goods in West Virginia. This, however, should be classified as an import-competing product and, therefore, the differential incidence and excess burden will rest on the factors of production employed in the import-competing industry and the same pattern of differential excess burden would be present as we analyzed earlier under the export and import-competing discussion of Cases 3 and 4.

Parenthetically, non-uniform pyramiding would be reduced and production organized more nearly along the lines of economic efficiency rather than along lines dictated by tax rates. It seems likely that

---

[1]See footnote 1, p. 210.

modification of the efficient factor mix due to future technological advances will not be accompanied by as many unneutral adjustments intended to reduce tax obligations, nor will those unneutral adjustments have the limiting effect on the growth of revenue. That is, to the extent that the patterns of factor employment are changed over time as technology advances, a value-added tax would continue to be levied on the value added created in the state, a result that is unlikely to be true under the multiple-classification turnover tax. "Challenges" or responses to the West Virginia turnover tax base are frequent. In 1967, the Interstate Carriers were successful in reducing their tax base by two-thirds.[1] In 1970, the Bethlehem Steel case was, according to estimates, the cause of the loss of millions in future tax revenue through a reduction in tax base.[2] Most recently, the turnover tax base for advertising of radio and television stations is being considered for elimination from the tax base on the grounds that it is interstate in character.[3]

Empirical Considerations

With respect to resource allocation among the export, import-competing, and domestic sectors, we have seen that no impairment of efficiency would be possible if one assumes fixed supplies of the factors of production. Further, if the marginal rate of substitution of capital for labor in West Virginia were equal to zero, there could be no excess burden with respect to changes in the relative price of capital and labor. If

---

[1]See State *ex rel*. Battle v Baltimore and O.R.R., 149 W.Va. 810, 143 SE 2d 331 (1965).

[2]See Bethlehem Mines Corp. v Haden W.Va. 172 S.E. 2d (1969).

[3]See Fanny Seiler, "House Eyes Alternate Vehicle," *Charleston (W.Va.) Gazette*, 28 February 1975, p. 1.

factors can move about among industries, however, there could be excess burdens within the broad sectors under both taxes. Thus, inefficiencies regarding both the sources and uses of income are possible if both factors of production are mobile. If either factor is fixed over the longer run, no excess burden may arise. Thus, given fixed factor proportions, only under Cases 4 and 8 is it possible to expect the existence of excess burdens. Even though such assumptions are heroic, it seems useful to employ such assumptions to estimate some components of the excess burdens under either tax. Even crude pioneering clues may facilitate judgments about whether the move to an income value-added tax may be considered an improvement in welfare.

With respect to all three broad sectors, we theorized that the structure of the turnover tax encouraged inefficiencies because of the inducements to vertically integrate, geographically disperse production facilities, and generate capital internally. With the shift to an income value-added tax, the artificial incentive to vertically integrate and to disperse production facilities to other states would be eliminated. In addition, it was argued that the tax-incentive to generate capital internally would be eliminated, but that there would still remain an incentive to import capital from outside the state, assuming that no equivalent taxes were levied on capital produced outside the state.

Unfortunately, because of the lack of data and models, we will not be unable to give empirical content to any of these three phenomena. We can, however, give clues to the possible differential excess burden which arises in the individual markets with the shift from a turnover to a value-added tax. The empirical method to be employed is one which has been widely used since its introduction by Harberger in 1959[1] and subsequent refinement.[2]

Excess Burden in Consumption/Production

The justification for the method rests on acceptance of the idea that the change in consumer (producer's) surplus is a useful way to approximate the excess burden effect of taxation. This method of describing and analyzing excess burden is vulnerable to the usual criticisms, but all attempts to measure excess burdens must assume that these shortcomings do not render the approach hopeless.[3] The approach is a partial equilibrium one, which in its simplest form is illustrated in Figure 3 Initially, the demand curve is BF. Let us assume that the economy is otherwise efficient (including the absence of taxes elsewhere) and an ad valorem tax (turnover tax) is levied on the production of exports in West Virginia equal to AB/OB and at the post-tax equilibrium equal to P_0P_t or T_G. The new "demand curve" becomes AF and represents the schedule of prices received by the producer net of the turnover tax. In addition, let us assume that the export sector is characterized by constant cost conditions in which the elasticity of substitution between capital and labor is zero. Under these conditions, the pre-tax equilibrium quantity and price will be equal to OQ_0 and OP_0, respectively and consumer

---

[1]Arnold C. Harberger, "The Corporate Income Tax: An Empirical Appraisal," Tax Revision Compendium, vol. 1. Submitted to the Committee on Ways and Means (Washington, D.C.: Government Printing Office, 1959) pp. 231-50.

[2]Arnold C. Harberger, Taxation and Welfare (Boston: Little, Brown and Co., 1974).

[3]For a discussion of these shortcomings and a rationale for the approach taken here, see Ibid., "Three Basic Postulates for Applied Welfare Economics: An Interpretive Essay," pp. 1-20.

FIGURE 3

ILLUSTRATION OF EXCESS BURDEN
UNDER AD VALOREM TAXATION

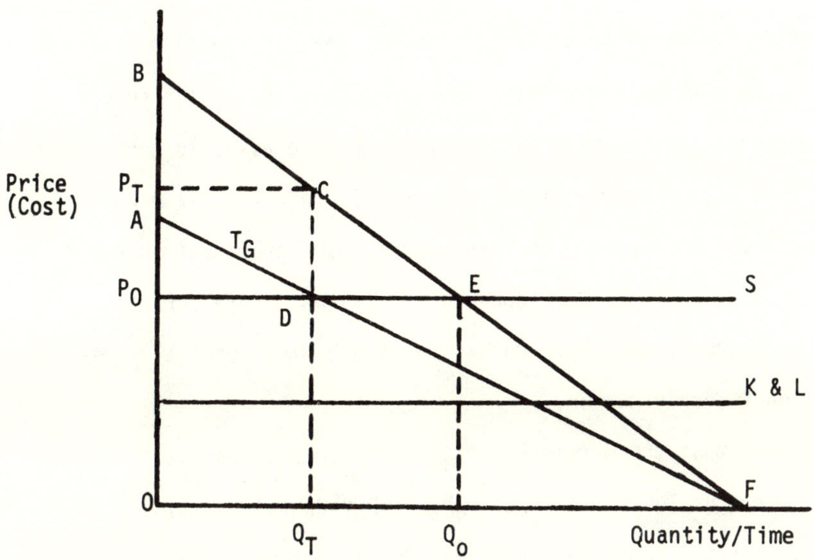

surplus is equal to the area P_0BE. Strictly speaking, these curves (compensated) are generally interpreted as aggregate demand by commodities and aggregate supply of factors of production in a closed economy. If a turnover or value-added tax were levied on all sectors in a closed economy, we would expect the supply curve to be relatively inelastic indicating the absence of alternative opportunities for the employment of the factors of production. In the open-economy setting in which we are working, we will want to relax this interpretation to reflect the idea (analogous to the <u>specific</u> excise tax model in a closed economy) that the level of aggregation is at the state (West Virginia) level and that the output supply curve may be relatively elastic or inelastic so long as it is consistent with the elasticity of supply of the factors of production from which it is derived. Thus, in Figure 3 we have superimposed the input supply curve (compensated) of labor (L) and capital (K) which are perfectly elastic. The aggregate supply curve is derived by the vertical summation of the two input supply curves.

Assuming that the marginal utility of income is constant, the tax reduces consumer surplus by the area P_0P_tCE, P_0P_tCD representing the resource transfer to the state. The area CDE represents a loss of consumer surplus in excess of that transferred to the state and, therefore, constitutes an excess burden in consumption. This is so, since theoretically the consumer would have been willing to pay $OBEQ_0$ if he were faced with the decision to purchase the units sequentially. Given linearity of the demand schedule over the relevant range, Harberger shows that the area CDE (excess burden) may be approximated by the formula[1] CDE = $-\frac{1}{2}(T_G \Delta Q)$,

---

[1]Ibid., p. 34.

where T is the tax revenue per unit and ΔQ is the change in the quantity consumed. He shows further that this expression is equivalent to the expression $-\frac{1}{2}\,\Sigma T_G \eta_d t_G$ where ΣT_G is equal to total revenue, η_d is the price elasticity of demand (in the original demand curve) and t_G is the percentage rate of the tax. This latter expression has an advantage over the former in that it does not require knowledge of the change in quantities sold and requires only that total revenue and tax rate be known. When this information is coupled with an assumption about the elasticity of demand, it permits the calculation of excess burden levels.

Ursula Hicks, who derived the equivalent measure in 1947, shows that the elasticity of demand function is a special case of a general expression in which constant costs prevail.[1] She shows that when the elasticity of supply η_s is allowed to vary with the elasticity of demand η_d expands to $\frac{\eta_d \eta_s}{\eta_d + \eta_s}$. The more general formulation, therefore, is

$$CDE = -\frac{1}{2}\,\Sigma T_G \frac{\eta_d \eta_s}{\eta_d + \eta_s} t_G$$

This may be illustrated by Figure 4 which shows that when the same tax is levied under increasing cost conditions, the burden of the tax is shared by both consumers and producers. The area CDE is equal to the total excess burden, with CFE representing the loss of consumer surplus and DFE the loss of producer's surplus. Using the general model described above and rearranging terms for ease of calculation, we will measure

---

[1]Ursula Hicks, Public Finance, 3rd ed (New York: Pitman Publishing Co., 1968), pp. 148-49.

FIGURE 4

CONSUMER'S AND PRODUCER'S SURPLUS MEASURE OF EXCESS BURDEN LEVELS WITH AD VALOREM TAXATION

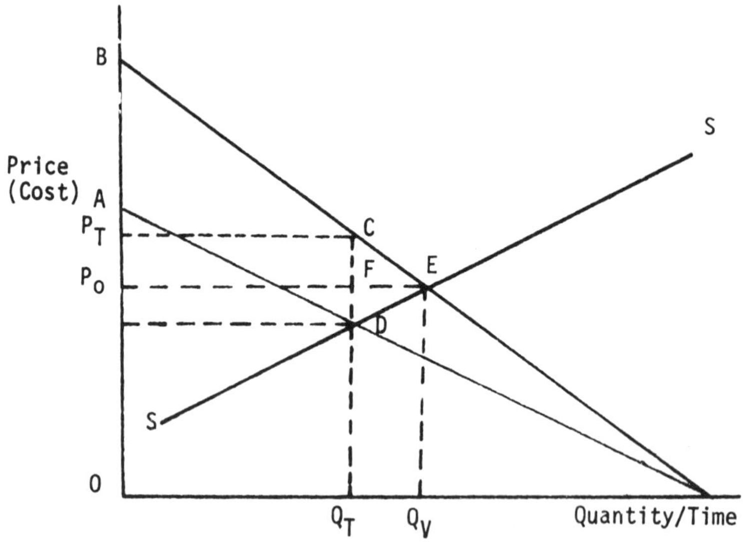

total excess burden in consumption (E.B.) under each of the two taxes as follows:

(1) Turnover Tax

$$E.B._G = -\tfrac{1}{2} \sum_{i=1}^{n} T_{G_i} t_{G_i} \frac{\eta_{d_i} \eta_{s_i}}{\eta_{d_i} + \eta_{s_i}}$$

(2) Value-Added Tax

$$E.B._V = -\tfrac{1}{2} \sum_{i=1}^{n} T_{V_i} t_{V_i} \frac{\eta_{d_i} \eta_{s_i}}{\eta_{d_i} + \eta_{s_i}}$$

The differential excess burden is equal to the algebraic difference between the two calculations, i.e., $E.B._V - E.B._G = \Delta E.B.$, and a negative value for $\Delta E.B.$ is to be interpreted as a reduction in excess burden. According to Harberger, there are two ways in which the tax rate (t) may be measured.[1] In the first view, the taxes paid by industry are seen as a percentage of the value-added contribution of that industry. In this way the demand for each industry's output is seen as a composite of both consumption and intermediate purchases, and permits a measure of the welfare loss in both production and consumption. The second view is to calculate the tax rate as the amount of tax embodied in a dollar of final demand. This would, however, have a leveling effect on the dispersion of the tax rates and, as a consequence, have the effect of eliminating the excess burden which may occur through the intermediate stage of production. In light of this, we will utilize the first method.

The data required for calculating the excess burdens may be split into two components, tax yield and tax rate $\sum_{i=1}^{n} (Tt)$ and the net elasticity

---

[1]See Harberger, "Corporate Income Tax," p. 232.

values $\frac{n_d n_s}{n_d + n_s}$. Table 25 contains the data for calculating the summed product of tax yield and effective tax rate under each of the taxes. Columns 2 through 5 relate to the turnover tax, while Columns 2, 6-8 relate to the replacement value-added tax. Column 2 shows that the estimated value added in West Virginia in 1967 for all firms is equal to $3.1 billion and is derived from our corporate sample of firms doing business in West Virginia. Column 3 shows the actual amount of turnover taxes collected by the West Virginia Tax Department for 1967 from each of the industries identified and amounts to $82.4 million. Column 4 shows the average effective rate of turnover tax per dollar of value added by all firms in the corporate sample. The number in parentheses is the value of three standard errors of the mean and provides an estimate of the confidence interval ± within which the population mean should fall at a 0.26 per cent significance level. Column 5 shows the product of Columns 3 and 4 and completes the dollar portion of the excess burden calculation under the turnover tax.

Column 6 shows the simulated amount of the tax that would be generated under an approximate equivalent yield value-added tax levied at a rate of 2.62 per cent of value added under the implicit assumption that the levels of output or value-added relationships do not change. Column 7 is the uniform rate levied on value added in each of the producing industries while Column 8 is the product of Columns 6 and 7 and provides the equivalent dollar portion of the excess burden calculation under the value-added tax.

TABLE 25

DATA SET FOR MEASURING DIFFERENTIAL EXCESS BURDENS
UNDER ALTERNATIVE BUSINESS TAXES
WEST VIRGINIA, 1967

Industry Identification	Estimated Value Added ($000)	Turnover Tax: Revenue T_G ($000)	Turnover Tax: Tax Rate t_G (Per cent)	Turnover Tax: $T_G t_G$ (Col 3 X 4) ($000)	Value-Added Tax: Revenue T_V ($000)	Value-Added Tax: Tax Rate t_V (Per cent)	Value-Added Tax: $T_V t_V$ (Col 6 X 7) ($000)
1	2	3	4	5	6	7	8
Coal Mining	257,604	11,123	4.04 0.87a	449	6,749	2.62	177
Crude Petroleum & Natural Gas	17,721	3,328	10.40 4.36	346	464	2.62	122
Contract Construction	174,181	9,782	7.34 3.47	718	4,564	2.62	120
Food & Kindred Products	30,191	743	1.91 0.67	142	791	2.62	21
Textile Mill, Apparel & Other Textiles	33,244	790	2.68 0.96	212	871	2.62	23
Chemicals & Allied Products	443,168	8,121	3.82 2.53	310	11,611	2.62	304
Glass & Glass Products	80,573	1,696	1.74 0.24	30	2,111	2.62	55
Stone & Clay Products	36,527	1,029	1.98 0.62	20	957	2.62	25
Primary Metals	442,443	6,635	1.77 0.46	117	11,592	2.62	304
Fabricated Metals	51,870	1,114	2.21 0.83	25	1,359	2.62	36

TABLE 25--Continued

Industry Identification	Estimated Value Added ($000)	Turnover Tax: Revenue T_G ($000)	Turnover Tax: Tax Rate t_G (Per cent)	Turnover Tax: $T_G t_G$ (Col 3 X 4) ($000)	Value-Added Tax: Revenue T_V ($000)	Value-Added Tax: Tax Rate t_V (Per cent)	Value-Added Tax: $T_V t_V$ (Col 6 X 7) ($000)
1	2	3	4	5	6	7	8
Machinery, Including Electrical	14,504	260	1.82 [0.92 a]	5	380	2.62	10
Transportation Equipment	18,359	327	1.76 [0.78 a]	6	481	2.62	13
All Other Manufacturing	55,305	1,300	2.92 [1.25 a]	38	1,449	2.62	38
Rail & Related Services	119,189	2,100	1.76 (N.C.)	37	3,123	2.62	82
Motor Freight, Related Services & All Other Transportation	27,610	1,081	5.22 [1.32 a]	56	724	2.62	19
Communication & Public Utilities	252,148	14,300	11.52 [2.69 a]	1,647	6,606	2.62	173
Wholesale Trade	252,778	2,757	2.29 [0.83 a]	63	6,623	2.62	174
Retail Trade	489,558	9,356	1.91 [0.30 a]	179	12,826	2.62	336
Finance	18,113	249	1.48 [0.14 a]	4	475	2.62	12
Real Estate	57,256	1,580	4.16 [3.10 a]	66	1,500	2.62	39
Services	288,668	4,737	2.07 [0.41 a]	98	7,563	2.62	198
Totals	3,161,000	82,409		4,250	82,819	2.62	2,170

[a]Three standard errors of the mean.

The second component of the excess burden formula has to do with the value of the elasticity coefficients. Since estimates of elasticity of demand or supply are not available for the West Virginia markets, we will assume a range of values consistent with those implied by our theoretical analysis in this chapter and the empirical analysis of Chapter IV. Table 26 shows the net elasticity coefficients to be applied to the derived data of Table 25. Utilizing Columns 5 and 8 of Table 25 together with the matrix of net elasticity coefficients from Table 26, we may now complete the calculation of possible excess burden under each of the taxes under the varying market conditions specified in our theoretical analysis. Our approach will be similar to that taken up in Chapter IV. We will begin by assuming that uniform elasticities apply to all industries and all consumers and estimate the possible level of excess burden in consumption and/or production using the characteristics of the short-run Simulation Models A, B, and C (Version 3).[1]

Simulation Model A. In the longer run, under Simulation Model A, we argued that with fixed proportions in production and Case 4 conditions applying, i.e., that the elasticity of demand was perfectly elastic, the excess burden would be a function of the elasticity of supply. The estimated level of excess burden is given in Table 27 below. Under the turnover tax, the long-run producer's excess burden is estimated to be between \$1.06 and \$3.19 million (Col. 2), given a range of elasticity of supply from 0.50 to 1.50 (Table 26, Row 5). Simulating the replacement of the turnover tax by a value-added tax and assuming that nothing else changes,

---

[1]We do not, however, need input-output to estimate these excess burdens since we are using a partial equilibrium approach.

TABLE 26

NET ELASTICITY COEFFICIENTS
UNDER A SELECTED SET
OF DEMAND AND SUPPLY ELASTICITY ASSUMPTIONS

$$\frac{\eta_d \eta_s}{\eta_d + \eta_s}$$

Elasticity of Demand η_d	Elasticity of Supply η_s 0	0.50	1.00	1.50	∞
	1	2	3	4	5
1. 0	---	0	0	0	0
2. 0.50	0	0.25	0.33	0.38	0.50
3. 1.00	0	0.33	0.50	0.60	1.00
4. 1.50	0	0.38	0.60	0.75	1.50
5. ∞	0	0.50	1.00	1.50	--

TABLE 27

PRODUCER'S EXCESS BURDENS UNDER ALTERNATIVE BUSINESS TAXES IN WEST VIRGINIA, SIMULATION MODEL A 1967

Elasticity Coefficients 100% Backward Shifting ($\eta_d = \infty$) η_s	Turnover Tax			Value-Added Tax			Differential Excess Burden		
	($000)	Per Cent of Revenue	Per Cent of Value Added	($000)	Per Cent of Revenue	Per Cent of Value Added	($000)	Per Cent of Revenue	Per Cent of Value Added
1	2	3	4	5	6	7	8	9	10
.50	1,062	1.29	0.04	542	0.66	0.02	- 520	0.63	0.02
1.00	2,125	2.58	0.07	1,085	1.32	0.03	-1,040	1.26	0.03
1.50	3,187	3.87	0.10	1,627	1.97	0.05	-1,560	1.89	0.05

yields a level of excess burden between $0.54 and $1.63 million (Col. 5) depending on the supply elasticity assumed. The differential excess burden (Col. 8) provides an estimated gain in welfare of approximately $0.52 to $1.56 million.

The reason for the reduction in excess burden is because the turnover tax rate (t) varies from one industry to another. This gives rise to a greater excess burden under the turnover tax since excess burdens vary with the square of the tax rate and a higher rate in one industry increases excess burden by more than a lower rate will reduce excess burden in another industry. With fixed proportions in production, if a uniform turnover tax were levied and subsequently a uniform equal-yield value-added tax replaced it, the level of excess burden would not change. Thus the differential excess burden estimated here is due solely to the existence of a differential rate structure under the turnover tax (ignoring other causes of turnover tax-induced inefficiencies such as pyramiding, spatial de-integration, and vertical integration).

In relative terms, the excess burden under the turnover tax ranges from 0.04 to 0.10 per cent of estimated value added (Col. 4) and in excess of 1 to almost 4 per cent of the revenue yield. With the value-added replacement, the relative excess burden as a percentage of estimated value added ranges from approximately 0.02 to 0.05 per cent (Col. 10) and as a per cent of revenue from 0.66 to almost 2.00 per cent (Col. 6). The reduction in excess burden under the value-added tax is approximately 50 per cent. Thus, an excess burden in production remains with the replacement value-added tax and the differential excess burden may be interpreted as the amount of excess burden eliminated by the removal of the differential rate structure under the turnover tax. In a sense these figures may be considered to be a conservative estimate of the differential excess burden with the replacement value-added tax since the estimates do not take account of the possible excess burden reduction associated with the vertical integration-price pyramiding, spatial de-integration, and internal capital generation phenomena. One should keep in mind, of course, that certain other components of excess burden are ignored or assumed away, and our oversimplifications inevitably make such estimates no more than rough clues.

Simulation Model B. Under Simulation Model B, given fixed factor proportions and perfect elasticity of supply (Case 8) such that the burden of the tax is borne entirely by the consumer, we noted that excess burden would be a function of the elasticity of demand. Under these conditions, the excess burdens are the same as under Simulation Model A since in Table 26 the net elasticity coefficients of Row 5 are identical to Column 5. As far as excess burden calculation is concerned, therefore, it does not matter if demand or supply is perfectly elastic. The only difference is that the excess burden now appears on the consumers of West Virginia's products rather than on producers as in Simulation Model A.

Simulation Model C. Under Simulation Model C, we assumed that for concentrated industries, the entire burden of the tax was passed forward, while in unconcentrated industries only 50 per cent of the burden was passed forward. The elasticities of demand and supply could vary so long as their combined effect permitted an equal sharing of the tax burden. In the calculations, the concentrated-industry supply coefficients (perfectly elastic) were paired with alternative demand coefficients ranging from 0.50 to 1.50 (Table 26, Col. 5). For the unconcentrated industries, we utilized those net elasticity coefficients which are the result of pairing elasticities of supply and demand whose values are the same, e.g., $\eta_d = 0.50 = \eta_s$. In Table 26 these net elasticity coefficients are those which come down the table beginning at Row 2, Column 2 and proceeding diagonally to Row 4, Column 4.

Table 28 provides the results and shows that the magnitude of change in excess burden is approximately the same as under the more restrictive conditions of Simulation Models A and B. There is, however, a slight dampening of the effect with the lowest differential excess burden equal to approximately $0.49 million (Col. 9) compared with the $0.52 million low estimate in Column 8, Table 27. As far as these projections are concerned, therefore, it seems that the effects associated with the shift from a turnover to a value-added tax are relatively insensitive to elasticity assumptions which attempt to distinguish between concentrated and unconcentrated industry groups.

Excess Burden in the Work-Leisure Choice

As noted earlier, excess burdens could arise with the work-leisure choice, but we do not add in estimates[1] prepared in this way since to do so would involve double-counting.[2] One may estimate excess burden on the output or the input side but they are not additive.

---

[1]Such estimates, prepared by the author, are on file in the Bureau of Business Research at West Virginia University and can be made available to those interested.

[2]Wisecarver, "Input-Market Distortions."

TABLE 28

EXCESS BURDENS UNDER ALTERNATIVE BUSINESS TAXES
IN WEST VIRGINIA, SIMULATION MODEL C
1967

Unconcentrated Industries 50% Forward Shifting $\eta_d = \eta_s$	Concentrated Industries 100% Forward Shifting ($\eta_s = \infty$) η_d	Excess Burden With Turnover Tax			Excess Burden With Value-Added Tax			Differential Excess Burden		
		($000)	As Per Cent of Revenue	As Per Cent of Value Added	($000)	As Per Cent of Revenue	As Per Cent of Value Added	($000)	As Per Cent of Revenue	As Per Cent of Value Added
1	2	3	4	5	6	7	8	9	10	11
0.50	0.50	955	1.66	0.03	506	0.61	0.02	- 488	0.54	0.01
1.00	0.50	1,062	1.29	0.03	542	0.66	0.02	- 520	0.63	0.02
1.50	0.50	1,200	1.46	0.04	579	0.70	0.02	- 621	0.75	0.02
0.50	1.00	1,802	2.19	0.06	985	1.20	0.03	- 818	0.99	0.03
1.00	1.00	1,910	2.32	0.06	1,021	1.24	0.03	- 889	1.08	0.03
1.50	1.00	2,017	2.45	0.06	1,058	1.28	0.03	- 959	1.16	0.03
0.50	1.50	2,650	3.22	0.08	1,454	1.76	0.05	-1,192	1.45	0.04
1.00	1.50	2,757	3.35	0.09	1,490	1.81	0.05	-1,267	1.54	0.04
1.50	1.50	2,870	3.48	0.09	1,527	1.85	0.05	-1,343	1.63	0.04

Concluding Observations

We have seen that with the replacement of the turnover tax, there can be no improvement of efficiency so long as either the factors of production or the demand is fixed. When these assumptions are relaxed, of course, excess burdens will arise under both taxes. With the aid of simplifying assumptions, we have theorized and estimated that the move to a value-added tax would reduce the magnitude of certain components of the excess burden. In addition, we discussed three phenomena which could give rise to additional excess burdens under the turnover tax, two of which would be eliminated entirely with the shift to a value-added tax. These two phenomena were vertical-integration-price-pyramiaing and spatial de-integration. The third phenomenon had to do with the methods of capital acquisition. Here we observed that since imports were not taxed, but domestic purchases were, that there would still be an incentive to acquire capital goods outside of the state. The choice between domestic purchases and internally generated capital, however, would no longer be biased in favor of the latter.

Some closing caveats are in order lest the impression be given that we take the numbers generated too seriously. A number of conditions which we assumed away, if present, could serve to alter the estimated effects. The most important of these is that we ignored all second-best considerations and also the conceivable externality-abatement effects of one or both taxes. Another heroic assumption comprised our guesses about elasticities, which neglect the basic uncertainties about them as well as the possible general equilibrium repercussions. For instance, supply elasticities would be shaped in part by locational advantages and economic rents which we know little about. Excess burden occurs, of course, only when we may observe changes in the decision to produce or consume and if the taxes do not induce this kind of response, then no excess burden may exist. In fact, the tax system may act to either correct implied inefficiencies or to transfer some of the rents to the public sector without adversely affecting resource allocation. In addition, for the purpose of this chapter we assumed that production was governed by fixed factor proportions. Though this is not always an unreasonable assumption in the short run, it does not represent a reasonable assumption for the long run. With variable proportions in the long run, we could expect changes in the relative mix of capital and labor employed. Finally, the data used for the simulations dealt with 1967 only and as such the numbers generated should be interpreted in terms of direction and relative magnitude, rather than precise estimates.

CHAPTER VI

TURNOVER VERSUS VALUE-ADDED TAXATION IN WEST VIRGINIA: REVENUE CONSIDERATIONS

In the preceding two chapters, we were concerned with the effect of the turnover and replacement value-added tax on burden-bearing and on efficiency in the economy. In this chapter we want to shift our focus and look at the tax change from the taxing authority's point of view. In particular, we will concentrate on the three revenue criteria--adequacy, stability-predictability, and administrative efficiency--which weighed heavily in prior legislative deliberations over the tax change. Of these three criteria, revenue adequacy was probably the most important issue in the debate, and, in fact, was instrumental in the defeat of the proposed change in 1967 and 1970.

We will begin, therefore, with a discussion of the adequacy criterion in general terms to see its relevance to the West Virginia situation. Following this, we will estimate revenues from a value-added tax in West Virginia, assuming no adjustments to the tax change by firms for the period 1967-1969. This does not mean that we may not observe other changes taking place, i.e., those due to conditions not associated with the tax change for the period 1967-1969. For the revenue implications after longer-run adjustments, we will resort to a speculative discussion in which we draw on some of the conclusions of the previous chapters.

Adequacy

Adequacy is the term generally used to describe the ability of a revenue system to finance anticipated growth in expenditures without having to resort to frequent rate changes or to other sources of revenue. This need for responsiveness of the revenue system has been especially important to state and local governments. State legislators and administrators have historically been faced with rates of growth in expenditures which, in the absence of rate changes or new sources of revenue, have exceeded the rate of growth of revenue from all sources. This may be an undesirable criterion if it reflects merely a desire on the part of public officials to ease their decision-making costs. Also such a criterion violates the general principle that expenditure decisions should be linked to revenue decisions. From this latter view, if the public wishes to buy public goods, then the necessary revenue should be provided through rate changes and/or new sources of revenue rather than from automatic increases in revenue. From either perspective, however, it is true that the rate of growtn in public expenditures for all states has historically grown at a faster rate than revenues when adjusted for rate changes and new taxes,[1] and that the current federal revenue sharing program with the states reflects a conscious decision to supplement state and local own revenue sources. And, in any event, decision makers are properly concerned with the amount of revenue that

---

[1]For a discussion of the past trends and their implication for the future, see the work of Lawrence R. Kegan and George P. Roniger, "The Outlook of State and Local Finance," Fiscal Issues in the Future of Federalism (New York: Committee for Economic Development, 1968), pp. 233-277.

should be expected from the tax structure in various circumstances.

It may be useful to compare an income elasticity of revenue (η_R) with an income elasticity of expenditures (η_E). Both the elasticity of revenues and expenditures require that an appropriate income base be taken into consideration. Thus, one might compare the per cent change of total revenue to the per cent change in personal income and derive an elasticity value. Similarly one might look at the per cent change in total expenditures relative to the per cent change in income to derive a value for the income elasticity of expenditures. We will term the ratio of these two elasticities the "adequacy elasticity of revenue (η_A)" as in equation 6-1.

$$\eta_A = \frac{\eta_R}{\eta_E} \qquad (6\text{-}1)$$

The adequacy elasticity measure may take the value of less than, equal to, or greater than one and the revenue system would be judged correspondingly as being less than adequate, adequate, or more than adequate with respect to meeting anticipated growth of expenditures.

Using this notation and applying it to the state of West Virginia, we find that West Virginia shared the same dilemma faced by other states. In 1968 a study of the adequacy of West Virginia's revenue system projected to 1975 estimated the income elasticity of turnover tax revenue to be 0.83. By way of contrast, the income elasticity of state revenue from all sources was projected to be 1.11. Relative to all revenue sources, one may judge the turnover tax as being only 75 per cent as effective in generating revenue from increments in income as all other sources combined. Further, in the absence of rate changes, the turnover tax would have less impact as a revenue source over time. For the same time period, the income elasticity of expenditures (which of course involves deliberate policy choices) was projected to be 1.66. The derived adequacy elasticity coefficient of 0.66 indicates an "inadequate" revenue structure, in the sense noted, since the state would be able to meet only 66 per cent of the expenditures that are likely to emerge--if no action were taken to increase existing tax rates and/or obtain new sources of revenue.[1]

Differential Elasticity of Revenue

We can also compare the "income elasticities" of two taxes. The ratio of their responsiveness for generating revenue from incremental income will be termed the "differential elasticity of revenue." Analogous in a sense to the notions of differential incidence and differential excess burden, this differential elasticity of tax revenue may be expressed as follows:

$$\Delta\eta_{r \cdot o} = \frac{\eta_r}{\eta_o} \qquad (6\text{-}2)$$

where the subscript o stands for the income elasticity of the original revenue source and the subscript r stands for the income elasticity of revenue from the replacement tax. The derived elasticity coefficient could take the value of greater than, equal to, or less than one, and the replacement tax would be judged correspondingly as contributing

---

[1]Dennis R. Leyden and Vance Q. Alvis, Fiscal Imperatives in 1975: A Current Perspective of West Virginia State Revenue and Expenditure Needs, West Virginia University Legislative Fiscal Studies, Vol. 1, No. 2, (Morgantown, W.Va.: West Virginia University, 1968), pp. 3, 13.

more than, the same as, or less than the original tax did to overall revenue growth. We will demonstrate below that while the adequacy elasticity of revenue requires that growth of an appropriate income base be taken into consideration, it is not necessary in differential elasticity of tax revenue considerations. This is so because the income base under the alternative tax remains the same and hence cancels out in the calculation. We are left, therefore, with an equation in which the only variables to be considered are those which affect tax revenue through changes in tax rates and tax base.

Consider, for example, that we are interested in knowing whether a proportional sales tax (s) is more or less productive over time than a proportional income tax (y). In differential elasticity terms, using personal income (p) as the income base, this may be measured as follows:

$$\Delta\eta_{s \cdot y} = \frac{\eta_s}{\eta_y} \tag{6-3}$$

Expanding and rearranging terms, 6-3 becomes 6-4:

$$\Delta\eta_{s \cdot y} = \frac{\Delta s_{t+1}}{s_t} \cdot \frac{p_t}{\Delta p_{t+1}} \cdot \frac{y_t}{\Delta y_{t+1}} \cdot \frac{\Delta p_{t+1}}{p_t} \tag{6-4}$$

Canceling common terms and reducing the remainder, equation 6-4 becomes 6-5:

$$\Delta\eta_{s \cdot y} = \frac{\%\Delta s}{\%\Delta y} \tag{6-5}$$

Thus, the problem reduces to an analysis of the comparative growth of revenue of alternative taxes in which the principal explanatory variables are those which explain changes in the tax bases and tax rates. We will try to examine this differential revenue elasticity of the value-added tax and the turnover tax.

Application to West Virginia

<u>No Output Adjustment to Value-Added Tax, 1967-1969</u>. We will initially limit our inquiry to those aspects of the two taxes which affect their relative productivity assuming no output adjustments to the change in tax. We will specify a model to estimate or simulate the change in revenue under each tax over the period 1967-1969. While before we assumed that all adjustments to the turnover tax had taken place, we now wish to observe West Virginia business' in a dynamic sense (by looking at changes in gross, value added, turnover tax base, and effective turnover tax rates) so that we may "explain" the changes in turnover tax revenue for the period 1967-1969. In addition, we will want to contrast these "explanations" with the ways in which value-added tax revenue may change. In this latter circumstance we assume that there are no additional changes in business activity for the period 1957-1969 because of the shift to the value-added tax. As in the other chapters, this is an extreme and probably unrealistic assumption, yet making even a crude start at estimating revenue possibilities seems to be important.

We also assume that the rate established for the value-added tax in the first year (1967) is one which yields the same revenue as under the turnover tax for the same year. This does not mean that revenue in 1968 and 1969 will also be equal, since we hold the 1967 value-added rate constant and observe its effects with the changes in gross and value added over the succeeding years, 1968, 1969. To be valid, this assumption for 1967 requires that the composition and level of real state government expenditures remain constant. One is faced at this point with the issues raised by Musgrave. He argues, if the assumption of equal money yield is used, there is a danger that the change in taxation ". . . may involve different transaction demands upon a constant money supply and thus involves price level changes."[1]

There are two aspects to this important observation that are pertinent here. First, is the tax change likely to alter prices nationally and thus affect import real expenditures by West Virginia government and, second, is the likely impact on domestic prices such as to lower domestic real expenditures by the West Virginia government?

In answer to the first question, Table 29 bears on the likely impact of the West Virginia economy on the national economy. Since West Virginia is estimated to have had only 1 per cent of the GNP in 1967 and an export level of 2/3 this amount, the possibility seems remote that the feedback effect would have a measurable effect on national price levels and thence on real state government import purchases.

The second question, however, does raise the possibility that real government domestic purchases will be reduced. This question is an empirical one, since there are some prices which will rise but others which will fall, _ceteris paribus_. The question becomes, "How will the change affect total state government domestic purchases?" One answer is provided in Table 30, where using the alternative Simulation

---

[1]Musgrave, _Theory of Public Finance_, p. 212.

TABLE 29

COMPARATIVE UNITED STATES AND WEST VIRGINIA
INCOME ACCOUNT STATISTICS
1965, 1967

	West Virginia			United States
	1965[a] ($000)	1967 ($000)	Per Cent U.S. GNP	1967 ($000)
Gross Industry Output	8,816,365	9,108,104[b]		
Gross State or National Product	6,966,092	7,197,000[d]	1.07	675,200,000[c]
State Exports	4,734,851	4,892,000[d]	0.72	
State Government Imports	39,148	40,443[d]	0.01	

Notes:

[a]William H. Miernyk and Kenneth L. Shellhammer, Simulating Regional Economic Development (Lexington: Mass.: D.C. Heath and Co., 1970), pp. 222-231.

[b]West Virginia State Tax Department, unpublished data.

[c]Survey of Current Business, Volume 51, No. 7, July 1971, p. 15.

[d]Estimated values were assumed to be the same proportion of Gross Industry Output in 1967 as in 1965.

For example:

$$\text{State Exports, 1967 (Estimated)} = \frac{\text{State Exports, 1965}}{\text{Gross Industry Output, 1965}} \cdot \text{Gross Industry Output, 1967}$$

TABLE 30

CHANGES IN OVERALL PRICE OF DOMESTIC STATE GOVERNMENT PURCHASES UNDER ALTERNATIVE SIMULATION MODELS WEST VIRGINIA, 1967

	Simulation Model	
Version	A	C
1	99.51	99.88
2	99.46	99.77
3	99.54	99.82

Models A and C of Chapter IV, we have calculated the price level change for domestic purchases of state government. The procedure is identical to that used to calculate the changes in overall price in the private export and domestic sectors.[1] Instead of weighting each industry's price index by its proportion of aggregate final private demand, we now weight each one by the proportion of state government purchases from that industry. The results show that under either simulation model (and for all versions) a price change of less than 1 per cent is indicated. Thus, our assumption of constant real government purchases seems to be a reasonable one.

Given these assumptions, we proceed by specifying a set of identities which will "explain" the change in revenue under each tax. In a broad aggregate sense, we may observe that under both taxes the change in revenue will be a function of change in the rate and the base:

(6-6) $$\Delta T = f(\Delta t, \Delta B)$$

In equation 6-6, T refers to total revenue, t refers to the tax rate, and B refers to the tax base. The tax rate (t) under the turnover tax may be viewed as a composite, consisting of the 16 different rates applied to the 30 classes of business activity. Any or all of the individual rates may change as a consequence of legislative action and together with the change in the base affect the change in revenue. Thus, equation 6-6 may be restructured as equation 6-7:

(6-7) $$\Delta t = g(\Delta t_1 \Delta B_1, \Delta t_2 \Delta B_2, \ldots t_n B_n)$$

---

[1]See discussion in Chapter IV, pp. 161-63, 180, as well as Appendix B for the details.

Since we are concerned with the relative productivity of the two tax measures, we will assume that statutory rates do not change. This does not mean that rates under the turnover tax will be invariant. The composite rate, Δt of equation 6-6, may also be affected by changes in the degree of vertical integration of individual firms. Since different tax rates apply to different classes of business activity, a firm which changed its degree of vertical integration from one period to another could have the effect of modifying the rate applicable to the same volume of business activity. For example, if a firm engaged in sand and gravel operations, which in 1967 was taxed at a rate of 3.95 per cent, decided to add another process--washing and grading--it is conceivable that the tax rate for this firm would drop from 3.95 (sand and gravel) to 0.40 per cent (manufacturing). A change in the composite rate may also occur as a consequence of misreporting of taxable base in a class subject to a different rate than the true class.[1] Thus, even though we assume that statutory rates do not change, we may find individual effective rates changing and as a consequence the composite rate as well. If this occurs, then the change in turnover tax revenue will likewise be affected and may be attributed to the structural characteristics of the tax.

Change in output under the turnover tax may be affected by structural considerations related to changes in the spatial de-integration phenomenon. If a firm shifts part of its productive capacity out of the state, it will reduce the value of output in West

---

[1]See discussion on page 208, including footnote 1 for an elaboration on this point.

Virginia even though the total value of the firm's output remains the same. Conversely, if the firm increases the amount of in-state production, it will tend to increase the value of output in West Virginia even though the total value of the firm's output does not change. We may also find the base changing as a consequence of the change in the socio-economic characteristics of the markets in which West Virginia's producers participate. We will assume that these socio-economic phenomena affect the value-added base in the same way and, hence, ignore them in our comparison of the differential elasticity of the alternative taxes.

The identity which shows these effects on revenue is given by equation 6-8 which indicates that the per cent change in turnover tax

(6-8) $$\%\Delta T_G = \%\Delta B_G + (\%\Delta t_G)(R_G)$$

revenue T_G over two time periods is equal to the per cent change in the tax base ($\%\Delta B_G$) over the same period plus the product of the per cent change in tax rate ($\%\Delta t_G$) and the ratio of the tax base in period 2 to the tax base in period 1 (R_G). Equation 6-8 permits us to separate the change in turnover tax revenue attributed to the change in base from that attributed to the change in effective rate over the period 1967-1969.

We move now to the relationship between changes in value-added tax revenue and the tax rate and base. Except for subscript notation, the general identity is the same as that for the turnover tax, i.e.,

(6-9) $$\%\Delta T_V = \%\Delta B_V + (\%\Delta t_V)(R_V)$$

with respect to the influence of rate change, we may note that since the value-added tax is uniform for all levels and classes of output, the only way the effective rate could change is through legislative action. Given our assumption that the statutory rate does not change, equation 6-9 reduces to 6-10:

$$\%\Delta T_V = \%\Delta B_V \tag{6-10}$$

Thus, the only changes which may occur in value-added tax revenue are those associated with changes in the base. The base of the value-added tax may change as a function of the employment of the factors of production, changes in depreciation levels, and changes in overall output. If there is a change in the proportion of import capital and/or intermediate purchases outside West Virginia, the aggregate value-added base would move in the opposite direction, given constant levels of output.

If intermediate import purchases per dollar of output increase, the effect would be immediate and would result in a reduction in the aggregate value-added base in the year of purchase. If intermediate domestic purchases increase per dollar of output, the effect would be to raise the aggregate value-added base in the year of purchase. Increases in the proportion of capital import purchases would be lagged as a function of depreciation schedules. For increases in the proportion of domestic capital purchases, the effect would be immediate since the sale would register immediately as an increase in aggregate output and would be offset in later years as a function of depreciation schedules.

These changes may also be seen as a function of the employment of the factors of production. With the assumptions made here, if out-of-state purchases of intermediate or capital goods per dollar of output change, then the relative employment of the factors of production must change also and in the opposite direction. We may use the ratio of value-added to gross to measure these phenomena. Beyond this, changes in the value-added base will be directly related to changes in the gross output of the state, given a constant value-added ratio. The manner in which these two factors influence total value-added revenue is shown by equation 6-11 where R_{VG} stands for the ratio of value-added to gross:

$$(6\text{-}11) \qquad \%\Delta B_V = \%\Delta B_G + \%\Delta R_{VG}$$

Substituting 6-11 into 6-9, we obtain the identity for measuring the change in value-added tax revenue:

$$(6\text{-}12) \qquad \%\Delta T_V = \%\Delta B_G + \%\Delta R_{VG}$$

As with the turnover tax identity, we may use equation 6-12 to separate out the changes in value-added tax revenue which may be attributed to changes in the gross base from that which may be attributed to changes in the ratio of value-added to gross.

Substituting equations 6-8 and 6-11 into equation 6-2, gives us equation 6-13:

$$(6\text{-}13) \qquad \Delta\eta_{V \cdot G} = \frac{\%\Delta T_V}{\%\Delta T_G} = \frac{\%\Delta B_G + \%\Delta R_{VG}}{\%\Delta B_G + (\%\Delta t_G)(R_G)}$$

In the simulation which follows, we will attempt to give empirical content to equations 6-8, 6-12, and 6-13. This requires that for 1967-1969 we provide the data base for our estimates of turnover tax base, revenue, and rate as well as the simulated estimate of the value-added tax base, revenue, and rate. We begin with the 1967 data. To estimate the total value-added base for all business activity in West Virginia, it was first necessary to adjust the value of gross reported to the West Virginia Tax Department by the multistate carriers (transportation). The reason for doing so is that the base under an income value-added tax is larger than under the turnover tax.[1] This adjustment is estimated to increase the tax base by some $283 million in 1967. Table 31 (Col. 3) shows that when this amount is included, the value of gross business activity in West Virginia in 1967 is estimated to have been approximately $9.1 billion.

With this adjusted gross base, we obtained an estimate of the value-added base by multiplying the sample-derived weighted ratios of value added to gross (Col. 2) by the total adjusted gross in all industries (Col. 3). We estimate that West Virginia's value added in 1967 amounted to 1/3 of the total gross or $3.1 billion (Col. 4). Of the six largest industries, comprising 80 per cent of the value added, the manufacturing industry is estimated to have generated the largest proportion of total value added in West Virginia (38 per cent) (Col. 4). This is 6 percentage points higher than its contribution to gross (32 per cent) (Col. 3). Interesting enough, the second largest

---

[1]Appendix C details the method employed to estimate the size of the tax base for the carriers doing business in West Virginia over the period 1967-1969. Evidence to support this adjustment is contained in Armco vs State of Michigan 102 NW 2D 552. In this case the court ruled that the Business Activities Tax (Value-Added Tax) was not a gross receipts tax and, therefore, not in violation of the Interstate Commerce Clause. By implication, it provided, however, that the state could begin with total receipts everywhere as a basis for apportionment of the value-added income of the multistate firm as defined by the Michigan Business Activities Tax. This particular case would appear to provide precedent for the same interpretation applying to the multistate carrier base for derivation of multistate value-added income.

TABLE 31

INCOME VALUE-ADDED BASE AND REVENUE ESTIMATE, WEST VIRGINIA, 1967

Rate = 0.0262

Industry Identification	Value Added / Gross[a]	Estimated Total Gross ($000)[b]	Value-Added Base ($000)[c]	Estimated Value-Added Revenue ($000)[d]	Turnover Tax Revenue CY 1967 ($000)[b]	Per Cent Change in Revenue With Turnover Tax Replaced[e]
1	2	3	4	5	6	7
Coal Mining	.30549	843,247 9.26f	257,604 8.15f	6,749	11,123 13.50f	- 39.23
Crude Petroleum & Natural Gas	.24802	71,448 0.78	17,721 0.56	464	3,328 4.04	- 86.06
Contract Construction	.36028	483,461 5.31	174,181 5.51	4,564	9,782 11.87	- 53.34
Manufacturing & Non-Metallic Minerals	.40943	2,945,983 32.36	1,206,174 38.16	31,602	22,016 26.71	43.54
Rail & Related Services	.48840	243,820 2.68	119,082 3.77	3,120	2,100 2.55	48.71
Motor Freight & Related Services	.52524	28,252 0.31	14,839 0.47	389	577 0.70	- 32.58
All Other Transportation	.56184	22,731 0.25	12,771 0.40	335	504 0.61	- 33.53

TABLE 31--Continued

Industry Identification	Value Added / Gross[a]	Estimated Total Gross ($000)[b]	Value-Added Base ($000)[c]	Estimated Value-Added Revenue ($000)[d]	Turnover Tax Revenue CY 1967 ($000)[b]	Per Cent Change in Revenue With Turnover Tax Replaced[e]
1	2	3	4	5	6	7
Communication & Public Utilities	.53776	468,886 5.14	252,148 7.98	6,606	14,300 17.35	- 53.80
Wholesale Trade	.19717	1,282,033 14.07	252,778 8.00	6,623	2,757 3.35	140.22
Retail Trade	.25522	1,918,182 21.06	489,558 15.49	12,826	9,356 11.35	37.09
Finance	.70610	25,652 0.28	18,113 0.57	475	249 0.30	90.76
Real Estate	.28152	203,380 2.23	57,256 1.81	1,500	1,580 1.92	- 5.06
Services	.50552	571,031 6.27	288,668 9.13	7,563	4,737 5.75	59.66
Total	.34705	9,108,106 100.00	3,161,000 100.00	82,819	82,409 100.00	0.50

[a]Derived from corporate sample.

[b]Furnished by West Virginia State Tax Department (unpublished).

[c]Col. 2 X Col. 3.

[d]Col. 4 X 0.0262

[e](1 - Col. 5 ÷ Col. 6)(100).

[f]Per Cent of Column Total.

contributor to value added in 1967 is the retail trade industry (16 per cent), followed by services (9 per cent), coal mining (8 per cent), and wholesale trade (8 per cent).

With a turnover tax yield of $82.409 million and an estimated value-added base of $3.1 billion, the effective rate would be 0.02607 per dollar of value added. To make sure the yield was at least equal to that under the turnover tax,this rate was rounded up to 0.0262 and yields approximately $82.819 million. This is approximately 1/4 of 1 per cent higher than the actual turnover tax yield (Col. 5). We should emphasize that the equal yield assumption applies only to the first year. For 1968 and 1969, we use the same rate and derive estimated value-added revenue which may be less, more than, or equal to the turnover tax revenue for the same year.

In percentage terms, the amount of change in revenue varies significantly among the different industries (Col. 7). The largest increase occurs in the wholesale trade industry (140 per cent) followed by finance (91 per cent), services (60 per cent), rail and related services (49 per cent), manufacturing (44 per cent), and retail trade (37 per cent) The largest decrease occurs in crude petroleum (-86 per cent) followed by communication and public utilities (-54 per cent), contract construction (-53 per cent), coal mining (-39 per cent), all other transportation (-34 per cent), motor freight and related services (-33 per cent), and real estate (-5 per cent). These percentage change figures are not to be interpreted as an indication of the percentage change in the level of taxes on individual firms within an industry.[1]

---

[1]See Appendix D.

The reason explained more fully below is that the sample-derived ratios of value added to gross in Column 2 of Table 31 are based on industry classifications of gross which included all activities of specific firms. The gross in Column 3, however, is based upon a classification of business activity by the West Virginia Tax Department which allocated the gross of each firm according to its tax class liability and, thereby, destroyed any linkage between tax base and impact on firms or industries.

An illustrative example of this problem may help to clarify the issue. Table 32 shows four hypothetical firms each with $100 of gross reported under the turnover tax. Firm A's principal business activity is in the mining of coal and, given the distribution of output, it would pay taxes on 80 per cent of the $100 of gross at the rate of 1.35 per cent. It also engages in some related manufacturing and services activity and, therefore, would be liable for a tax of 0.40 per cent on the manufacturing portion and 1.05 per cent on the services portion. For the purpose of our investigation, this firm would have been assigned to the coal mining industry and its entire gross and value added would be assigned to that industry. The Tax Department, however, would have assigned $80 to the coal mining industry, $5 to crude petroleum, $10 to manufacturing, and $5 to services. The same difference in treatment would apply to the remaining three firms. The result is that our study would have shown four industries--coal mining, manufacturing, retail trade, and crude petroleum with $100 gross for each. In contrast, the Tax Department would have shown eight industries with gross value of production as shown by the bottom row of the table.

TABLE 32

ILLUSTRATIVE COMPARISON OF THE DIFFERENCE BETWEEN STUDY AND STATE TAX DEPARTMENT TREATMENT OF INDIVIDUAL FIRM STATISTICS WEST VIRGINIA

		Industry Classification for Tax Purposes							
Firm	Total Gross	Coal Mining	Crude Petroleum	Contract Construction	Manufacturing	Retail Trade	Wholesale Trade	Services	Industry Classification by Study
1	2	3	4	5	6	7	8	9	10
A	$100	$80	$ 5	---	$10	---	---	$ 5	Coal Mining
B	$100	---	---	---	$75	---	$15	$10	Manufacturing
C	$100	---	---	---	---	$80	$10	$10	Retail Trade
D	$100	---	$50	$30	---	---	---	$20	Crude Petroleum
Total	$400	$80	$55	$30	$85	$80	$25	$45	

This difference in treatment means that if the gross assigned by the Tax Department to the classes of business activity whose value-added-to-gross ratio is less than the industry of assignment by the study, we will have understated the value-added base and overstated the rate required. We believe that this is, in fact, the case, since we estimated the rate required to be 2.52 per cent in an earlier study in which the Tax Department gross <u>was</u> allocated according to the major business activity of individual firms.[1] Thus, the value-added rate (2.62 per cent) is to be interpreted only as a rough average figure which permits us to simulate an equal revenue yield in the aggregate and not as an indicator of the actual rates or the impact on individual firms or industries. The effect of this is to understate the revenue yield with a given rate and therefore introduces a conservative bias to our estimates of revenue under the value-added tax.

Figure 5 below shows the effect of the size of the tax base on the rate required to yield a given amount of tax revenue. Illustrative iso-revenue curves are superimposed to show how the rate declines as the tax base increases for given levels of revenue yield. This includes an iso-revenue curve for the 1967 required yield of $82.409 million.[2]

To obtain revenue estimates and changes in revenue for the period 1967-1968 and 1968-1969, we developed Tables 33 and 34 in a

---

[1]Leyden, "Some Empirical Observations," p. 526.

[2]This graph may also be used to estimate the effect of growth in the tax base for a given rate. By extending a vertical line from a selected rate one can identify the possible revenue gains associated with alternative growth rates.

FIGURE 5

VALUE ADDED ISO-REVENUE GRAPH
OF
BASE AND RATE

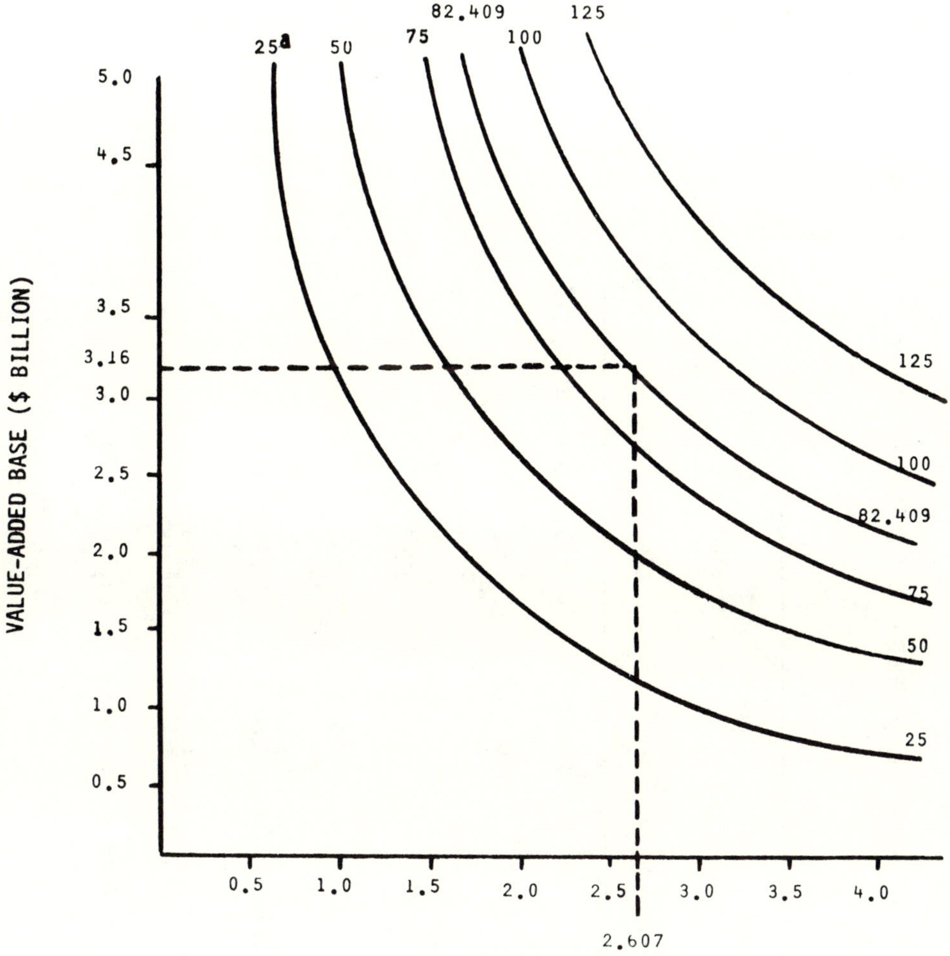

*Contour lines measure equal amounts of revenue in millions of dollars.

TABLE 33

INCOME VALUE-ADDED BASE AND REVENUE ESTIMATE, WEST VIRGINIA, 1968

Rate = 0.0262

Industry Identification	Value Added / Gross[a]	Estimated Total Gross ($000)[b]	Value-Added Base ($000)[c]	Estimated Value-Added Revenue ($000)[d]	Turnover Tax Revenue CY 1968 ($000)[b]	Per Cent Change in Revenue With Turnover Tax Replaced[e]
1	2	3	4	5	6	7
Coal Mining	.27886	749,633 8.06[f]	209,043 6.90[f]	5,477	10,261 11.70[f]	- 46.27
Crude Petroleum & Natural Gas	.38462	58,885 0.63	22,648 0.75	593	3,343 3.81	- 82.26
Contract Construction	.33107	469,609 5.05	155,473 5.13	4,073	10,529 12.00	- 61.32
Manufacturing & Non-Metallic Minerals	.36066	3,153,938 33.84	1,137,499 37.52	29,802	26,564 30.29	14.40
Rail & Related Services	.48884	242,776 2.61	118,679 3.91	3,109	558 0.64	457.17
Motor Freight & Related Services	.53822	28,719 0.31	15,457 0.51	405	630 0.72	- 36.44
All Other Transportation	.55718	26,260 0.28	14,632 0.48	383	468 0.53	- 18.16

TABLE 33--Continued

Industry Identification	Value Added / Gross[a]	Estimated Total Gross ($000)[b]	Value-Added Base ($000)[c]	Estimated Value-Added Revenue ($000)[d]	Turnover Tax Revenue CY 1968 ($000)[b]	Per Cent Change in Revenue With Turnover Tax Replaced[e]
1	2	3	4	5	6	7
Communication & Public Utilities	.51886	461,297 4.96	239,349 7.90	6,271	14,156 16.14	- 62.81
Wholesale Trade	.17772	1,448,056 15.56	257,349 8.49	6,743	3,553 4.05	89.90
Retail Trade	.27546	1,923,988 20.67	529,982 17.48	13,886	10,022 11.43	38.63
Finance	.70954	21,177 0.23	15,026 0.50	394	244 0.28	61.48
Real Estate	.23111	146,868 1.58	33,943 1.12	889	1,672 1.91	- 45.75
Services	.49125	574,935 6.18	282,436 9.32	7,400	5,707 6.51	30.37
Total	.32575	9,306,141 100.00	3,031,516 100.00	79,426	87,707 100.00	- 9.81

Notes See notes bottom of Table 31.

TABLE 34

INCOME VALUE-ADDED BASE AND REVENUE ESTIMATE, WEST VIRGINIA, 1969

Rate = 0.0262

Industry Identification	Value Added / Gross[a]	Estimated Total Gross ($000)[b]	Value-Added Base ($000)[c]	Estimated Value-Added Revenue ($000)[d]	Turnover Tax Revenue CY 1969 ($000)[b]	Per Cent Change in Revenue With Turnover Tax Replaced[e]
1	2	3	4	5	6	7
Coal Mining	.30355	741,836 7.00[f]	225,184 6.50[f]	5,900	9,883 10.61[f]	- 39.73
Crude Petroleum & Natural Gas	.35597	58,215 0.55	20,723 0.60	543	3,672 3.94	- 85.21
Contract Construction	.38475	571,829 5.39	220,011 6.37	5,764	11,008 11.82	- 47.64
Manufacturing & Non-Metallic Minerals	.35330	3,613,624 34.09	1,278,500 36.90	33,497	28,389 30.49	20.60
Rail & Related Services	.48884	250,235 2.36	122,325 3.53	3,205	630 0.68	408.73
Motor Freight & Related Services	.55628	40,215 0.38	22,371 0.65	586	835 0.90	- 29.82
All Other Transportation	.56550	31,547 0.30	17,840 0.51	467	520 0.56	- 10.19

TABLE 34--Continued

Industry Identification	Value Added / Gross[a]	Estimated Total Gross ($000)[b]	Value-Added Base ($000)[c]	Estimated Value-Added Revenue ($000)[d]	Turnover Tax Revenue CY 1969 ($000)[b]	Per Cent Change in Revenue With Turnover Tax Replaced[e]
1	2	3	4	5	6	7
Communication & Public Utilities	.49425	523,033 4.93	258,509 7.46	6,773	15,681 16.84	- 65.40
Wholesale Trade	.18312	1,635,931 15.43	299,572 8.64	7,849	3,438 3.69	128.45
Retail Trade	.26909	2,302,833 21.72	619,669 17.88	16,235	10,691 11.48	0.05
Finance	.66505	22,958 0.22	15,268 0.44	400	239 0.26	67.36
Real Estate	.27682	154,327 1.46	42,721 1.23	1,119	1,576 1.69	- 27.60
Services	.49407	653,369 6.16	322,810 9.31	8,458	6,557 7.04	31.36
Total	.32694	10,599,952 100.00	3,465,503 100.00	90,796	93,119 100.00	- 2.86

Notes: See notes bottom of Table 31.

manner similar to that of Table 31. The reader is reminded that the tables reflect changes in the level and composition of output which occurred under the turnover tax during the period 1967-1969 and do <u>not</u> reflect any adjustments by firms to the change to a value-added tax. This is an extreme assumption, but it is believed to be conservative since we do not expect as many opportunities for tax avoidance under the value-added tax as exists under the turnover tax.

Given our assumptions, a comparison of Column 2 of Tables 31 and 33 reveals that over the period 1967-1968, significant declines occurred in the gross business of coal mining, crude petroleum, contract construction, and rail and related services as well as declines in the value-added-to-gross ratios of coal mining, contract construction, communication and public utilities, and wholesale trade. Overall, industries which increased their output levels exceeded those declining, such that overall gross output increased from \$9.1 billion to \$9.3 billion. This was not true, however, for the ratio of value added to gross since the composite ratio declined from 0.34705 to 0.32575. The combined effect of the change in gross base and the change in value-added ratio is estimated to have caused a decline in the value-added base of \$129 million and a resulting decline in estimated revenue of \$3.4 million. The turnover tax yield for the same period, after adjusting for statutory tax rate changes, increased from \$82.419 million to \$84.332 million, leaving a net loss of \$4.906 million with the change to a value-added tax.

We have constructed Table 35 in order to establish the average differential revenue elasticity for the period 1967-1968 and to

TABLE 35

CHANGES IN BASE, RATE, REVENUE AND DIFFERENTIAL REVENUE ELASTICITY UNDER ALTERNATIVE TAXES WEST VIRGINIA, 1967-1968

Part	Turnover Tax ($000)	Value-Added Tax ($000)
A. Revenue Measures		
Average Revenue ($\bar{T}$)[a]	83,371	81,123
(1) Change in Revenue (ΔT)[b]	1,923	-3,391
(2) Per Cent Change ($\%\Delta T$)[c]	2.31	-4.18
B. Base Measures		
(1) Average Base ($\bar{B}$)[d]	9,207,122	3,096,287
(A) Change in Base (ΔB)[e]	198,032	-129,426
(B) Per Cent Change ($\%\Delta B$)[f]	2.15	-4.18
(2) Average Value-Added/Gross ($\bar{R}_{VG}$)[g]	.336405	
(A) Change in Ratio (ΔR_{VG})[h]	.021290	
(B) Per Cent Change ($\%\Delta R_{VG}$)[i]	-6.33	

C. Change in Revenue and Differential Elasticity of Tax Change

(1) Change in Turnover Tax Revenue

(6-8) $\%\Delta T_G = \%\Delta B_G + (\%\Delta t_G)\ (R_G)$

$$\%\Delta t_G = \frac{2.31 - 2.15}{1.0215} = 0.16$$

$$\%\Delta T_G = 2.15 + (0.16)\ (1.0215) = 2.31$$

TABLE 35--Continued

Part	Turnover Tax ($000)	Value-Added Tax ($000)
C. Continued		
(2) Change in Value-Added Revenue		
(6-12) $\%\Delta\overline{T}_V = \%\Delta\overline{B}_G + \%\Delta\overline{R}_{VG}$		
$\%\Delta T_V = 2.15 + (-6.33) = -4.18$		
(3) Differential Elasticity of Tax Change		
(6-13) $\Delta\eta_{V \cdot G} = \frac{\%\Delta B_G + \%\Delta R_{VG}}{\%\Delta B_G + (\%\Delta t)(R_G)}$		
$\Delta\eta_{V \cdot G} = \frac{2.15 + (-6.33)}{2.15 + (0.16)(1.0215)} = -1.81$		

Notes:

a $\overline{T} = \frac{T_{67} + T_{68}}{2}$

b $\Delta T = T_{68} - T_{67}$

c $\%\Delta T = \frac{\Delta T}{\overline{T}} \cdot 100$

d $\overline{B} = \frac{B_{67} + B_{68}}{2}$

e $\Delta B = B_{63} - B_{67}$

f $\%\Delta B = \frac{\Delta B}{\overline{B}} \cdot 100$

g $\overline{R}_{VG} = \frac{R_{VG_{67}} + R_{VG_{68}}}{2}$

h $\Delta R_{VG} = R_{VG_{68}} - R_{VG_{67}}$

i $\%\Delta R_{VG} = \frac{\Delta R_{VG}}{\overline{R}} .100$

explore analytically the contribution of the base and rate change to the overall change in revenue (using the average elasticity concept). Part A of the table identifies the average revenue under both taxes and the absolute change in revenue to arrive at a per cent change. Part B provides comparable information on the average and absolute changes in the component bases of gross and value added as well as average and absolute changes in the value-added ratio. Part C provides our estimates of the changes in turnover and value-added tax revenue, respectively, as well as the differential revenue elasticity of the tax change.

For the turnover tax, the 2.31 per cent change in revenue is attributed to the 2.15 per cent change in the base and the 0.16 per cent change in effective rate. For the value-added tax the 4.18 per cent decline in revenue is attributed to the 6.33 per cent decline in the value-added ratio which was partially offset by a 2.15 per cent increase in the base. This gives us a differential revenue elasticity of -1.81 for the period 1967-1968 and indicates that, in the aggregate, the value-added tax would not have contributed as much to revenue growth as the turnover tax and, in fact, had an opposite sign. Note too that we are neglecting several adjustments that firms might make to reduce their value-added tax bills. If the data are at all accurate, the results suggest that legislators would be less than enthusiastic about the revenue prospects with a shift to a value-added tax.

To put this in perspective, we should emphasize that we are looking at value-added relationships under an existing turnover tax and are not, at this point, attempting to identify what would happen with the change to a value-added tax. One appropriate question at this point is, "What caused this significant change in both value-added ratios and gross among the various classes of business activity?"

There are a number of possible explanations which may be examined by disaggregating the tax changes according to individual industries as we have done in Table 36. The first possibility was the 1968 increase in the turnover tax rate on manufacturing from 0.40 to 0.80 per cent and on the communication and public utilities, and other transportation industries from 1.50 to 3.00 per cent. In the absence of tax avoidance there should have been an approximate doubling of the effective turnover tax rate in the manufacturing, communication and public utilities, and other transportation industries with some rate increases in other industries. The extent of this latter increase in effective rates would depend on the proportion of manufacturing, communication and public utilities, and other transportation activity engaged in by firms whose principal business activity was other than manufacturing, communication and public utilities, or other transportation.

An examination of Column 3 reveals that instead of an approximate doubling of the effective rate under the turnover tax, the rate increased by only 11.12 per cent in manufacturing, 7.02 per cent in motor freight, 0.63 per cent in communication and public utilities, and -18.89 per cent in other transportation. The effective rates did increase in all other industries which suggested that there was less tax avoidance with respect to rate changes than in the industries which experienced the statutory rate change. Our next question is, "How might this have been accomplished?"

TABLE 36

CHANGES IN BASE, RATE, AND REVENUE UNDER ALTERNATIVE TAXES BY INDUSTRY
WEST VIRGINIA, 1967-1968

Industry Identification	Turnover Tax $\%\Delta\overline{B}_G$ +	$((\%\Delta\overline{t}_G)$	$(R_G))$	= $\%\Delta\overline{T}_G$	Value-Added Tax $\%\Delta\overline{B}_G$ +	$\%\Delta R_{VG}$	= $\%\Delta\overline{T}_V$
1	2	3	4	5	6	7	8
Coal Mining	-11.75	4.15	.8890	- 8.06	-11.75	- 9.01	-20.76
Crude Petroleum & Natural Gas	-19.28	23.93	.8242	0.45	-19.28	43.18	23.90
Contract Construction	- 2.91	10.57	.9713	7.36	- 2.91	- 8.45	-11.36
Manufacturing & Non-Metallic Minerals	6.82	11.12	1.0706	18.72	6.82	-12.67	- 5.85
Rail & Related Services	N.C.	N.C.	.9957	-116.03	N.C.	N.C.	N.C.
Motor Freight & Related Services	1.64	7.02	1.0165	8.78	1.64	2.44	4.08
All Other Transportation	14.41	-18.89	1.1553	- 7.41	14.41	- 0.83	13.58
Communication & Public Utilities	- 1.63	0.63	.9838	- 1.01	- 1.63	- 3.38	- 5.01
Wholesale Trade	12.16	11.57	1.1295	25.23	12.16	-10.38	1.78
Retail Trade	0.30	6.56	1.0030	6.87	0.30	7.63	7.93
Finance	-19.11	20.69	.8255	- 2.03	-19.11	0.49	-18.62
Real Estate	-32.27	52.53	.7221	5.66	-32.27	-19.67	-51.94
Services	0.68	17.78	1.0068	18.58	0.68	- 2.86	- 2.18
Total	2.15	0.16	1.0215	2.31	2.15	- 6.33	- 4.18

The immediate reaction to the higher tax rate by multistate firms could have been to shift part of their labor-using operations to plants outside the state. As we discussed in Chapter III, multistate gross income is apportioned to the state on the basis of the proportion of labor in West Virginia to the amount of labor everywhere. The effect of this would be to reduce the turnover tax base in West Virginia. It would have also lowered the value-added ratio because the value added of multistate firms is apportioned to the state on the basis of two factors--labor and capital. The magnitude of reduction in the turnover tax base would necessarily have been greater than the magnitude of change in the value-added base. If correct, we should observe a per cent decline in the turnover tax base accompanied by a smaller per cent decline in the value-added ratio. Column 7 of Table 36 shows a decline in the value-added ratio of 12.67 per cent, which could be consistent with our observation, but Column 2 shows an increase in the base of 6.82 per cent. Thus, the data appear to be contradictory. We believe that part of the explanation is due to the difference in reactions by multistate and domestic firms which created offsetting effects. A more complete analysis, beyond the scope here, would require that estimates of revenue and differential revenue elasticity be separately developed for the multistate and domestic firms so as to isolate these offsetting effects in the combined multistate-domestic data presented in Table 36. A preliminary scan of the multistate and domestic data indicates that with two exceptions, the ratio of value added to gross for multistate firms nationwide and industry by industry is greater than the comparable value-added ratio in West Virginia. Second, the value-added ratio of domestic firms (West Virginia) in the aggregate increased over the period 1967-1968 and, except for finance, real estate, and services, the value-added ratios by industry for West Virginia were either stable or increasing. Finally, the data indicate that in general the nationwide value-added ratios for multistate firms fluctuate considerably from one year to the next and that this fluctuation is even more pronounced in West Virginia. It is difficult to draw any conclusions about these changes, but West Virginia obviously contributes less value added per dollar of gross than its sister industries in other states. Further, this may be due, in part, to the overall tax structure in West Virginia. With respect to the data presented in Table 36, it seems likely that some tax avoidance is involved, but because of the cross-effects of domestic and multistate activities, it is impossible to establish the specific pattern of tax avoidance.

Let us look at the period of change from 1968-1969 under the same assumption that while we may observe changes in base, effective rates, and revenues, they are not attributable to the shift to a value-added tax. Table 37 has been constructed in the same way as Table 35 except that it shows the tax changes for the period 1968-1969. In Part A, we may observe that turnover tax revenue increased by 6.22 per cent while estimated value-added revenue increased by 13.36 per cent. Part B shows that the turnover tax base increased by 13.00 per cent while the value-added base increased by 13.36 per cent. Part C shows that the positive increase of 13.00 per cent in the turnover tax base was offset by a decline in the effective rate ($\overline{t}_G$) of 5.96 per cent which, when multiplied by the turnover base ratio (R_G), results in a decline in

TABLE 37

CHANGES IN BASE, RATE, REVENUE AND DIFFERENTIAL REVENUE ELASTICITY UNDER ALTERNATIVE TAXES WEST VIRGINIA, 1968-1969

Part	Turnover Tax ($000)	Value-Added Tax ($000)
A. Revenue Measures		
Average Revenue ($\bar{T}$)[a]	87,038	85,111
(1) Change in Revenue (ΔT)[b]	5,412	11,370
(2) Per Cent Change ($\%\Delta T$)[c]	6.22	13.36
B. Base Measures		
(1) Average Base ($\bar{B}$)[d]	9,953,046	3,248,538
(A) Change in Base (ΔB)[e]	1,293,816	433,929
(B) Per Cent Change ($\%\Delta B$)[f]	13.00	13.36
(2) Average Value-Added/Gross ($\bar{R}_{VG}$)[g]	.32635	
(A) Change in Ratio (ΔR_{VG})[h]	.00118	
(B) Per Cent Change ($\%\Delta R_{VG}$)[i]	0.36	
C. Change in Revenue and Differential Elasticity of Tax Change		
(1) Change in Turnover Tax Revenue		

(6-8) $$\%\Delta T_G = \%\Delta B_G + (\%\Delta t_G)(R_G)$$

$$\%\Delta t_G = \frac{6.22 - 13.00}{1.1391} = -5.96$$

$$\%\Delta T_G = 13.00 + (-5.96)(1.1391) = 6.22$$

Part	Turnover Tax ($000)	Value-Added Tax ($000)
C. Continued		
(2) Change in Value-Added Revenue		
(6-12) $\%\Delta\bar{T}_V = \%\Delta\bar{B}_G + \%\Delta\bar{R}_{VG}$		
$\%\Delta T_V = 13.00 + 0.36 = 13.36$		
(3) Differential Elasticity of Tax Change		
(6-13) $\Delta\eta_{V \cdot G} = \dfrac{\%\Delta B_G + \%\Delta R_{VG}}{\%\Delta\bar{B}_G + (\%\Delta t)(\bar{R}_G)}$		
$\Delta\eta_{V \cdot G} = \dfrac{13.00 + 0.36}{13.00 + (-5.96)(1.1391)} = 2.15$		

Notes:

Except for the change in years, the formulas are the same as for the comparable lettered notes in Table 35.

total revenue of 6.78 per cent attributable to the decline in effective turnover tax rate. The increase of 13.36 per cent in value-added tax revenue is attributed to a 13.00 per cent increase in the base of the turnover tax (B_G) and a 0.36 per cent increase in the ratio of value added to gross (R_{VG}). The differential revenue elasticity value of 2.15 indicates that for the period 1968-1969, a value-added tax would have contributed more than twice the contribution of the turnover tax to overall revenue, given our restrictive assumptions. Thus, there is a reversal of the trend indicated for 1967-1968. Instead of a negative differential tax elasticity, we find it to be positive and higher than in 1967-1968. Just as there were circumstances which may have led to a response by the business firms to the change in the business tax structure in 1968, so there was no doubt a response to events which took place in 1969. In 1969 the sales and use tax was extended to cover business purchases over the period April 1, 1969-March 13, 1970 to cover an anticipated budget deficit. This was strongly opposed by the business community and may have led to widespread deterioration in the reporting of taxable value under the turnover tax to compensate for their increased tax liability under the extended sales and use tax provision. In addition, they may have avoided making certain purchases given the temporary nature of the tax. If these responses in fact occurred, we should observe an increase in the ratio of value added to gross for each industry and a decline in the effective turnover tax rates.

Table 38 shows changes in base, rate, and revenue for the two taxes. Column 3 shows that 10 of the 13 industries had declines in

TABLE 38

CHANGES IN BASE, RATE, AND REVENUE UNDER ALTERNATIVE TAXES BY INDUSTRY
WEST VIRGINIA, 1968-1969

Industry Identification	Turnover Tax $\%\Delta\overline{B}_G$ +	$((\%\Delta\overline{t}_G)$	$(R_G))$ =	$\%\Delta\overline{T}_G$	Value-Added Tax $\%\Delta\overline{B}_G$ +	$\%\Delta R_{VG}$ =	$\%\Delta\overline{T}_V$
1	2	3	4	5	6	7	8
Coal Mining	- 1.05	- 2.73	.9896	- 3.75	- 1.05	8.48	7.43
Crude Petroleum & Natural Gas	- 1.14	10.64	.9886	9.38	- 1.14	- 7.74	- 8.88
Contract Construction	19.63	-12.47	1.2177	4.45	19.63	15.00	34.63
Manufacturing & Non-Metallic Minerals	13.58	- 4.68	1.1457	8.21	13.58	- 1.92	11.66
Rail & Related Services	3.03	8.82	1.0307	12.12	3.03	0.00	3.03
Motor Freight & Related Services	33.35	- 3.83	1.4003	27.99	33.35	3.30	36.65
All Other Transportation	18.29	- 6.46	1.2013	10.53	18.29	1.48	19.77
Communication & Public Utilities	12.54	- 2.04	1.1338	10.22	12.54	- 4.86	7.68
Wholesale Trade	12.18	- 2.91	1.1297	- 3.29	12.18	2.99	15.17
Retail Trade	17.93	- 9.58	1.1969	6.46	17.93	- 2.34	15.59
Finance	8.07	- 9.35	1.0841	- 2.07	8.07	- 6.47	1.60
Real Estate	4.95	-10.34	1.0508	5.91	4.95	18.00	22.95
Services	12.77	0.96	1.1364	13.86	12.77	0.57	13.34
Total	13.00	- 5.96	1.1391	6.22	6.22	0.36	13.36

effective turnover tax rates ranging from 12.47 (contract construction) to 2.04 (communication and public utilities). Also 7 of the 13 industries show increases in their ratio of value added to gross (Col. 7). This suggests that the response on the part of firms was largely to limit their tax liability through vertical integration and/or reporting of taxable value under the turnover tax in a class and rate lower than might otherwise have been the case. Again we should mention that the evidence about what was happening is inconclusive because we cannot separate the performance of domestic from multistate firms.

Over the entire period, revenue under the simulated value-added tax fell short of the revenue under the turnover tax by $3.44 million. This is shown in Table 39 where we have indicated growth of estimated revenue under the two taxes. Thus, in 1968, total revenue of $84.332 million under the turnover tax is comprised of the $82.409 million of 1967 plus the increased income of $1.923 million in 1968. For 1969, the total revenue of $89.744 million is comprised of the base for 1967 of $82.409 million plus the sum of the changes in 1968 and 1969 of $1.923 and $5.412 million, respectively.

These changes may be largely responses to changes in the business tax climate which occurred over the period 1967-1969, as the business community tried legally to limit their tax liabilities by seeking ways in which the taxable value could be classified so as to lower effective tax rates.

Long-Run Considerations, 1967-1980. In the long run, or with more adjustments permitted, we concluded in Chapter IV that on balance there is a chance that overall output and employment would increase

TABLE 39

TOTAL TAX RECEIPTS
UNDER ALTERNATIVE TAXES
WEST VIRGINIA, 1967-1969
($000)

Year	Contribution to Base From 1967		1968		1969		Total Revenue	Change in Revenue
A. TURNOVER TAX								
1967	$ 82,409					=	$ 82,409	
								$ 1,923
1968	82,409	+	$1,923			=	84,332	
								5,412
1969	82,409	+	1,923	+	$5,412	=	89,744	
Total 1967-1969	$247,227	+	$3,846	+	$5,412	=	$256,485	
B. VALUE-ADDED TAX (SIMULATED)								
1967	$ 82,819					=	$ 82,819	
								- 3,391
1968	82,819	-	$3,391			=	79,428	
								11,370
1969	82,819	-	3,391	+	$11,370	=	90,798	
Total 1967-1969	$248,457	-	$6,782	+	$11,370	=	$253,045	
C. REVENUE SHORTFALL (SIMULATED)							-$ 3,440	

with the shift to a value-added tax given the state of the economy over the period 1967-1969 and beyond. As indicated in Chapter V, the tax change might well result in an increase in efficiency and output in comparison with the turnover tax, depending on demand and supply conditions. Also, if the revenue elasticities are as suggested above, the increase in revenue due to the growth of output (B_G) will be greater under the value-added than the turnover tax. The magnitude of the differential in growth attributed to this improvement is of course related to the possible reduction of excess burden.

We may, therefore, estimate this potential gain in output by associating it with the possible reduction in excess burden identified in Chapter V.[1] In Figure 6, the output (net of taxes) measured at factor costs (OADE) is the same proportion of total tax revenue (ABCD) as the output loss (net of taxes) at factor cost (DFGE) is of twice the excess burden (2CDF = DCHF).

$$\text{(6-14)} \qquad \frac{\text{OBCE} - \text{ABCD}}{\text{ABCD}} = \frac{\text{DFGE}}{2(\text{CDF})}$$

Solving for DFGE yields:

$$\text{(6-15)} \qquad \text{DFGE} = \frac{2(\text{CDE})(\text{OBCE} - \text{ABCD})}{\text{ABCD}}$$

If so, then we can measure the value of output loss at factor cost for both the turnover and value-added taxes with the difference between them (DJEI) measuring the net gain in output with the shift to a value-added tax. Using the same notation as before, these output losses (O) may be

[1]As we did in Chapter V, we wish to emphasize that this technique for measuring excess burden is vulnerable to criticism, but we assume that the shortcomings do not render this approach hopeless. See Harberger, "Three Postulates."

A. TURNOVER TAX

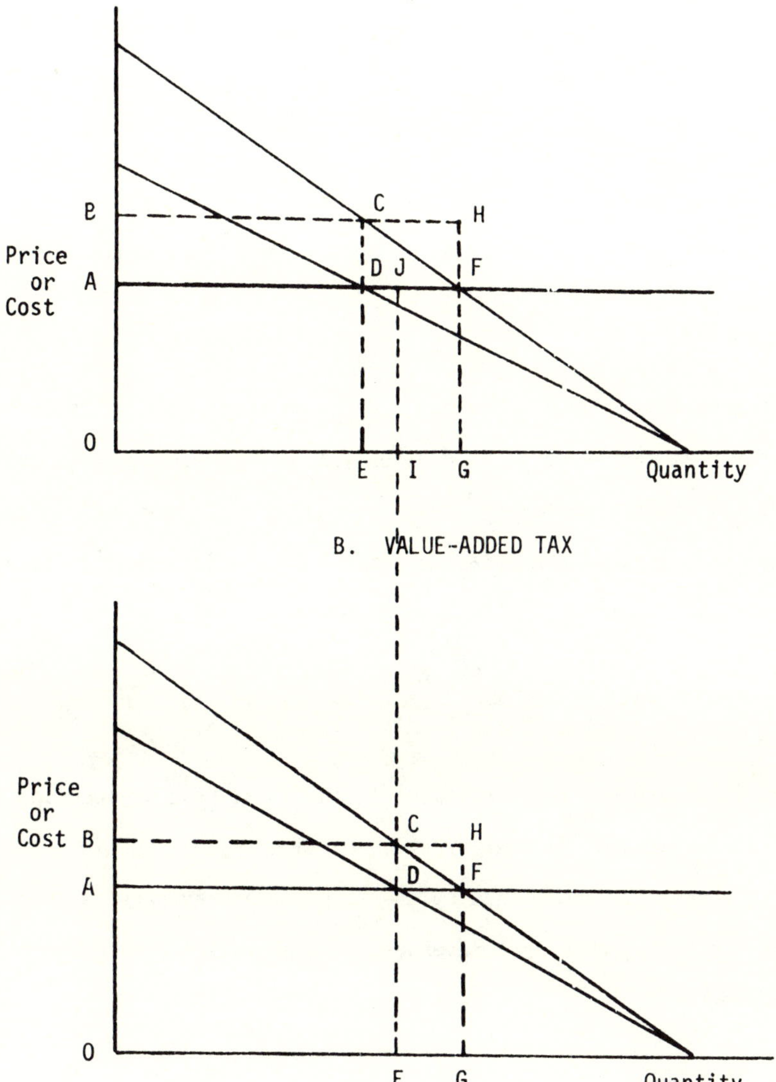

FIGURE 6

ILLUSTRATIVE GAIN IN OUTPUT ASSOCIATED
WITH EFFICIENCY GAINS
WEST VIRGINIA, 1967

expressed as follows for the turnover and value-added taxes:

$$(6\text{-}16) \qquad O_G = \frac{(2)(E.B._G)(B_V - T_G)}{T_G}$$

$$(6\text{-}17) \qquad O_V = \frac{(2)(E.B_V)(B_V - T_V)}{T_V}$$

By netting out the difference in the two values, we can also obtain a measure of the differential change in output ($\Delta O_{V \cdot G}$) as shown in equation 6-18:

$$(6\text{-}18) \qquad \Delta O_{V \cdot G} = O_V - O_G$$

If we express this change in output ($\Delta O_{V \cdot G}$) as a per cent of total output measured at factor costs in a given year (t) and assume that this per cent will hold true for the year (t + n) in which the efficiency gains are realized, we can obtain a measure of the increment to total base in the same year.

$$(6\text{-}19) \qquad \Delta O_{V \cdot G_{t+n}} = \frac{\Delta O_{V \cdot G_t}}{(B_G - T_G)_t} (B_G - T_G)_{t+n}$$

Finally, if we project this increment to the total base at some appropriate rate of growth (i) over a period of time (p) and multiply the resulting successive increments by the value-added tax rate, we can simulate the magnitude of net revenue gains ($\Delta T'$) with the change to a value-added tax:

$$(6\text{-}20) \qquad \Delta T'_{V \cdot G_p} = \sum_{j=1}^{p} (\Delta O_{V \cdot G_{t \cdot n}})(1 + i)^{n+j}(t_V)$$

To estimate the possible long-run effect of the differential output gain ($\Delta O_{V \cdot G}$), we begin with the simulated potential efficiency losses under either tax. Table 40, Part A shows the potential output loss under the turnover tax (O_G) in 1967 as measured by equation 6-16, while Part B shows the potential output loss (O_V) under the value-added tax as measured by equation 6-17. These possibilities are shown for each of the simulation models and for the set of assumed demand and supply elasticity coefficients (discussed in Chapter V). Column 4 shows the estimated output loss under the turnover tax ranging from as low as 2.26 to as high as 7.53 per cent of 1967 output. Under the value-added tax the output loss ranges from 1.20 to 3.85 per cent of output. The net gain in output with the shift to a value-added tax ($\Delta O_{V \cdot G}$) is shown in Column 5 and ranges from 1.06 per cent to 3.68 per cent of 1967 output. With these data we can now project the revenue gain under either tax and by subtraction obtain the net gain in revenue (equation 6-20). To do so we must make a number of assumptions.

Let us assume, therefore, that output gains ($\Delta O_{V \cdot G}$) are not fully realized until 1970 and that the range of gains in output in Table 40 are the appropriate ones to apply to the estimated base in 1970. (All these calculations should be regarded only as being suggestive, for, to repeat an earlier refrain, we are ignoring second-best considerations, possible externality-changes, certain components of total excess burden, and numerous alternative assumptions.) Finally, let us assume that for the period 1970 to 1980, real growth in the tax base is at a constant rate of 3 per cent per year. Given these assumptions and using the range of output gains under Simulation Models A and B as examples, we can calculate the net addition to revenue for the 13-year period 1967-1980. This is accomplished by multiplying

TABLE 40

ESTIMATED ABSOLUTE AND DIFFERENTIAL OUTPUT LOSSES
UNDER ALTERNATIVE TAXES, MODELS A, B, AND C
WEST VIRGINIA, 1967

Elasticity Coefficients		2(Excess Burden)[a] ($000)	Output Loss ($000)[b]	Output Loss Per Cent of Total Output[c]	Net Gain In Output Per Cent[d]
1		2	3	4	5
		A. TURNOVER TAX			
Models A and B					
All Industries[e]					
.50		-2,125	- 79,385	-2.51	
1.00		-4,250	-158,769	-5.02	
1.50		-6,374	-238,116	-7.53	
Model C					
Unconcentrated Industries	Concentrated[f] Industries				
.50	.50	-1,910	- 71,353	-2.26	
1.00	.50	-2,124	- 79,347	-2.51	
1.50	.50	-2,400	- 89,658	-2.84	
.50	1.00	-3,604	-134,636	-4.26	
1.00	1.00	-3,820	-142,706	-4.51	
1.50	1.00	-4,034	-150,700	-4.77	
.50	1.50	-5,300	=197,995	-6.26	
1.00	1.50	-5,514	-205,989	-6.52	
1.50	1.50	-5,740	-214,432	-6.78	

TABLE 40--Continued

Elasticity Coefficients		2(Excess Burden)[a] ($000)	Output Loss ($000)[b]	Output Loss Per Cent of Total Output[c]	Net Gain In Output Per Cent[d]
1		2	3	4	5
B. VALUE-ADDED TAX					
Models A and B					
All Industries[e]					
.50		-1,084	- 40,498	-1.28	1.23
1.00		-2,170	- 81,091	-2.56	2.46
1.50		-3,254	-121,569	-3.85	3.68
Model C					
Unconcentrated Industries	Concentrated[f] Industries				
.50	.50	-1,012	- 37,808	-1.20	1.06
1.00	.50	-1,084	- 40,498	-1.28	1.23
1.50	.50	-1,158	- 43,263	-1.37	1.47
.50	1.00	-1,970	- 73,599	-2.33	1.93
1.00	1.00	-2,042	- 76,289	-2.41	2.10
1.50	1.00	-2,116	- 79,054	-2.50	2.27
.50	1.50	-2,908	-108,643	-3.44	2.82
1.00	1.50	-2,980	-111,333	-3.52	3.00
1.50	1.50	-3,054	-114,097	-3.61	3.17

TABLE 40--Continued

[a]Derived from Table 27, Columns 2, 5 for Models A and B and Table 28, Columns 3, 6 for Model C.

[b]Output Loss (Equations 6-16 and 6-17) = $(2)(E \cdot B.)\ \frac{B_V - T}{T}$

$= (\text{Col. } 2)\ (0.3736)$

[c]Per Cent of Output = $\frac{\text{Col. } 3}{B_V}\ (100)$

[d]Net Gain in Output (Per Cent)

$$\frac{O_{V \cdot G}}{B_V}\ (100) = \frac{O_V - O_G}{B_G}\ (100)$$

[e]See Table 27 for the interpretation of the elasticities.

[f]See Table 28 for the interpretation of the elasticities.

the value-added base in 1969 by: (1) 103 per cent to reflect real growth in 1970; (2) 1.23 and 3.68 per cent alternatively to reflect the increment in 1970 output attributable to the efficiency gains; and (3) by 2.62 per cent to reflect the increment to total revenue associated with the gain in efficiency. The resulting value is then compounded at an annual rate of 103 per cent to arrive at the cumulative increment to total revenue through 1980.

Table 41 presents the detailed results for Simulation Models A and B and the summary results for Simulation Model C. Under A or B, when we use the smallest output gain of 1.28 per cent, a cumulative breakeven point in revenue would have been reached by 1972. By 1980, the state would have accumulated $10.908 million in additional revenue over and above the turnover tax with identical secular changes. If we use the largest gain in output figure of 3.68 per cent, the breakeven point is reached by 1971 and by 1980, the state would have accumulated $39.488 million in additional revenue.

Thus, under Model A or B, we estimate an increment to revenue growth of between $10 and $40 million, with a probable value of approximately $20 million through the period 1980. Under Simulation Model C, with a low output gain equal to 1.06 per cent, the cumulative increment to total revenue is $8.924 million and with a high output gain of 3.17 per cent, the cumulative increment is $33.539 million.

In the absence of any other changes, we conclude that the shift to a value-added tax may initially result in short-term losses in revenue. In the long run, however, these losses will not only be recovered in subsequent years but there will also be a positive

TABLE 41

SIMULATION OF THE NET GAIN IN REAL REVENUE DUE TO EFFICIENCY GAINS UNDER A VALUE-ADDED TAX WEST VIRGINIA, 1967-1980 ($000)

SIMULATION MODELS A AND B

Efficiency Gain in 1970

	Minimum, 1.28 Per Cent		Maximum, 3.68 Per Cent	
Year	Revenue Increment	Revenue Cumulative	Revenue Increment	Revenue Cumulative
1967	410	410	410	410
1968	-4,904	- 4,494	-4,904	- 4,494
1969	1,054	- 3,440	1,054	- 3,440
1970	1,120	- 2,320	3,352	- 88
1971	1,153	- 1,167	3,452	3,368
1972	1,189	22	3,556	6,920
1973	1,224	1,246	3,663	10,583
1974	1,261	2,507	3,772	14,355
1975	1,299	3,806	3,886	18,241
1976	1,337	5,143	4,002	22,243
1977	1,378	6,521	4,122	26,365
1978	1,419	7,940	4,246	30,611
1979	1,462	9,402	4,373	34,984
1980	1,506	10,908	4,504	39,488

SIMULATION MODEL C

Minimum Cumulative Revenue, 1967-1980[a]	$ 8,924
Maximum Cumulative Revenue, 1967-1980[b]	$33,539

[a]Minimum efficiency gain, 1970, (1.06 per cent).

[b]Maximum efficiency gain, 1970, (3.17 per cent)

contribution to overall revenue growth.

Further, we believe that these simulated estimates are conservative inasmuch as we have not included any of the positive effects on output associated with the gains from uneconomic vertical integration and spatial de-integration. Thus, in general, we conclude that when the change to a value-added tax is judged in terms of adequacy, it will over the long run contribute more to overall revenue growth than the turnover tax. The magnitude of the differential contribution to revenue we would judge to be approximately $24 million over a 13-year period. Needless to say, though, these exercises and the resulting estimates are far from conclusive for reasons mentioned earlier.

Stability-Predictability

From private industry's point of view, the term "predictability" refers to the ability to predict future tax liabilities with a fair degree of accuracy. From the state government's view, stability refers to the ability of a revenue system to provide a stable source of revenue in the face of economic fluctuations associated with the business cycle. Since the business cycle is largely a function of forces outside the control of any one state, the criterion calls for overall revenue growth to be fairly inelastic with respect to the business cycle. A strict application of this criterion would be in conflict with the criterion of "adequacy," which requires that the revenues be related to expenditures rather than be merely stable. Ideally, state governments would like revenue to be elastic in the growth phase of the business cycle, but inelastic in the declining phase of the cycle. This would require a tax structure which shifted from high to low elasticity sources over the business cycle. Thus, some trade-offs are necessary between the goals implied by the two criteria.

When we try to apply the stability-predictability criterion (however defined) to a _change_ in tax, we seek to judge whether the _change_ contributes to the overall stability-predictability of the revenue system. That is, we are concerned with the differential stability-predictability of alternative revenue sources. We will attempt to establish a basis for judging whether the change to a value-added tax will result in more or less stability and predictability.

With respect to the predictability of the two taxes from the producer's point of view, there have been, under the turnover tax, frequent and seemingly capricious rate changes which have created a great deal of uncertainty about future tax liabilities. This uncertainty has handicapped future planning on the part of firms for capital expansion and new plant development. Historic patterns of change in tax rates under the turnover taxes may be best characterized as a process of "who's going to get it in the neck this year."

Table 42 demonstrates better than words this pattern of rate change. Businessmen faced with decisions on new plant investment and/or capital expansion of existing plants face major uncertainties about costing a venture out because of the difficulty of predicting future tax liabilities: more than one industrial prospect has turned West Virginia down for this reason--tax instability. This is not, of course, a disadvantage of the turnover tax per se, but the nature of this tax makes it more vulnerable to non-uniform and frequent rate changes through shifting political pressures. It may also be

TABLE 42

CHANGE IN TURNOVER TAX RATE
WEST VIRGINIA, 1951-1971

Industry Classification	Rate 1951	Rate 1971	Per Cent Change
	(Per Cent)		
Coal	1.00	3.50	250
Limestone, Sandstone	1.50	2.20	57
Oil	3.00	4.34	45
Natural Gas	6.00	8.63	44
Blast Furnace	3.00	3.95	45
Sand, Gravel	3.00	4.34	45
Timber	1.50	2.20	47
Other Natural Resources	2.00	2.86	43
Manufacturing	0.30	0.88	176
Selling			
Retail	0.50	0.55	10
Wholesale	0.15	0.27	80
Utilities			
Electric Railway	1.00	1.40	40
Water	4.00	4.40	10
Electric Light & Power Domestic & Commercial	4.00	5.72	43
All Other Electric Light & Power	3.00	4.29	43
Natural Gas	3.00	4.29	43
Toll Bridges	2.00	4.29	115
All Other Utilities	2.00	2.86	43
Contracting	2.00	2.20	10
Amusements	0.50	0.71	42
All Other Services	1.00	1.15	15
Rentals	1.00	1.15	15
Financial Institutions	--	1.15	---

attributed, in part, to a response on the part of state government to the tax avoidance behavior on the part of individual firms, discussed earlier.[1] The problem which arises is that with a choice of 16 rates and 30 classes, the tax change operates differentially on business firms depending on the types of production in which they engage. Thus, if all firms attempt to avoid taxes and the state adjusts by raising rates selectively, some firms may be successful in their tax avoidance effort while others are penalized for the same effort.

The capriciousness of these tax changes would be considerably lessened with the shift to a value-added tax. This is so since any value-added tax rate change would apply to all classes of business activity rather than to individual industries as in the past. Businessmen may consequently, with appropriate assumptions about future revenue goals, predict with a greater degree of certainty the likely change in rates required to meet their share of any projected future increase in revenue.

From the state's view of stability, it is difficult to make a judgment of the differential stability of the turnover versus the value-added tax. The issue would turn on judgments and data related to changes in gross versus changes in value added with changes in the business cycle. No such information is available at the present time. In an *a priori* sense, if gross sales change less rapidly than employment of the factors of production over the business cycle, then the turnover tax would be judged the more stable tax instrument. This, of

---

[1]See Chapter V, pp. 201ff for an elaboration on this point.

course, assumes that effective tax rates do not change with either tax. We know, however, from our analysis of the 1967-1969 period, that effective turnover tax rates vary considerably from one year to the next and hence it would be hazardous to judge that the turnover tax is the more stable revenue source in periods of economic fluctuation.

Administrative Efficiency

Administrative cost is an important criterion of a desirable tax. Administrative costs ranging from 1 to 2 per cent of revenue are often considered reasonable. We have no evidence at this time which would provide a comparison of the costs of administering the tax per dollar of revenue collected under either tax. We do, however, know that when a type of value-added tax was levied in the state of Michigan, the administrative costs per $100 of revenue were 77 cents or 3/4 of 1 per cent of total revenue for the first year of operation.[1] Presumably the costs per dollar of revenue would decline over successive years. We also know that in 1974, the cost per $100 of turnover tax revenue was 43 cents[2] or roughly 1/2 or 1 per cent of total tax revenue. Both of these figures fall within the acceptable range of administrative costs. On balance, we would judge that over the course of two or three years, the administrative efficiency of the value-added tax would be approximately the same as the turnover tax.

---

[1]Papke, "Theory and Practice," p. 73.

[2]Unpublished data furnished by the West Virginia Tax Department, April 3, 1974.

Concluding Observations

This chapter completes our analysis of the economic effects of a value-added tax alternative to the current system of turnover taxation on business enterprises in West Virginia. In this chapter, we were concerned with the differential effects of the tax change as judged by the criteria--adequacy, stability-predictability, and administrative efficiency. We found that a revenue short-fall might have occurred over the period 1967-1969 with a value-added tax, assuming that there was no response to the tax change. This assumption rests on shaky grounds, however, since we found that substantial tax avoidance took place in both tax periods of change which affected both positively and negatively the contributions of revenue growth of the value-added tax. If efficiency gains are possible in the long run, the differential contribution to revenue by the value-added tax would be positive. The judgment that gains might be forthcoming was reinforced by the fact that we did not take account of other positive gains in efficiency such as those associated with the reduced incentive to uneconomic vertical integration and spatial de-integration and other tax avoidance behavior. On balance, we conclude that the value-added tax would be more rather than less responsive in terms of adequacy. We were unable to say much about the comparative stability-predictability and administrative efficiency of the two taxes, but on the basis of limited information we concluded that the value-added tax would probably bring improved predictability of tax liability. Finally, we speculated that the state would find the administration of the value-added tax about as efficient as the turnover tax.

CHAPTER VII

TURNOVER VERSUS VALUE-ADDED TAXATION IN WEST VIRGINIA: SUMMARY AND CONCLUSIONS

Though value added has been used for over a century as a conceptual framework for measuring income flows to the factors of production, its use as a base for the taxation of business enterprises has been of relatively recent origin, dating back to the 1920's. Following World War II and especially since the late 1960's, there has been an acceleration of interest in or adoption of a value-added tax by more and more governments at the state and national levels. A case in point is its recent consideration (1967 and 1970) by the West Virginia legislature as a replacement for the current system of turnover taxation in the state.

In an attempt to reduce the degree of uncertainty about the effects of the tax, this study seeks to trace out relevant effects of a proposed value-added tax in West Virginia, compare these effects with those of the existing turnover taxes, and contribute to the preparation of estimates or judgments about differential incidence, differential excess burdens, and other consequences. The relevant effects include impacts on: (1) prices in the short run; (2) distribution, i.e., "who bears the burden?"; (3) excess burdens, i.e., departures from economic efficiency; and (4) the adequacy and stability of revenues, and administrative efficiency in collecting the revenues.

Price Effects and Incidence

Using a competitive partial equilibrium model, we analyzed incidence and price effects of the turnover tax in three broad sectors (export, import-competing, and domestic) in two time periods--the immediate market period in which the factors of production were assumed to be fixed and a longer-run period in which we explored eight possible combinations (cases) of demand and supply conditions which might apply in one or more of the three sectors. Following this we extended the analysis by exploring possible general equilibrium implications of the partial equilibrium findings. This in turn was followed by an analysis of the differential incidence and price effects of the shift to an income value-added tax.

Theoretical Considerations

The incidence of the turnover tax and the differential incidence of the income value-added tax depended, of course, on the time period of analysis and the assumptions made with respect to demand, production functions, supplies of the factors of production, and the markets for which West Virginia firms produce.

In particular, in the "immediate run" or market period, the turnover tax would fall on the fixed factors of production in West Virginia under conditions of perfect elasticity of demand for exports and supply of import products. If the demand for West Virginia's exports and supply of its import products were perfectly inelastic, the entire incidence of the tax would fall on the consumers of West Virginia's exports and import-competing products. With the elasticity of demand for exports and supply of import products being greater than zero but less than infinity, the burden would fall on both the consumers of, and the factors of production employed in, the West Virginia export and import-competing industries, unless the supply of exports and import-competing products was perfectly inelastic. If the latter circumstances were true, the turnover tax would fall on the factors of production in West Virginia.

Obviously, if the supplies of the factors were fixed and production governed by fixed technical coefficients, no output change would occur nor would there be any resource migration. Because factor supplies are not really fixed, some output declines could occur in the short run as well as some reduction in the employment of the factors of production. Assuming an "adaptive monetary-fiscal policy" at the federal level, the unemployment would elicit monetary expansion and overall prices would rise until full employment was re-established, shifting part of the burden to consumers unless factor supplies ended up where they started. We also expected no output declines if there were locational advantages to producing in West Virginia which were reflected in economic rents paid to the factors of production and the rents in each of the firms did not exceed the taxes levied under the turnover tax.

Because of the differentiated rate structure of the turnover tax, any changes in final demand prices, employment of the factors of production, or output would not be uniform within the industries, however. Those factors and consumers whose activities and consumption were taxed at above average rates would experience relatively high tax burdens while factors and consumers whose activities were taxed at below average rates would experience relatively low tax burdens. Further adjustments depend on cross-elasticities and repercussions.

As for the longer-run incidence of the turnover tax, it depends not only on demand conditions but also on the form of the production function and the elasticities of supply of labor and capital. We identified eight possible cases in which the incidence of the tax could be assessed. For example, if the supply of capital was perfectly elastic and the supply of labor was fixed, the entire burden of the producer's portion of the tax would shift to labor. Further, output would decline if the operative production function was a Cobb-Douglas type, but if the production function was a fixed proportion type, no output effects would occur. In the latter circumstances, the return to labor would be less than under the Cobb-Douglas form. If both capital and labor were mobile in the long run, then both employment of the factors of production and output would decline in West Virginia and increase in the non-taxed areas.

From a general equilibrium view, other changes would also take place. On the use of income side, the change in relative prices as between the export, import-competing, and domestic markets would cause some realignment of consumption as would changes in the relative prices of West Virginia exports and competing non-taxed goods. Without migration, income effects on the uses side would be small (arising only from income losses due to excess burdens), given our assumption of equal marginal propensities to spend by the different income recipients. On the sources of income side, changes in the prices received by the factors of production in West Virginia would result in shifts in the demand for import-competing and domestic goods, but ignoring excess burdens, no change in the pattern of demand would occur given our assumption of equal marginal propensities to spend. If excess burdens were present, we could expect output declines, higher tax rates to be imposed to maintain the same real level of expenditures by state government, and some repercussions on the pattern of demand.

With regard to differential incidence, the income value-added tax would shift some burden away from factors employed by and customers of low value-added firms to those connected with high value-added firms. (A high value-added firm is one which experiences higher tax bills under the value-added tax than under the turnover tax and comes about as the result of having a higher than average level of value added relative to gross and/or a less than average amount of taxes paid per dollar of gross under the turnover tax. The converse would be true for low value-added firms.) This does not mean, however, that all of the burden would be shifted. Some burden would still remain on the low value-added consumers and producers. Patterns of consumption would follow the changes in relative prices in the product markets, and changes in employment of the factors of production would follow the changes in the relative prices paid to them. Again, we assume equal marginal propensities to spend, and similar expenditures patterns, by all income recipients including government.

Empirical Considerations

Given these directional influences of possible effects on prices in consumer and factor markets, we then attempted, with the aid of assumptions that may often be unrealistic, to estimate the price effects associated with the tax change. This was accomplished by simulating the West Virginia economy under one of the alternative sets of assumptions made in the theoretical analysis. This simulation employed an input-output model of the West Virginia economy together with data obtained from a stratified sample of tax returns of corporations doing business in West Virginia during the period 1967-1969. The familiar shortcomings of input-output analysis (e.g., those arising from the assumptions of fixed coefficients) limit the applicability of the results.

In particular, three simulation models were used: (1) Model A--which assumed perfectly inelastic demand (burden on consumers); (2) Model B--which assumed perfectly elastic demand (burden on factors); and (3) Model C--which assumed that some industries could only pass 50 per cent of the tax changes forward (burden on consumers and factors). Under Model A we employed three value-added tax base versions: (1) Version 1--which used a gross value-added base against which price distortions associated with the turnover tax and income value-added tax could be contrasted; (2) Version 2--which used an income value-added base as estimated by the input-output model; and (3) Version 3--which treated the value-added tax as an exogenous factor based on our estimates using the sample corporate tax return data.

Model A. The principal measure used to trace through the percentage changes in prices was a tax-change coefficient which included both direct and indirect effects and represented the total change in the amount of taxes paid per dollar of delivery to final demand. By comparing the estimated value-added taxes paid per dollar of delivery to final demand under Version 1 with the estimated taxes paid under the turnover tax and under Versions 2 and 3 of the value-added tax, we obtained clues to the potential relative distortions of prices paid by West Virginia industry consumer groups. Under Version 1, our estimates showed no distortions in relative prices inasmuch as the amount of direct and indirect taxes paid per dollar of delivery to final demand was 1.13¢ for all industries. By contrast, the standard deviation of direct and indirect turnover taxes paid per dollar of delivery to final demand was estimated to be 1.29¢. The comparable standard deviation with the move to an income value-added tax was estimated to be 0.42¢ (Version 2) and 0.79¢ (Version 3). Thus, under Model A, our simulation suggests that the distortion in relative prices among industry consumer groups would be reduced by 2/3 (Version 2) or 1/3 (Version 3) with the shift to an income value-added tax.

Using the tax coefficients to estimate price changes in each industry's market, we found that 13 industries would be classified as high value added with 11 of the 13 industry groups experiencing price increases of less than 1 per cent. Eleven industries were classified as low value added and 6 of the 11 industry consumer groups were estimated to experience price declines of greater than 1 per cent and the remaining 5 industry consumer groups would experience price declines of less than 1 per cent.

Finally, under Model A we estimated the overall price effects in each of the two broad consuming export and import-competing and domestic sectors and found that the overall price level of exports would decline slightly by 6/100 of 1 per cent under Version 2 and by 1/100 of 1 per cent under Version 3. In the domestic market (including the import-competing sector), we estimated that overall prices would fall by 1/100 of 1 per cent (Version 3) or increase by 8/100 of 1 per cent (Version 2). Given these results, we judged that the relative competitive position of the state vis-a-vis the rest of the country would not be greatly changed in the market period with the shift to a value-added tax and under the assumptions of Model A.

Model B. In this simulation we assumed that the burden of the tax change would rest on the factors of production and attempted to assess the impact on the payments to the factors of production under three alternative sets of assumptions about factor mobility and wage flexibility. In the first two sets, we assumed that the factors of production were fixed and assumed alternatively wages were flexible or inflexible. In the third set we assumed that labor was fixed, but capital was mobile.

With fixed factor supplies, flexible wages, and the switch from the turnover to the value-added tax, only three of the high value-added industries would experience reductions in payments to labor and capital that exceeded 1 per cent: primary metals, wholesale trade, and finance. In low value-added industries, gains in the return to the factors of production in excess of 1 per cent were estimated for crude petroleum, contract construction, communication and public utilities, coal mining, motor freight, and other transportation.

Alternatively, when we assumed wages were institutionally fixed in the market period and both factors fixed in supply, the burden of the tax change would fall on capital. Our estimates showed marked gains in the payment to capital in low value-added industries, while high value-added industries by contrast were estimated to have significant declines in the payments to capital--in, for example, finance, transportation equipment, and primary metals. These various results of shifting to the value-added tax stem, of course, from the assumptions indicated.

Finally, when we assumed the supply of capital to be mobile and that of labor as fixed, the entire differential burden of the tax switch would fall on labor. Under these conditions, the payments to labor were estimated to increase by 24.88 per cent in the crude petroleum industry and 7.21 per cent in the communication and public utility industry. Other less dramatic gains would accrue to labor employed in contract construction, coal mining, motor freight, other transportation, and stone and clay products, and real estate. Among the high value-added industries, the largest per cent declines in payments to labor (1-3 per cent) were estimated to be in the manufacturing industries of chemicals, primary metals, and machinery; railroads; wholesale trade; and finance and services. Labor employed in food, textiles, glass, fabricated metals, transportation equipment, other manufacturing, and retail trade were estimated to experience losses of less than 1 per cent in income.

Model C. Under Model C we attempted to estimate the effects with an intermediate set of assumptions in which some portion of the change in tax was assumed to be shifted to the prices of intermediate goods and thence to the price of final goods. The remaining portion of the tax change would be borne by the factors of production. In order to accomplish this type of simulation, we used the input-output model for the price effects and the corporate sample simulation for the factor return effects. With respect to the effect on prices to specific industry consumer groups, the Simulation C results differed, industry-by-industry, from those of Simulation A by less than 1 per cent, suggesting that prices are rather insensitive to modest variations in the shifting assumptions for these two taxes. (Part of the reason for this insensitivity is, of course, the fact that in Simulation C we still assumed 100 per cent forward shifting in 14 of the 24 industries.) In the broad sectors the overall price level of exports would decline by 3/100 of 1 per cent and domestic sector price levels would decline by 5/100 of 1 per cent. This represented a difference in overall relative prices of 8/100 of 1 per cent in favor of exports. We concluded from these results that the price effect on the uses of income of consumers of West Virginia products would not be significantly different from those suggested under Model A, or under a moderate range of shifting assumptions.

The portion of the tax not passed forward brought income gains to factors employed in contract construction and motor freight transportation, with matching income losses of 1/2 of 1 per cent experienced in the manufacturing industries of food, textiles, glass and glass products, fabricated metals, and other manufacturing.

The estimates provided by these simulations of price and incidence were of course highly dubious and, therefore, only limited conclusions could be drawn. In fact, we were reluctant to speculate beyond the bounds of the models themselves, since other assumptions and other models might have led to different conclusions. This was the first time, however, that anyone had tried to explore for even crude clues to the incidence and price effects of a regional value-added tax.

Impacts on Excess Burden

Turnover Tax

All taxes (except a hypothetical head tax) may impose excess burdens. Our objective in this part of the study was to explore the conditions under which the turnover tax may interfere with the attainment of efficiency and whether under the same conditions the substitution of an income value-added tax would reduce the degree of excess burden. In addition, we wanted to develop estimates of the magnitude of these excess burdens. The theoretical analysis was limited to four of the eight cases previously examined for incidence and price effects. These were cases in which, among other conditions, we assumed that the production function was governed by fixed proportions and that, at one extreme, the price elasticity of demand was perfectly elastic. We assumed that the economy in West Virginia and elsewhere was otherwise efficient before the imposition of the turnover tax and that there were no externalities in production or consumption in the private market. In addition, we assumed that owners of the factors of production employed in West Virginia and the state government and consumers of West Virginia products had the same marginal propensity to spend and the same income-compensated elasticity of demand for each of the composite goods produced in West Virginia--export, import-competing, and domestic. Finally, we assumed that production was governed by fixed proportions of factors in West Virginia and that initially the supplies of the factors of production, labor and capital, were fixed.

Export and Import-Competing Sectors. If one assumes perfect elasticity of demand for export and import-competing products, no impairment of efficiency occurs on the use of income side. Further, in the market period, no inefficiency is possible so long as the supply of the factors of production is fixed and the elasticity of substitution is zero even though the imposition of the tax lowers the prices received by capital and labor. In subsequent time periods, however, excess burden would arise when both factors are assumed to be mobile but not when labor supply is said to be fixed. In general, we concluded that with fixed proportions in production and a ratio of capital to labor in excess of one, the burden of the tax would be disproportionately shared by the factor having the lower supply elasticity, and the greater the divergence between capital and labor supply elasticities, the less would be the output effect (excess burden). Also this excess burden in production was the kind likely to be present <u>within</u> each of the broad sectors, if a uniform turnover tax was levied. This was not the case in West Virginia, however, which had a differentiated rate structure made up of 16 different rates applied to 30 classes of business activity. We argued that because of the differentiated rate structure the excess burdens were likely to be larger than with a uniform turnover tax levy.

<u>Export and Domestic Sectors</u>. When the elasticity of demand was assumed to be less than perfect, no impairment of efficiency was possible so long as the factors of production were assumed to be fixed, e.g., in the "immediate run" or market period. If the same demand conditions applied in the longer run in which factors were not fixed, excess burdens could be present in connection with both the uses and sources of income. In general, the burden would be shared by producers and consumers in proportion to the relative elasticities of demand and supply.

On the use of income side, efficiency would be impaired as a consequence of the distortion in relative prices as between exports and non-taxed export-competing products and as between domestic and import-competing products. The presence of these price differences would cause shifts in consumption away from export and domestic products and toward export and import-competing products.

Export, Import-Competing, and Domestic Sectors. Beyond the excess burdens noted above, three other sources of inefficiency under the turnover tax could arise in all three sectors. These were the inducement to engage in uneconomic vertical integration, uneconomic spatial de-integration, and uneconomic import purchases of capital goods.

Value-Added Tax

With the shift to a value-added tax, we focused attention on the cases which raised possibilities of induced inefficiency. With an equal-yield value-added tax replacing the turnover tax, excess burdens would still exist with factor mobility and perfectly elastic demand, but the level of excess burden would be less than under the West Virginia turnover tax since the value-added tax would be a uniform levy, and, therefore, the excess burden associated with the differentiated rate structure would be removed.

With less than perfect elasticity of demand and supply, the differential incidence of the value-added tax would shift from consumers and producers of low value-added products to consumers and producers of high value-added products: Excess burden should be reduced since the uniform value-added levy would reduce the relative price difference between high and low value-added goods within each of the markets.

Offsetting this effect would be the increase in the relative price spread between high value-added export and domestic products and non-taxed export-competing and import products. Conversely, the relative price spread between low value-added exports and domestic products and non-taxed export-competing and import products would narrow. Whether excess burdens would be increased or decreased depended, therefore, on the relative cross-elasticities of demand for export-competing and import products in response to the change in the price of high and low value-added goods.

As for the excess burdens associated with tax-induced vertical integration, spatial de-integration, and capital acquisition, the shift to a value-added tax should eliminate the first two induced responses to the turnover tax. Capital goods acquisition from outside the state would still be favored, but the tax-induced incentive to produce capital within the firms in West Virginia would be reduced. Because of the lack of data and models, we were not able to make any measurements of these phenomena. We were able, however, to provide clues to some other parts of the differential excess burden that would arise with the shift from a turnover to a value-added tax.

Drawing on the Harberger model on the use of consumer and producer surplus to approximate the excess burden of taxation, we prepared estimates of differential excess burden under the three Simulation Models A, B, and C. The estimated reduction of excess burden under all three models was similar--the welfare loss being approximately 50 per cent less under the value-added tax than under the turnover tax.

Some closing caveats are in order lest the impression be given that we take the numbers that were generated too seriously. A number of considerations which we assumed away could, if present, alter the estimated effects. We ignored all second-best considerations and also the conceivable externality-abatement effects of one or both taxes. Another heroic assumption comprised our guesses about elasticities, which neglect the basic uncertainties about them as well as many possible general equilibrium repercussions. In addition, for part of the study, we assumed that production was governed by fixed factor proportions. Though this is not always an unreasonable assumption in the short run, it does not represent a reasonable assumption for the long run. With variable proportions in the long run, we could expect changes in the relative mix of capital and labor employed. Finally, the data used for the simulations dealt with 1967 only and as such the numbers generated should be interpreted in terms of direction and relative magnitude, rather than as precise estimates.

Adequacy, Stability and Predictability, and Administrative Efficiency

Adequacy

To explore the responsiveness of revenues to the two taxes under changing conditions, we derived a differential elasticity of revenue measure analogous in a sense to the nature of differential incidence and differential excess burden. To apply this measure to West Virginia for the period 1967-1969, we assumed no output adjustment to the tax switch (i.e., we assumed that the changes observed in gross, value added, and turnover tax bases, and in effective turnover tax rates, were attributable to events other than the shift to a value-added tax). As in our other analyses, this was an extreme and probably unrealistic assumption, yet making even a crude start at estimating revenue possibilities seemed to be important. Using our corporate sample and other data furnished by the West Virginia State Tax Department, we estimated changes in revenue for the period 1967-1968 and 1968-1969 under the turnover and the proposed value-added tax.

During the period 1967-1968, significant declines occurred in the gross sales of coal mining, crude petroleum, contract construction, and rail and related services as well as declines in the value-added-to-gross ratios of coal mining, contract construction, communication and public utilities, and wholesale trade. Overall, industries which increased their output levels exceeded those declining, such that overall gross output increased from $9.1 billion to $9.3 billion. The composite ratio of value-added-to-gross declined, however, from .35 to .33. The combined effect of the change in base and the change in all industry value-added ratio caused an estimated decline in the value-added base of $129 million and in simulated value-added revenue of $3.4 million. The turnover tax yield for the same period, after adjusting for statutory tax rate changes, increased from roughly $82 million to $84 million, leaving a net loss of $5 million with the change to a value-added tax.

The 2.31 per cent change in turnover tax revenue was attributable to a 2.15 per cent change in the base and a 0.16 per cent change in the effective turnover tax rate. For the value-added tax the 4.18 per cent decline in revenue was attributable to a 6.33 per cent decline in the value-added ratio, which was partially offset by a 2.15 per cent increase in the value-added base. The net effect was an estimated differential revenue elasticity of -1.81 for the period 1967-1968 indicating that, in the aggregate, the value-added tax would not have contributed as much to revenue growth as the turnover tax and in fact had an opposite sign. It should be noted also that we neglected the adjustments that firms might make to reduce their value-added tax bills. If the data are at all accurate, the results suggested that legislators would be less than enthusiastic about such revenue prospects with the shift to a value-added tax, for rates would have to be increased over time to obtain the same revenue.

We then attempted to answer the question "What caused this significant change in both value-added ratios and gross among the various classes of business activity over the period 1967-1968?" It seemed likely that much of this decline was due to the actual changes in turnover tax rates on manufacturing, communication and public utilities, and transportation industries in the latter half of 1967, which induced some tax avoidance behavior. The explanation could not be more conclusive because of the differences in reaction by multistate and domestic firms, which created offsetting effects.

For the period 1968-1969, however, we found that turnover tax revenue increased only 6.22 per cent while estimated value-added revenue increased by 13.36 per cent. Further, the turnover tax base increased by 13.00 per cent while the value-added base increased by 13.36 per cent. The differential revenue elasticity was 2.15 indicating that for the period 1968-1969, a value-added tax would have contributed more than twice as much as the turnover tax to overall revenue, given our restrictive assumptions. Thus, in 1968-1969, instead of the negative differential tax elasticity of 1967-1968, there was a positive (and higher) differential revenue elasticity.

Just as business firms may have responded to the change in the business tax structure in 1968, so there was no doubt a response to events which took place in 1969. In 1969 the sales and use tax was extended to cover business purchases over the period April 1, 1969-March 31, 1970 to cover an anticipated budget deficit. This was strongly opposed by the business community, which may have helped cause widespread under-reporting of taxable value under the turnover tax to compensate for their increased tax liability under the extended sales and use tax provision. In addition, businessmen may have avoided making certain purchases, given the temporary nature of the latter tax. If these responses in fact occurred, one should observe an increase in the ratio of value added to gross in _many_ industries and a decline in the effective turnover tax rates. The data seem to confirm this proposition inasmuch as 10 of the 13 major industry groups had declines in effective turnover tax rates and 7 of the 13 industry groups had increases in their ratios of value added to gross. These findings suggested that businessmen may have avoided their tax liability through vertical integration and/or reporting of taxable value under the turnover tax in a class and rate lower than might otherwise have been the case. Again, the evidence about what was happening was inconclusive because we could not separate the performance of domestic from multistate firms. Over the entire period 1967-1969, revenue under the simulated value-added tax fell short of the revenue under the turnover tax by $3.44 million. (In the earlier analyses of differential incidence and excess burden, the equal yield assumption applied only to 1967. In the examination of revenues during 1967-1969, the 1967 value-added tax rate--2.62--was held constant for 1968 and 1969. Hence, it was possible for total revenue to diverge under the two taxes over the period 1967-1969.)

On the assumption that total excess burden would be reduced by the switch to a value-added tax, we estimated the change in revenue which might be attributed to such improvement in efficiency (again drawing on the "Harberger model"). Using our earlier simulation models we estimated that the net gain in output with the shift to a value-added tax ranged from 1.06 to 3.68 per cent of 1967 output. Using these ranges and assuming that they were not realized until 1970, we estimated various break-even points in cumulative revenue to the year 1980. For example, using a net efficiency gain of about 1.3 per cent we estimated that a break-even point in cumulative revenue would have been reached by 1972. By 1980, the state would have collected about $10.9 million more than with the turnover tax, given identical changes in the economy.

These figures did not include any of the potential gains from reducing uneconomic vertical integration and spatial de-integration. Thus, it seems reasonable to believe that the change to a value-added tax would contribute more to overall revenue growth than the turnover tax in the long run. Needless to say, though, these exercises and the resulting estimates were far from conclusive.

Stability and Predictability

From private industry's point of view, the ability of firms to predict future tax liabilities with a fair degree of accuracy is a matter of some concern. From the state government's view, the ability of a revenue system to provide stable revenues in the face of economic fluctuations is important.

With respect to the predictability of producer's tax bills, there have been, under the turnover tax, frequent and seemingly capricious rate changes which have created a great deal of uncertainty about future tax liabilities. This uncertainty has handicapped future planning by firms for capital expansion and new plant development. More than one industrial prospect has turned West Virginia down for this reason--tax instability. This is not, of course, a disadvantage of the turnover tax per se, but the nature of this tax seems to make it more vulnerable to shifting political pressures for non-uniform and frequent rate changes. Rate changes may arise partly because of firms' efforts to avoid taxes in view of the options presented by the turnover tax provisions. With 16 rates and 30 classes, each tax change operates differentially on business firms depending on the types of production in which they engage. Thus, if all firms attempt to avoid taxes and the state adjusts by raising rates selectively, some firms may be successful in their tax avoidance effort while others are penalized for the same effort.

The capriciousness of tax changes would probably be lessened with the shift to a value-added tax. The reason is that any value-added tax rate change would apply to all classes of business activity rather than to the individual industries as in the past. Businessmen could consequently predict with a greater degree of certainty the likely change in rates required to meet their share of any projected future increase in revenue.

Regarding the state's interest in revenue stability, we could not develop any evidence on the differential stability of the turnover versus the value-added tax. The issue would turn on judgments and data related to changes in value added with cyclical fluctuations in the economy. No helpful data are available at the present time.

Administrative Efficiency

Administrative cost is an important criterion of a desirable tax. Administrative costs ranging from 1 to 2 per cent of revenue are often considered reasonable. We had no evidence which would provide a comparison of such costs per dollar of revenue collected under the two taxes. When one type of value-added tax was levied in the state of Michigan, however, the administrative costs amounted to 3/4 of 1 per cent of total revenue for the first year of operation. Presumably the costs per dollar of revenue declined over successive years. We also know that in 1974, the administrative costs in West Virginia were roughly 1/2 of 1 per cent of total turnover tax revenue. It seems likely that, over the course of two or three years, the administrative efficiency of the value-added tax would be no worse than that of the turnover tax.

Concluding Observation

On balance, these arguments and simulations suggest that the value-added tax does deserve consideration at the sub-national level--that is, in an open economy--if the tax it would replace were a turnover tax such as that levied in West Virginia, or a tax which had comparable distorting effects.

BIBLIOGRAPHY

Aaron, Henry A. "The Differential Price Effects of a Value-Added Tax." National Tax Journal 21 (June 1968):162-75.

Adams, Thomas S. "Fundamental Problems of Federal Income Taxation." Quarterly Journal of Economics 35 (August 1921):527-56.

Advisory Commission on Intergovernmental Relations. State-Local Taxation and Industrial Location, Report A-30. Washington, D.C.: Government Printing Office, April 1967.

Alvis, Vance Q. "Turnover Taxation in West Virginia." Sales Taxation. West Virginia University Legislative Fiscal Studies, vol. 1, no. 3. Morgantown, W.Va.: West Virginia University, 1970, pp. 1-49.

Bethlehem Mines Corp. v Haden W.Va. 172 S.E. 2d., 1969.

Bonsar, Charles F. "Analysis of Major Business Taxes Levied by Indiana." Business Taxation in Indiana. Indianapolis: Indiana Commission on State Tax and Financing Policy, 1966, pp. 9-135.

__________ "State Taxation of Interstate Commerce." Business Taxation in Indiana. Indianapolis: Indiana Commission on State Tax and Financing Policy, 1966, pp. 69-96.

Bossons, John. "The Economic and Redistributive Effects of a Value-Added Tax." Proceedings of the Sixty-First Annual Conference on Taxation of the National Tax Association, 1971. 1972:254-65.

Buchanan, James M. The Public Finances, rev. ed. Homewood, Ill.: Richard D. Irwin, 1965.

Butler, E. B. "Britain and the Continental Value-Added Tax--III." Bankers' Magazine of Australasia (July 1968):39-45.

Business Taxation, Report of the President's Task Force on Business Taxation. Washington, D.C.: Government Printing Office, 1970.

Carson, Howard, ed. West Virginia Blue Book, 1973. Charleston, W.Va.: West Virginia State Senate, 1974.

Charleston (W.Va.) Gazette. Statement of House Minority Leader George H. Seibert, Jr., 5 February 1970.

Cohen, Edwin J. "Foreign Experience with a Value-Added Tax." National Tax Journal 24 (September 1971):399-402.

Committee for Economic Development, Research and Policy Committee. Better Balance in Federal Taxes on Business. New York: Committee for Economic Development, 1966.

Cragg, John G. Current Problems and Issues in State Taxation of Interstate Commerce. Government Finance Brief No. 3 (new series). New York: Tax Foundation, Inc., 1966.

Dailey, Richard L. 1975-76 Budget Hearings. House Finance Committee, West Virginia Legislature. 28 February 1975.

Davis, Claude J.; Elkins, Eugene R.; Frasure, Carl M.; Reeves, Mavis Mann; Ross, William R.; and Sturm, Albert L. West Virginia State and Local Government. Morgantown, W.Va.: West Virginia University, 1963.

"Delegates Approve Democrats' Taxes." Morgantown (W.Va.) Sunday Dominion Post, 1 February 1970.

"Dem Tax Plan Seen Falling Short of Need." Letter of Charles H. Haden. Charleston (W.Va.) Daily Mail, 3 February 1970.

Dorfman, Robert; Samuelson, Paul A.; and Solow, Robert M. Linear Programming and Economic Analysis. New York: McGraw-Hill Book Co., 1958.

Due, James F., and Friedlander, Ann. Government Finance, 5th ed. Homewood, Ill.: Richard D. Irwin, 1965.

Due, John F. "Proposal for a Federal Value-Added Tax." Illinois Business Review 27 (June 1970):6.

__________ "Studies of State-Local Tax Influence on Location of Industry." National Tax Journal 14 (September 1961):163-73.

__________ "The Value-Added Tax." Western Economic Journal 3 (June 1965):165-71:

__________ "Value-Added Tax Proposals in the United States." Essays in Honor of C. Ward Macy. Edited by Paul Kleinsorge. Eugene, Ore.: University of Oregon Books, 1966, pp. 111-26.

Ebel, Robert D. An Evaluation of a Value Added Tax for the State of Hawaii. Honolulu, Hawaii: University of Hawaii, 1973.

__________ The Michigan Business Activities Tax: Value-Added Taxation in the Subnational Economy. MSU Business Studies. East Lansing, Mich.: Michigan State University, 1972.

Eckstein, Otto. "Comparison of European and United States Tax Structures and Growth Implications." The Role of Direct and Indirect Taxes in the Federal Revenue System. A Conference Report of the National Bureau of Economic Research and the Brookings Institution. Princeton, N.J.: Princeton University Press, 1964, pp. 217-93.

Eldridge, Douglas H. "Equity Administration and Compliance, and Intergovernmental Fiscal Aspects." The Role of Direct and Indirect Taxes in the Federal Revenue System. A Conference Report of the National Bureau of Economic Research and the Brookings Institution. Princeton. N.J.: Princeton University Press, 1964, pp. 141-216.

Floyd, Robert H. "The Very Controversial Tax on Value-Added." Monthly Review. Atlanta: Federal Reserve Bank (July 1972).

Fifteenth Biennial Report of the West Virginia Tax Commissioner. Charleston, W.Va.: State of West Virginia.

Forte, Francesco. "On the Feasibility of a Truly General Value-Added Tax: Some Reflection on the French Experience." National Tax Journal 19 (December 1966):337-61.

Friedman, Milton. Price Theory: A Provisional Text, rev. ed. Chicago: Aldine Publishing Co., 1966.

Great Britain, Commission on Turnover Taxation. Report, 1964. London: Her Majesty's Stationery Office, March 1964.

Gordon, Nathan N. "Tax Harmonization in the Common Market and U.S. Tax Policy." Proceedings of the Fifty-Eighth Annual Conference on Taxation of the National Tax Association, 1965. 1966:393-400.

The Governor's Commission on State and Local Finances. Tax Facts in West Virginia: The State Tax and Revenue Structure. Charleston, W.Va.: State of West Virginia, 1954.

Greenhut, Melvin D., and Colberg, Marshall. Factors in the Location of Florida Industry. Tallahassee: The Florida State University, 1967.

Guerard, Michele. "The Brazilian State Value-Added Tax." IMF Staff Papers 20 (March 1973):118-169.

Hamilton, Charles E., Executive Director, West Virginia Manufacturing Associations. "Tax Stability Backbone of Producers." Charleston (W.Va.) Sunday Gazette-Mail, 25 January 1970.

Harberger, Arnold C. "Let's Try a Value-Added Tax." Challenge (November-December 1966).

__________ "The Incidence of the Corporate Income Tax." The Journal of Political Economy 70 (September 1962):215-40.

__________ Taxation and Welfare. Boston: Little, Brown and Co., 1974.

__________ "The Corporate Income Tax: An Empirical Appraisal." Tax Revision Compendium. vol. 1. Submitted to the Committee on Ways and Means, Washington, D.C.: Government Printing Office, 1959, pp. 231-50.

Harriss, C. Lowell. "State-Local Taxation of Interstate Commerce: Progress and Problems." Proceedings of the Fifty-Ninth Annual Conference on Taxation of the National Tax Association, 1966. 1967:294-307.

Hellerstein, Jerome R. "State Taxation, Interstate Business: Reflections on Legislative Directions." Federal-State-Local Fiscal Relationships. Princeton, N.J.: Tax Institute of America, 1968, pp. 257-67.

Hicks, Ursula. Public Finance, 3rd ed. New York: Pitman Publishing Co., 1968.

Hirsch, Werner Z. The Economics of State and Local Government. New York: McGraw-Hill Book Co., 1971.

Hoffman, Harry. "In the Dark and Yelling." Charleston (W.Va.) Gazette, 3 February 1970.

____________, editorial. "Tax Stability Needed." Charleston (W.Va.) Gazette, 2 May 1969.

____________, editorial. "Time for Greatness." Charleston (W.Va.) Gazette, 10 February 1970.

House Taxation Committee Substitute for House Bill No 4640, House of Representatives, East Lansing, Mich.: State of Michigan, April 1975.

Internal Revenue Service, Statistics of Income 1967, 1968, 1969 Corporation Income Tax Returns. Washington, D.C.: Government Printing Office, 1971, 1972, 1973.

Ito, Hanya. "The Value-Added Tax in Japan." The Annals of the Hitotsubashi Academy 1 (January 1950):43-59.

Kegan, Lawrence R., and Roniger, George P. "The Outlook of State and Local Finance." Fiscal Issues in the Future of Federalism. New York: Committee for Economic Development, 1968, pp. 231-83.

Kimura, Motokazu. "An Unrealized Plan: The Value-Added Tax in Japan." The Annals of the Hitotsubashi Academy 13 (January 1958):113-26.

Krauss, Mel, and O'Brien, Peter. "Some International Implications of Value-Added Taxation." National Tax Journal 23 (December 1970): 435-40.

____________ and Bird, Richard M. "The Value Added Tax: Critique of a Review." Journal of Economic Literature 9 (Decmeber 1971):1167-73.

Kust, Leonard E. "A New Venture in Federalism." Tax Review 31 (December 1970):51-4.

"Legislative Tax Plan Endorsed." Statement of Miles C. Stanley. Charleston (W.Va.) Gazette, 28 January 1970.

Lent, George E. "Value-Added Taxes." IMF Survey 1 (February 1972).

Leyden, Dennis R., and Alvis, Vance Q. Fiscal Imperatives in 1975: A Current Perspective of West Virginia State Revenue and Expenditure Needs. West Virginia University Legislative Fiscal Studies, vol. 1, no. 2. Morgantown, W.Va.: West Virginia University, 1968.

Leyden, Dennis R. "Some Empirical Observations on the Differential Impact of a Turnover Versus Value-Added Taxation at the Sub-National Level." Proceedings of the Sixty-Fourth Annual Conference on Taxation of the National Tax Association, 1971. 1972:502-31.

Lindholm, Richard W. "Adaption of Tax Policy to International and Great Society Requirements (Especially the Value-Added Tax)." Tax Changes for Shortrun Stabilization. Subcommittee for Fiscal Policy, Joint Economic Committee. Washington, D.C.: Government Printing Office, 1966, pp. 88-91.

__________. "The French Value-Added Tax." Oregon Business Review (February 1968).

__________. "The Value-Added Tax: A Short Review of the Literature." Journal of Economic Literature 12 (December 1970): 1178-89.

McLure, Charles E. Jr. "Commodity Tax Incidence in Open Economies." National Tax Journal 17 (June 1964):187-204.

__________. "The Inter-regional Incidence of General Regional Taxes." Public Finance 24 (September 1969):457-84.

__________. "The Tax on Value Added: Pros and Cons." Value Added Tax: Two Views. Washington, D.C.: American Enterprise Institute for Public Policy Research, 1972, pp. 1-68.

Marsh, Don. "Value-Added Tax Bill Gets Approval of House." Charleston (W.Va.) Gazette, 1 February 1970.

"Michigan Governor Seeks Value-Added Tax." State Tax Review 32 (April 1971).

Miernyk, William H,; Shellhammer, Kenneth L.; Brown, Douglas M.; Coccari, Ronald L.; Gallagher, Charles J.; and Wineman, Wesley H. Simulating Regional Economic Development. Lexington, Mass.: D.C. Heath and Co., 1970.

Mieszkowski, Peter M. "On the Theory of Tax Incidence." Journal of Political Economy 75 (September 1967):250-62.

Missorten, Walter. "Some Problems in Implementing a Tax on Value Added." National Tax Journal 21 (December 1968):396-411.

Morss, Elliot R. "An Evaluation of the Report on State Taxation." National Tax Journal 18 (September 1965):297-303.

Mueller, Eva, and Morgan, James N. "Location Decisions of Manufacturers." American Economic Review: Papers and Proceedings of the Seventy-Fourth Annual Meeting, 1961. 52 (June 1962):206-17.

Musgrave, Richard A., and Richman, Peggy Brewer. "Allocation Aspects, Domestic and International." The Role of Direct and Indirect Taxes in the Federal Revenue System. A Conference Report of the National Bureau of Economic Research and Brookings Institution. Princeton, N.J.: Princeton University Press, 1964, pp. 81-131.

Musgrave, Richard A., and Musgrave, Peggy B. Public Finance in Theory and Practice. New York: McGraw-Hill Book Co., 1973.

Musgrave, Richard A. The Theory of Public Finance. New York: McGraw-Hill Book Co., 1959.

National Bureau of Economic Research and Brookings Institution. The Role of Direct and Indirect Taxes in the Federal Revenue System. A Conference Report of the National Bureau of Economic Research and Brookings Institution. Princeton, N.J.: Princeton University Press, 1964.

National Bureau of Economic Research. 54th Annual Report (September 1974): 44-45.

Neumark Report of the Fiscal and Financial Committee on Tax Harmonization in the Common Market. Chicago: Commerce Clearing House, 1963.

Oakland, William H. "The Theory of the Value-Added Tax: II, Incidence Effects." National Tax Journal 20 (September 1967):270-81.

Official of Conway Research, Inc. Publishers of "17th Annual Site Selection Handbook, 1974." Industrial Development and Manufacturers Record. Telephone conversation, 25 May 1975.

Oldman, Oliver, and Schoettle, Ferdinand P. State and Local Taxes and Finance. Mineola, N.Y.: The Foundation Press, Inc., 1974.

Papke, James A. "The Consumer Sales Tax Credit or Rebate." Report presented to the Joint Committee on Government and Finance of the West Virginia Legislature. Charleston, W.Va., 22 August 1966.

________. "General Outline of Gross Margins Tax." Report presented to the Joint Committee on Government and Finance of the West Virginia Legislature. Charleston, W.Va., 17 August 1966.

________. "The Incidence of State-Local Taxes in West Virginia: Distribution of Tax Payments Among Resident Household Income Groups." Report presented to the Joint Committee on Government and Finance of the West Virginia Legislature. Charleston, W.Va., 8 August 1966.

________. "Michigan's Value-Added Tax After Seven Years." National Tax Journal 13 (December 1960):350-63.

______________ "Objectives of a Tax Program for West Virginia." Report presented to the Joint Committee on Government and Finance of the West Virginia Legislature. Charleston, W.Va., 10 July 1966.

______________ "Revenue Effects of Alternative Tax Structure Adjustments." Report presented to the Joint Committee on Goverment and Finance of the West Virginia Legislature. Charleston, W.Va., 8 August 1970.

______________ "The State Business Tax Structure: A Quantitative Analysis for Policy Deliberation." Report presented to the Joint Committee on Government and Finance of the West Virginia Legislature. Charleston, W.Va., 12 September 1966.

______________ "The Theory and Practice of Value-Added Taxation." Ph.D. dissertation, Cornell University, 1959.

Peckman, Joseph A., and Okner, Benjamin A. Who Bears the Tax Burden? Studies of Government Finance. Washington, D.C.: The Brookings Institution, 1974.

Point Pleasant (W.Va.) Register, Statement of Senate President Lloyd Jackson, 13 January 1970.

"Proposed New Tax Wouldn't Do What It Was Supposed To!" Observation of Charles S. Armstead. Morgantown (W.Va.) Post, 7 June 1967.

Ray, Cadwell L. "An Analysis of Value-Added Taxation with Special Reference to the State of Texas." Ph.D. dissertation, University of Texas, 1967.

Rolph, Earl R. "The Economic Effects of a Federal Value-Added Tax." Public Finance and Fiscal Policy. edited by Joseph Scherer and James A. Papke. Boston: Houghton Mifflin Co., 1966, pp. 143-53.

Saunders, Robert J. The Spatial Concentration of Industry in Appalachia: An Analysis of Potential for Import Substitution. Washington, D.C.: Appalachian Regional Commission, 1969.

Seibert, George H., Jr. "Tax Measures Handed Moore." Charleston (W.Va.) Daily Mail, 5 February 1970.

Seiler, Fanny. "House Eyes Alternative Vehicle." Charleston (W.Va.) Gazette. 28 February 1975.

Shoup, Carl S. "Consumption Tax, and Wages Type and Consumption Type of Value-Added Tax." National Tax Journal 21 (June 1968):153-61.

______________ "Experience with the Value-Added Tax in Denmark and Prospects in Sweden." Finanzarchiv (March 1969):236-52.

______________ Public Finance. Chicago: Aldine Publishing Co., 1969.

_____________ "Theory and Background of the Value-Added Tax." Proceedings of the Forty-Eighth Annual Conference on Taxation of the National Tax Association, 1955. 1956:7-19.

Shoup Mission. Report on Japanese Taxation. 4 vols. Tokyo: Supreme Commander for the Allied Powers, 1949.

_____________ Second Report on Japanese Taxation. Tokyo: Japan Tax Association, 1950.

Siegel, Sidney. Nonparametric Statistics. New York: McGraw-Hill Book Co., 1956.

Slitor, Richard E. "The Value-Added Tax as an Alternative to Corporate Income Tax." Alternatives to Present Federal Taxes. Princeton, N.J.: Tax Institute of America, 1964, pp. 35-54.

Sixteenth Biennial Report of the West Virginia Tax Commissioner. Charleston, W.Va.: State of West Virginia.

Smit, Hans and Herzog, Peter E. The Law of the European Economic Community: A Commentary on the EEC Treaty. New York: The Matthew Bender and Company, Inc., 1976, Vol. 3, pp. 425ff.

Smith, Dan T. "The Value-Added Tax as an Alternative to the Corporate Tax." Proceedings of the Fifty-Seventh Annual Conference on Taxation of the National Tax Association, 1963. 1964:424-30.

_____________ "When-if-we have the VAT." Harvard Business Review 51 (January 1973):6-18ff.

"Stability--That's What Matters for Business." Charleston (W.Va.) Gazette, 23 December 1969.

State Tax Study Commission. Final Report of State Tax Study Commission: West Virginia Taxes: (State and Local). Charleston, W.Va.: State of West Virginia, 1960.

State Tax Study Commission. First Report of State Tax Study Commission: West Virginia Taxes: (State and Local). Charleston, W.Va.: State of West Virginia, 1959.

State ex rel. Battle v Baltimore and O.R.R., 149 W.Va. 810, 143 SE 2d 331 (1965).

State of West Virginia. "Executive Message No. 16." The Journal of the House of Delegates. West Virginia: 1970.

State of West Virginia. "House Bill 588." The Journal of the House of Delegates. West Virginia: 1970.

Studenski, Paul. "Toward a Theory of Business Taxation." Journal of Political Economy 48 (May 1940):621-54.

Sullivan, Clara K. The Search for Tax Principles in the E.E.C. Harvard Law School International Program in Taxation. Chicago: Commerce Clearing House, 1963.

________________. The Tax on Value-Added. New York: Columbia University Press, 1965.

Survey of Current Business. February 1974.

Tax Foundation. "Taxation of Interstate Business." Proceedings of the Tax Foundation Seminar. New York: Tax Foundation, Inc., 1970.

Thompson, James H. Methods of Plant Site Selection Available to Small Manufacturing Firms. Small Business Management Research Reports. Morgantown, W.Va.: West Virginia University, 1961.

Ture, Norman B. "Economics of the Value-Added Tax." Value Added Tax: Two Views. Washington, D.C.: American Enterprise Institute for Public Policy Research, 1972, pp. 69-97.

U.S. Congress. House. Committee of the Judiciary, Special Subcommittee on State Taxation of Interstate Commerce. State Taxation of Interstate Commerce. 88th Cong. 2nd sess., 1964-1965, vols. 1-4.

U.S. Congress. House. Committee on Ways and Means. "The Economic Effects of a Federal Value-Added Tax." Excise Tax Compendium, by Earl R. Rolph. Washington, D.C.: Government Printing Office, 1964, pp. 99-107.

"Value-Added Package Deserves State Test." Charleston (W.Va.) Gazette, 11 February 1970.

"Value-Added Tax Business Killers, Says Businessman." Remarks of William Bright of Bright, Inc. Charleston (W.Va.) Daily Mail, 4 February 1970.

West Virginia Code of 1966. Charlottesville, Va: Michie Co., 1966 and Cumulative Supplements for 1967-1969.

West Virginia State Tax Department Thirty-Second Report, 1967-1968. Charleston, W.Va.: State of West Virginia, 1968.

Welch, Ronald V. "Equity, Administration and Compliance, and Intergovernmental Fiscal Aspects: Comment." The Role of Direct and Indirect Taxes in the Federal Revenue System. A Conference Report of the National Bureau of Economic Research and the Brookings Institution. Princeton, N.J.: Princeton University Press, 1964, pp. 209-15.

Wisecarver, Daniel. "The Social Costs of Input-Market Distortions." The American Economic Review 64 (June 1974):359-72.

Williams, William V. "A Measure of the Impact of State and Local Taxes on Industry Location." Journal of Regional Science 7 (January 1967):49-59.

APPENDIX A

TURNOVER AND VALUE-ADDED TAX BASES: SAMPLING PROCEDURES AND RESULTS

APPENDIX A

TURNOVER AND VALUE-ADDED TAX BASES: SAMPLING PROCEDURES AND RESULTS

The empirical base chosen was the corporate sector of West Virginia business enterprises since it is only in this sector that adequate information is available for estimating the effect of the tax change. Agreement was obtained from the West Virginia State Tax Department to obtain a stratified sample of tax returns on corporations doing business in West Virginia during the period 1967-1969.

Since there is a fairly skewed distribution of turnover tax payments by corporations in West Virginia, we decided to use a stratified-judgment sample, with care exercised to obtain as close to a 100 per cent sample of the large corporations and a random sample of all other corporations within each stratification. The stratification was based on industry classifications as defined for tax purposes by the Internal Revenue System, U.S. Treasury Department under the so-called "Standard Enterprise Classification System" (SEC). This stratification together with the comparable SEC classes under the West Virginia Turnover Taxes is provided in Table 43. The codes assigned for purposes of this study are also noted in Columns 3 and 4.[1] From a tax department computer printout of a stratified listing of all corporations registered in West Virginia, with appropriate safeguards to prevent identity of the firms, the large taxpayer was identified and isolated. The remaining firms were then used as a base for the draw of a random sample of 1 per cent or 35,

---

[1]The code for non-metallic minerals was changed from 3 to 5.10 because most of the firms report their largest gross in the manufacturing processing industries. Communications (Study Code 7) was merged with public utilities (Code 8) because of disclosure problems.

TABLE 43

WEST VIRGINIA INDUSTRY CODE EQUIVALENTS
1967-1969

West Virginia Turnover Tax Code Description	Standard Enterprise Classification[a] Code	West Virginia Turnover Tax Code[b]	Industry Study Code Initial	Industry Study Code Final
Minerals				
Coal Mining	1100-1199	1	1	1
Crude Petroleum & Natural Gas	1300-1399	3, 4	2	2
Non-Metallic Minerals	1400-1499	2, 5	3	5.10
Contract Construction		6, 7	4	4
Building	1510-1519		4.01	4.01
Highway & Street Construction	1520-1529	16, 17	4.02	4.02
Special Trade Contractors	1530-1539		4.03	4.03
Manufacturing			5	5
Food & Kindred Products	2000-2199		5.01	5.01
Textile Mill, Apparel & Other Textiles	2200-2399		5.02	5.02
Chemicals & Allied Products	2800-2899		5.03	5.03
Glass & Glass Products	3210-3219		5.04	5.04
Stone & Clay Products	3240-3298		5.05	5.05
Primary Metals	3300-3399	8	5.06	5.06
Fabricated Metals	3400-3499		5.07	5.07
Machinery, Including Electric Machinery	3500-3699		5.08	5.08
Transportation Equipment	3700-3799		5.09	5.09
All Other Manufacturing Not Elsewhere Classified	2400-2799 2900-3200 3800-3999		5.10	5.10

TABLE 43--Continued

West Virginia Turnover Tax Code Description	Standard Enterprise Classification[a] Code	West Virginia Turnover Tax Code[b]	Industry Study Code	
			Initial	Final
Transportation			6	6
Rail & Related Services	4010-4019	30	6.01	6.01
Motor Freight & Related Services	4030-4039	24, 25	6.02	6.02
All Other Transportation Not Elsewhere Classified	4020-4029 4040-4069, 4098	22, 23 28, 29	6.03	6.03
Communication & Public Utilities				8
Communication	4810-4898	26, 27	7	8
Public Utilities	4910-4940	11, 12, 13 14, 15	8	8
Wholesale & Retail Trade				
Wholesale	5010-5098	10	9	9
Retail	5210-5298	9	10	10
Finance & Real Estate				
Banks & Trusts, Credit Agencies Other Than Banks, Security and Commodity Brokers, Holding & Other Investment Companies	6010-6048	21	11	11
Real Estate	6510-6598	19, 20	12	12
Services				
All Services	7010-8098	18, 19	13	13

TABLE 43--Continued

[a]Internal Revenue Service, Statistics of Income, 1967, U.S. Business Tax Returns, (Washington, D.C.: Government Printing Office).

[b]West Virginia State Tax Department.

whichever was larger. The results of this process, displayed in Table 44 (Cols. 4-6) show that there were 557 large firms and 1,110 smaller corporations included in the initial sample request of the tax department. This scheme proved to be fine for the large taxpayer but not so for the small taxpayer since the list of firms from which the random sample subset was selected included both active and non-active corporations. To compensate for this, agreement was reached with the tax department that for every inactive corporation selected in the random set, an active corporation of comparable industry and size would be substituted.

Beyond this initial problem, we encountered a problem in the usability of the returns received. A number of firms had to be rejected because they did not do business for the entire time period (1967-1969), were illegable subchapter S corporations, did not provide sufficient information to perform the various calculations, or were duplicates of returns furnished previously (See Col. 8). Still others were rejected by a process used to screen out those firms which met an initial non-reject criterion and placed on computer tape, but which were subsequently discovered to be duplicates of other returns or contained spurious data which could not possibly be sustained as reasonable given the tax return set (See Cols. 9-11). A final problem encountered was the fact that although most of the corporation's filed on a calendar year base, there were a fair number in the sample which filed on a fiscal year base which ranged over the entire 11-month period. This required that four years of data (1967-1970) be provided so that calendar year returns could be constructed. The details by which the sample returns were processed are described in the following section.

TABLE 44
WEST VIRGINIA VALUE-ADDED STUDY SAMPLE RESULTS
1967-1969

Industry Study Code	Standard Enterprise Classification Code	Industry Identification	Initial Universe Identification Large	Initial Universe Identification Small	Total	Sample Request Large	Sample Request Small	Total Request	Total Received	Rejected	Disposition of Returns Override 1967	Disposition of Returns Total Not Used 1967	Usable 1967
		MINERALS											
1	1100-1199	Coal Mining	76	274	350	76	35	111	210	69	16	85	125
2	1300-1399	Crude Petroleum & Natural Gas	20	157	177	20	35	55	87	36	16	52	35
4		CONTRACT CONSTRUCTION											
4.01& 4.02	1510,1520	Building, Highway & Street Construction	86	204	290	86	35	121	176	59	4	63	113
4.03	1331,1532 1538	Special Trade Contractors	42	382	424	42	35	77	104	30	5	35	69
5 & 3		MANUFACTURING											
5.01	2000-2199	Food & Kindred Products	25	163	188	25	35	60	66	16	0	16	50
5.02	2200-2399	Textile Mill, Apparel & Other Textiles	9	25	34	9	25	34	25	5	3	8	17
5.03	2800-2899	Chemicals & Allied Products	25	218	243	25	35	60	44	4	11	15	29
5.04	3210-3219	Glass & Glass Products	13	41	54	13	35	48	36	4	1	5	31
5.05	3240-3298	Stone & Clay Products	6	48	54	6	35	41	40	7	2	9	31
5.06	3300-3399	Primary Metals	13	34	47	13	34	47	35	9	4	13	22
5.07	3400-3499	Fabricated Metals	18	92	110	18	35	53	56	11	3	14	42
5.08	3500-3699	Machinery, Incl. Electrical	14	130	144	14	35	49	45	7	11	18	27
5.09	3700-3799	Transportation Equipment	8	29	37	8	29	37	17	9	1	10	7
5.10 3	2400-2799 2900-3200 3800-3999*	All Other Manufacturing Plus Non-Metallic Minerals*	42	535	577	42	53	95	141	49	2	51	90
6		TRANSPORTATION											
6.01	4011-4019	Rail & Related Services	4	18	22	4	18	22	6	1	5	5	0
6.02	4030	Motor Freight & Related Services	4	124	128	4	35	39	11	0	6	6	5
6.03	4020-4029 4040-4069 4098	All Other Transportation	6	129	135	6	35	41	54	6	13	19	35
7 & 8		COMMUNICATION & PUBLIC UTILITIES											
	4800-4999	Communication & Public Utilities	23	198	221	23	35	58	213	26	107	133	80
		WHOLESALE & RETAIL TRADE											
9	5000-5099	Wholesale	29	735	764	29	76	105	145	24	13	37	108
10	5211-5298	Retail	67	1,610	1,677	67	161	228	209	41	14	55	154
		FINANCE & REAL ESTATE											
11	6000-6049	Financial Institutions**	3	320	323	3	35	38	38	9	12	21	17
12	6500-6599	Real Estate	3	1,238	1,241	3	124	127	63	9	45	54	9
13		SERVICES											
	7000-8099	Services	21	988	1,009	21	100	121	180	48	19	67	113
		TOTAL	557	7,692	8,249	557	1,110	1,667	1,954	479	313	792	1,209

*Non-Metallic Minerals were included in Other Manufacturing because the firms operating in West Virginia generally declare their largest activity in manufacturing processing.

**Does not include banks because they were not subject to state business taxation for the period 1967 through 1969.

Program Configuration for Processing Sample Data

The attached flow chart (Figure 7) should assist the reader in understanding how the tax data was finally processed. The sample selection process described above represented a request to the tax department for the corporate data. They responded by furnishing the requested tax return set for each corporation covering the three-year period. These were then logged in and given an arbitrary set of numbers to keep track of them. All of the variables to be keypunched were assigned "variable numbers."[1] Each tax return set was then put through a pre-screening process which consisted of checks to insure that: returns were numbered; the data was arithmetically accurate; and complete data was furnished. If a tax return set passed the pre-screening, it was sent forward for keypunching (#2). If the set did not pass the pre-screen, that is, if there were some materials missing from the set furnished by the tax department, it was placed in a separate file to be held for additional data. A request was sent to the tax department indicating that information was lacking. One of two things happened in response to the request: either the additional data was furnished, in which case the flow was completed and it went through the pre-screen again and thence to keypunch; or the tax department indicated that they had no further information for that firm and that nothing more could be done. In this latter case, the particular account was rejected and placed in storage. As the returns were keypunched, cards were furnished to the programmer and the original data returned to the storage file. The keypunched returns were separated

---

[1]They are on file in the Bureau of Business Research at West Virginia University and may be made available to interested parties.

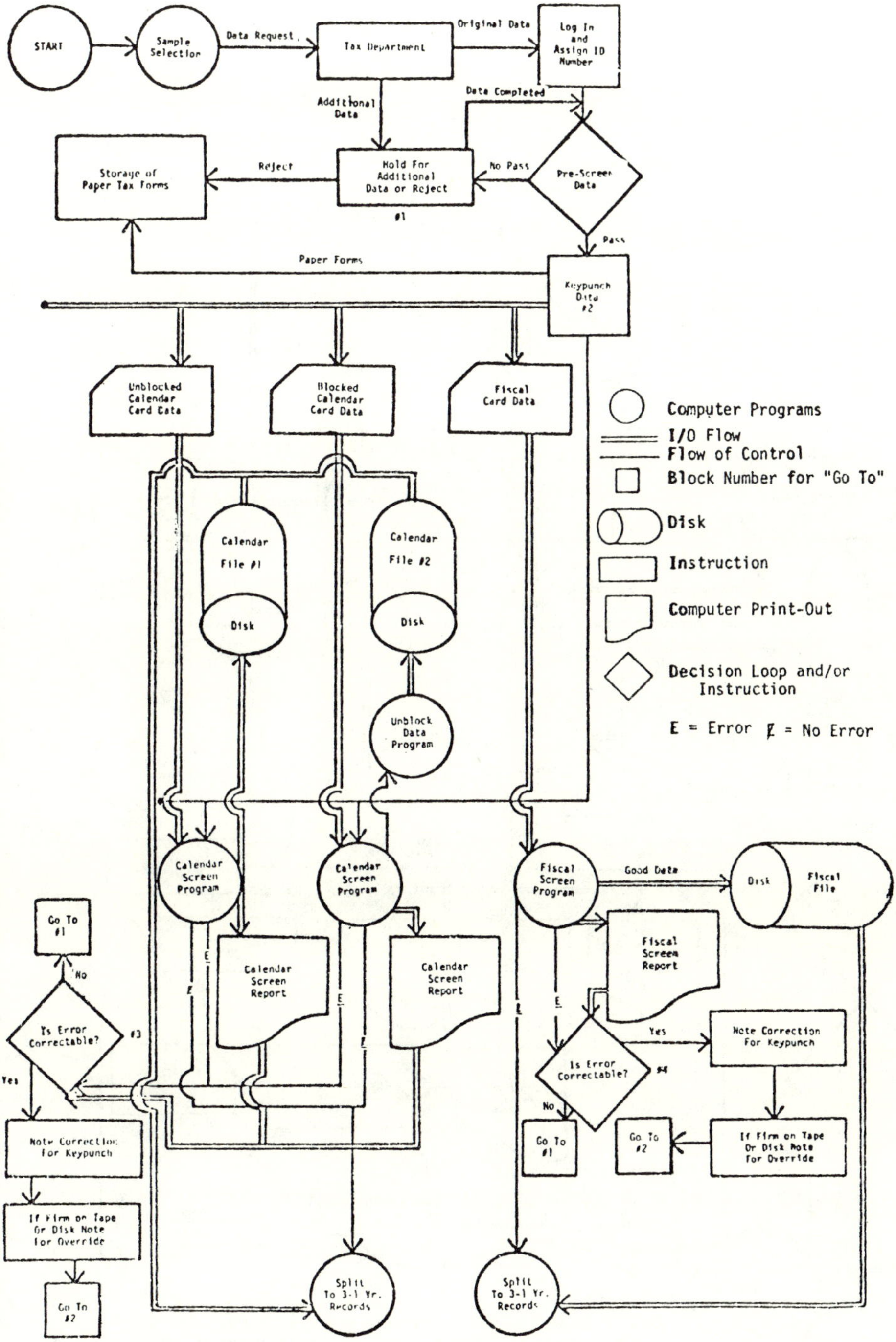

FIGURE 7: DATA PROCESS FLOW CHART

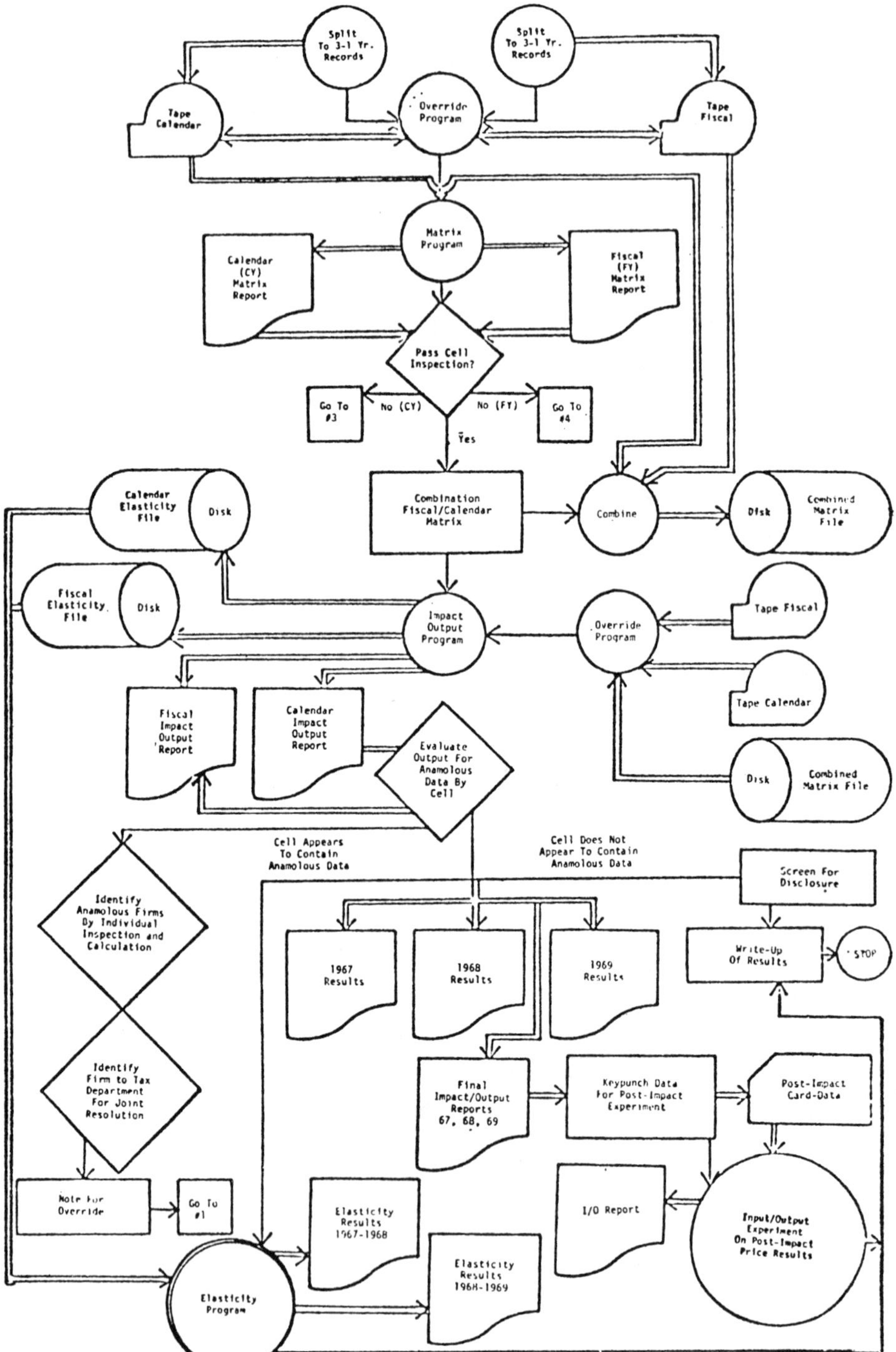

FIGURE 7--Continued

into three tax return decks--fiscal year, unblocked calendar year, and blocked calendar year. The three data decks were then processed through a computer screen program to check for keypunch errors, arithmetic errors, and industry coding errors as follows:

List of Errors[1]--

1. Federal Taxable Income on the 1120 equal to Federal Taxable Income on the WV 112.
2. WV 112 Schedule B or C Addition Checks.
3. WV 112 Wage and Salary Percentage Check.
4. WV 112 Property Percentage Check.
5. Agreement of B & O and Carrier Taxes paid with Schedule D, WV 112 credit for BOCT paid.
6. US 1120 Arithmetic Checks.
7. Agreement of Business SEC Codes on All Three Years on US 1120 and Turnover Tax Codes on All Three Years.
8. Agreement of Business SEC Codes on 1120 with Business Code Activity Noted on B & O and Carrier Returns.

A computer report was furnished which indicated whether or not a firm passed all of these screen checks. It should be noted that errors 1 and 5 were not used to screen out, but simply to provide information to the tax department. If they did not pass the screen report, that is, they were not accepted, the firm was identified and information furnished as to the nature of the error. Returns so identified were pulled from their storage location and the identified errors were checked against the return. In this way, a check could be made both for errors in terms of

---

[1]A detailed statement of the screened-for errors is on file in the Bureau of Business Research at West Virginia University and may be made available to interested parties.

the return and with respect to the keypunching of the returns. If the errors were correctable, they were returned to #2, i.e., the materials were re-keypunched. If they were not correctable, they were returned to #1 and notification made to the tax department. The loop was then re-entered depending upon whether the information was forthcoming or not. Having passed through the screen report, the unblocked calendar year returns were considered acceptable and placed on disc (Calendar File #1). The blocked calendar year firm and the fiscal year firm required additional manipulations before they could be considered ready for the next step in the data processing sequence.

The blocked accounts were a means used by the tax department to insure the confidentiality of some of the largest taxpayers. These large accounts were forwarded with two or more other accounts added to them and were presented as one firm. In this case, there was also furnished the amount of gross sales as shown in line 1 of the 1120s for each of the firms represented in the block, as well as the amount of gross that was declared under the turnover tax for each one of the returns. This information was used as a basis for deblocking the set received. For example, if the blocked return contained three firms and the total gross declared on line 1 of the 1120 was 25 per cent assigned to Firm 1, 50 per cent assigned to Firm 2, and 25 per cent assigned to Firm 3, three dummy firms 1120's and 112's were created by allocating all of the items on the blocked return to each of the three in proportion to their percentages of 1120 gross. The same procedure was used for deriving a comparable set of dummy turnover tax returns by using the distribution of turnover gross in West Virginia. Having accomplished this task, the deblocked-screened firms were considered acceptable and placed on disc (Calendar Year File #2).

At this juncture, a routine was written to merge the two disk-calendar-year files into one and split into three one-year records for 1967, 1968, and 1969. This was then loaded on a calendar-year tape.

The fiscal-year return which passed the screen check needed to conform in time to the three calendar years 1967, 1968, and 1969. To accomplish this for each fiscal-year account, fiscal 1970 returns were obtained and an allocation technique (split to three one-year records) was used to create three calendar-year returns from the four fiscal-year returns, according to the following steps:

<u>Step 1</u>.

Assign a month code to each set of returns depending on the ending fiscal-year month recorded on the original tax return as per the following:

Code	Period Covered
1	11/1 - 12/31
2	1/1 - 2/28
3	3/1 - 4/30
4	5/1 - 6/30
5	7/1 - 8/31
6	9/1 - 10/31

<u>Step 2</u>.

Create a calendar-year return for each of three years, 1967-1969 by applying an appropriate proportion to each of the relevant variables on the four fiscal-year returns.

At this juncture, a fiscal and a calendar tape were created which were used as input to a matrix program, the purpose of which was to provide an estimate of the wages and salaries for those corporations which did all of their business in West Virginia (domestic corporations). This procedure was necessary because domestic corporations are not required by the tax department to report wages and salaries on their West Virginia

Corporation Tax Return (WV 112). They do, however, report on the U.S. Corporation Return (line 2) a "Cost of Goods Sold" figure--which includes wage and salaries paid, cost of materials, and inventory adjustments. The multistate corporation is, however, required to report its wages and salaries both in West Virginia and everywhere. The multistate wages and salaries everywhere relative to cost of goods sold (multistate ratio) was placed in an industry-by-size matrix and used to estimate the domestic corporation wages and salaries. This was done by multiplying the multistate ratio by the sum of the domestic firm's line 2 (cost of goods sold) and lines 12 and 13 (wages and salaries not elsewhere deducted). This procedure was performed for each year on both the fiscal- and calendar-year tapes. After inspection/correction for anomalous data, we merged all three years into a combined matrix because the number of observations in any one year by industry proved to be relatively small. This maximized the number of observations but at the cost of diminished sensitivity to annual wage and salary fluctuations, since the effect was to average out some changes which may have occurred inter-year for domestic corporations.

We now had three tapes: (1) a fiscal tape containing data for all of the fiscal year filers; (2) a calendar tape for calendar year filers; and (3) a matrix tape for estimating wages and salaries for domestic corporations. With the completion of these three tapes, it was possible to move to the substantive portion of the analysis, except that any error or anomalous data which might still exist in any corporate file could no longer be corrected without creating new tapes. To accommodate to this possibility, an override program was written which was inserted to intercept output data from the calendar-and fiscal-year tapes, but before the matrix tape. This override sub-routine caused the data output from any firm identified to be overridden in any subsequent run and provision made, as explained below, for correcting the data by creating a new firm.

From this point on, analytical programs were written to provide the basis for the analysis contained in Chapters IV-VI. At each stage, the output of the analytical programs were evaluated to ascertain whether anomalous data existed in the output. When such a condition seemed to be true the firms which made up the cell containing the anomalous data were identified and a resolution made as to the reasons for the anomalous data. Once the appropriate firms were identified, they were then forwarded to the tax department for resolution, i.e., returned to #4 and notification given of the problem. At the same time an override instruction was provided and if the error was correctable, the firms were re-keypunched with a new I.D. number and re-entered into the data set.

Finally, all of the output was evaluated for disclosure and either aggregated or omitted so as to meet the government restriction on disclosing information which would permit the identification of any individual firm.

Representativeness of Sample

To show the portions of the business sector represented by the sample, the dollar amount of gross business identified in the sample is compared with the known dollar amount of gross declared on tax returns by all businesses in West Virginia (see Table 45). The sample from Industry Code 12--real estate, includes only 1.26 per cent of the gross actually declared. This is explained by the fact that the sample firms were classified by their Standard Enterprise Classification Code on their

TABLE 45

COVERAGE OF SAMPLE DATA

Industry Study Code	Industry Identification	Sample West Virginia Gross CY 1967 ($000)	Number of Firms in Sample	Total West Virginia Gross CY 1967 ($000)	Sample Per Cent of Total Gross
1	Coal Mining	650,809	125	843,247	77.18
2	Crude Petroleum & Natural Gas	21,263	35	71,448	30.29
4	Contract Construction	171,692	182	483,461	35.51
5	Manufacturing & Non-Metallic Minerals	2,842,645	346	2,945,983	96.49
6	Transportation	55,121	56	75,217	73.28
8	Communication & Public Utilities	367,722	80	435,722	84.39
9	Wholesale Trade	324,510	108	1,282,033	25.31
10	Retail Trade	455,480	154	1,918,182	23.75
11	Finance	4,514	17	25,652	17.60
12	Real Estate	2,559	9	203,380	1.26
13	Services	68,584	113	571,031	12.01
	Total	4,964,899	1,225	8,824,709	56.26

federal return and where there was conflict with the industry identification on the turnover tax return, the firm was assigned to the turnover tax industry with the largest gross. In most cases, this was not a problem, but in this industry, there are firms whose principal classification is in an industry other than real estate which for turnover tax purposes includes royalties and fees other than real estate. Thus, the universe gross overstates the true real estate gross by including gross which properly belongs in the coal, oil and gas, and service industries. In all the other industries, it appears that the sample contains adequate representation of the volume of business done in West Virginia.

APPENDIX B

DESCRIPTION OF INPUT-OUTPUT MODEL FOR SIMULATING PRICE EFFECTS AND INCIDENCE OF THE SHIFT FROM A TURNOVER TO AN INCOME VALUE-ADDED TAX IN WEST VIRGINIA, 1967

This appendix describes the mathematical form of the input-output model used to develop the simulated effects on prices on each industry and on the broad export and domestic (domestic and import-competing) sectors. The specific programs used for the calculations are on file in the Bureau of Business Research at West Virginia University and can be made available upon request.

APPENDIX B

DESCRIPTION OF INPUT-OUTPUT MODEL FOR SIMULATING PRICE EFFECTS AND INCIDENCE OF THE SHIFT FROM A TURNOVER TO AN INCOME VALUE-ADDED TAX IN WEST VIRGINIA, 1967

In matrix notation, the basic equation in an open economy is as follows:

(1) $X - AX = Y' + Y''$

where X is a column vector representing the output of n industries, composed of the elements x_i where $i = 1, 2, \ldots n$,

and A is an n X n matrix of direct coefficients which expresses the assumption that sales from the ith sector to the jth sector is a constant proportion of the jth's sector's output x_j, i.e.,

$a_{ij} = x_{ij}/x_j$

for $i = 1, 2, \ldots n$,
$j = 1, 2, \ldots n$,

and Y' is a column vector representing the ith's sector exports composed of the elements y'_i, where $i = 1, 2, \ldots n$,

and Y'' is a column vector representing the ith's sector shipment to domestic final demand composed of the elements y''_i where $i = 1, 2, \ldots n$.

Factoring equation (1) for X yields equation (2)

(2) $(I - A)X = (Y' + Y'')$

where I is an identity matrix of the same order as A. The direct coefficient matrix A when subtracted from the identity matrix I yields a Leontief matrix which when multiplied by the output vector yields the vector of value of shipments to final demand, $(Y' + Y'')$.

Solving for X yields equation (3)

(3) $$X = (I - A)^{-1}(Y' + Y'') = (I - A)^{-1}Y' + (I - A)^{-1}Y''$$

where $(I - A)^{-1}$ is the inverse of the Leontief matrix representing the direct and indirect requirements per dollar of delivery to final demand and is further expressed as the direct and indirect requirements from all sectors per dollar of delivery to final export demand and final domestic demand by the ith sector.

Introducing taxation into the system: (4) for turnover taxation;

(4) $$T_g = t_g X$$

where $T_g = (T_{gi})$, $i = 1, 2, \ldots n$,

a vector representing the turnover tax (yield) imposed on the gross output of the ith sector

$$\text{and } t_g = \begin{bmatrix} t_{g1} & 0 & \cdots & 0 \\ 0 & t_{g2} & & 0 \\ \cdot & & \cdot & \cdot \\ \cdot & & \cdot & \cdot \\ \cdot & & \cdot & \cdot \\ 0 & 0 & \cdots & t_{gn} \end{bmatrix}$$

a diagonal matrix whose diagonal is composed of the rate of the gross output of the ith sector defined as T_{gi}/X_i, and is assumed to be a constant proportion of the gross output of the ith sector,

Thus,

$$\begin{bmatrix} T_{g1} \\ T_{g2} \\ \cdot \\ \cdot \\ \cdot \\ T_{gn} \end{bmatrix} = \begin{bmatrix} t_{g1} & 0 & \cdots & 0 \\ 0 & t_{g2} & & 0 \\ \cdot & & \cdot & \cdot \\ \cdot & & \cdot & \cdot \\ \cdot & & \cdot & \cdot \\ 0 & 0 & \cdots & t_{gn} \end{bmatrix} \begin{bmatrix} X_1 \\ X_2 \\ \cdot \\ \cdot \\ \cdot \\ X_n \end{bmatrix}$$

for value-added taxation

(5) $T_V = t_V V$

where $T_V = (T_{Vi})$, i = 1, 2, . . . n,

a vector representing the value-added tax (yield) imposed on the value added of the ith sector.

$$\text{and } t_V = \begin{bmatrix} t_{v1} & \cdots & 0 \\ \cdot & t_{v2} & \cdot \\ \cdot & \cdot & \cdot \\ \cdot & \cdot & \cdot \\ \cdot & \cdot & \cdot \\ 0 & \cdots & t_{vn} \end{bmatrix}$$

a diagonal matrix whose diagonal is composed of the elements representing the rate of tax imposed on the ith's sector value added. By definition this rate is the same for all sectors.

Thus,

$$\begin{bmatrix} T_{v1} \\ T_{v2} \\ \cdot \\ \cdot \\ \cdot \\ T_{vn} \end{bmatrix} = \begin{bmatrix} t_{v1} & 0 & \cdots & 0 \\ 0 & t_{v2} & & 0 \\ \cdot & & \cdot & \cdot \\ \cdot & & \cdot & \cdot \\ \cdot & & \cdot & \cdot \\ 0 & 0 & \cdots & t_{vn} \end{bmatrix} \begin{bmatrix} V_1 \\ V_2 \\ \cdot \\ \cdot \\ \cdot \\ V_n \end{bmatrix}$$

and V = a vector representing the value added of the jth sector which for purposes of this study may be defined in three ways, i.e.,

(5a) $V_j^{(1)} = [V_j]$, j = 1, 2, . . . n is an n-tuple vector

$$\text{where } V_j = X_j - \sum_{i=1}^{n} a_{ij}X_i$$

is a vector composed of the elements $V_j^{(1)}$ (value added in sector (j) j = 1, 2, . . . n) where value added in sector j is defined as equal to total output X_j minus purchases from all industries.

This is the typical definition of value added for input-output purposes and is equivalent to the base identified under the gross value-added tax form.

(5b) $$V_j^{(2)} = [X_j - \sum_{i=1}^{n} a_{ij}X_j - M_j - D_j]$$

a vector yielding the income value added for a sub-national area where M_j represents industry j's import purchases and D_j represents depreciation expenses in industry j.

(5c) $$V_j^{(3)} = V_j^{(2)}$$

where $V^{(3)}$ is a vector representing the income value added of sector j as in (5b) except where j = tax exempt sectors. In this particular case the proposed statute (House Bill 588) exempts agriculture, banks, and insurance companies.

We now have the elements of a model for deriving the differential incidence of the move from a turnover tax to an income value-added tax.

(6) $$\Delta T = (T_v - T_g)(S)$$

$$\text{where } \Delta T = \begin{bmatrix} \Delta T_1 \\ \Delta T_2 \\ \cdot \\ \cdot \\ \cdot \\ \Delta T_n \end{bmatrix}$$

the vector composed of element ΔT_i representing the differential change in tax yield in industry i accompanying the change from a turnover to an income value-added tax which is passed forward to final demand. ΔT_i is equivalent to the differences in tax rate, Δt_i, times output of industry X_i.

$$\text{and } S = \begin{bmatrix} S_1 \\ S_2 \\ \cdot \\ \cdot \\ \cdot \\ S_n \end{bmatrix}$$

is a vector representing the assumed proportion of the differential tax change which has passed forward to final demand by the ith sector.

Thus,

$$\Delta T = \begin{bmatrix} \Delta T_1 \\ \Delta T_2 \\ \cdot \\ \cdot \\ \cdot \\ \Delta T_n \end{bmatrix} = \begin{bmatrix} T_{v1} - T_{g1} & 0 & \cdots & 0 \\ 0 & T_{v2} - T_{g2} & \cdots & 0 \\ \cdot & \cdot & \cdot & \cdot \\ \cdot & \cdot & \cdot & \cdot \\ \cdot & \cdot & \cdot & \cdot \\ 0 & 0 & \cdots & T_{vn} - T_{gn} \end{bmatrix} \begin{bmatrix} S_1 \\ S_2 \\ \cdot \\ \cdot \\ \cdot \\ S_n \end{bmatrix}$$

Multiplying both sides of equation (3) by a n x n diagonal matrix, $\frac{\Delta T}{X}$, (composed of elements, $\Delta t_i = \frac{\Delta T_i}{X_i}$ along the diagonal and zeros elsewhere) yields a column vector of changes in tax payments by the ith industry.

(7) $$\Delta T = \frac{\Delta T}{X} X = \frac{\Delta T}{X} [(I - A)^{-1}Y' + (I - A)^{-1}Y''] = \Delta T^{(1)} + \Delta T^{(2)}$$

where,

$$\Delta T^{(1)} = \frac{\Delta T}{X} (I - A)^{-1}(Y')$$

a column vector of final tax payments to the ith sector for i = 1, 2, . . . n, attributable to all sector's exports.

$$\Delta T^{(2)} = \frac{\Delta T}{X} (I - A)^{-1}(Y'')$$

a column vector of final tax payments by the ith sector for i = 1, 2, . . . n, attributable to all sector's deomstic sales.

Substituting (6) into (7) gives

$$\Delta T = \left(\frac{\Delta T}{X}\right)\left((I - A)^{-1}Y' + (I - A)^{-1}Y''\right)$$
$$= \frac{(T_v - T_g)S}{X} (I - A)^{-1} Y' + \frac{(T_v - T_g)S}{X} (I - A)^{-1} Y''$$

(8)

$$\Delta T = \begin{bmatrix} \Delta T_1 \\ \Delta T_2 \\ \cdot \\ \cdot \\ \cdot \\ \Delta T_n \end{bmatrix} = \begin{bmatrix} \frac{(T_{v1} - T_{g1})S_1}{X_1} & 0 & \cdots & 0 \\ 0 & \frac{(T_{v2} - T_{g2})S_2}{X_2} & . & 0 \\ . & . & . & . \\ . & . & . & . \\ . & . & . & . \\ 0 & 0 & \cdots & \frac{(T_{vn} - T_{gn})S_n}{X_n} \end{bmatrix}$$

$$\begin{bmatrix} C_{11}, C_{12} & \cdots & C_{1n} \\ C_{21} \quad . & \cdots & C_{2n} \\ . \quad . & . & . \\ . \quad . & . & . \\ . \quad . & . & . \\ C_{n1} \quad C_{n2} & \cdots & C_{nn} \end{bmatrix} \begin{bmatrix} Y'_1 \\ Y'_2 \\ . \\ . \\ . \\ Y'_n \end{bmatrix} +$$

$$\begin{bmatrix} \frac{(T_{v1} - T_{g1})S_1}{X_1} & 0 & \cdots & 0 \\ 0 & \frac{(T_{v2} - T_{g2})S_2}{X_2} & . & . \\ . & . & . & . \\ . & . & . & . \\ . & . & . & . \\ 0 & 0 & \cdots & \frac{T_{vn} - T_{gn} (S_n)}{X_n} \end{bmatrix}$$

$$\begin{bmatrix} C_{11}, C_{12} & \cdots & C_{1n} \\ C_{21} \quad . & \cdots & C_{2n} \\ . \quad . & . & . \\ . \quad . & . & . \\ . \quad . & . & . \\ C_{n1} \quad C_{n2} & \cdots & C_{nn} \end{bmatrix} \begin{bmatrix} Y''_1 \\ Y''_2 \\ . \\ . \\ . \\ Y''_n \end{bmatrix}$$

where the matrix of C's is equal to our $(I - A)^{-1}$, i.e.,

$$(I - A)^{-1} = [C_{ij}], \quad \begin{matrix} i = 1, \ldots n \\ j = 1, \ldots n \end{matrix}$$

The matrix obtained by the operation

$$\frac{\Delta T}{X}(I - A)^{-1} = \frac{T_x - T_g}{X} S (I - A)^{-1}$$

is a matrix of tax coefficients (ΔTc_{ij}) which represent the change in tax payments by the ith industry attributable to one dollar of delivery to final demand by industry j, for all i, j.

Thus,

$$\Delta TC_{ij} = \begin{bmatrix} \frac{T_{v1} - T_{g1}}{X_1} S_1C_{11} & \frac{T_{v1} - T_{g1}}{X_1} S_1C_{12} & \cdots & \frac{T_{v1} - T_{g1}}{X_1} S_1C_{1n} \\ \frac{T_{v2} - T_{g2}}{X_2} S_2C_{21} & \frac{T_{v2} - T_{g2}}{X_2} S_2C_{22} & \cdots & \frac{T_{v2} - T_{g2}}{X_2} S_2C_{2n} \\ \vdots & \vdots & \vdots & \vdots \\ \frac{T_{vn} - T_{gn}}{X_n} S_nC_{n1} & \frac{T_{vn} - T_{gn}}{X_n} S_nC_{n2} & \cdots & \frac{T_{vn} - T_{gn}}{X_n} S_nC_{nn} \end{bmatrix}$$

Summing each of the j columns in the matrix of tax coefficients yields a vector of tax coefficient ΔTc_j which represent the total change in tax payments by all sectors per dollar of delivery of final demand by the jth industry,

where,

(9) $$\Delta Tc_j = \sum_{i=1}^{n} \frac{Tv_i - Tg_i}{X_i} S_iC_{ij}, \; j = 1, \ldots n$$

To put these coefficients in index terms the following operation is required:

(9a) $$\Delta I_{Tc_j} = (1 + \Delta Tc_j) \cdot (100), \; j = 1, \ldots n$$

To establish an index of differential price change by final demand sector, the vector of converted summed tax coefficients ΔTc_j is weighted by the proportion of sales by industry j to final demand. The resultant vector is then summed to arrive at the aggregate effect on prices in each of the markets.

The effect on overall price in the export market ($\Delta Ip'$) is as follows:

(10a)

$$\Delta Ip'_j = \begin{bmatrix} (1 + \Delta Tc_1) \\ (1 + \Delta Tc_2) \\ \cdot \\ \cdot \\ \cdot \\ (1 + \Delta Tc_n) \end{bmatrix} \begin{bmatrix} \frac{Y'_1}{\sum_{j=1}^{n} Y'_j} \\ \frac{Y'_2}{\sum_{j=1}^{n} Y'_j} \\ \cdot \\ \cdot \\ \cdot \\ \frac{Y'_n}{\sum_{j=1}^{n} Y'_j} \end{bmatrix} = \begin{bmatrix} \Delta Ip'_1 \\ \Delta Ip'_2 \\ \cdot \\ \cdot \\ \cdot \\ \Delta Ip'_n \end{bmatrix}$$

(10b)

$$\Delta I_p' = \sum_{j=1}^{n} \Delta Ip' \cdot 100$$

The effect on overall price in the domestic market ($\Delta Ip''$) is as follows:

(11a)

$$\Delta Ip''_j = \begin{bmatrix} (1 + \Delta Tc_1) \\ (1 + \Delta Tc_2) \\ \cdot \\ \cdot \\ \cdot \\ (1 + \Delta Tc_n) \end{bmatrix} \begin{bmatrix} \frac{Y''_1}{\sum_{j=1}^{n} Y''_j} \\ \frac{Y''_2}{\sum_{j=1}^{n} Y''_j} \\ \cdot \\ \cdot \\ \cdot \\ \frac{Y''_n}{\sum_{j=1}^{n} Y''_n} \end{bmatrix} = \begin{bmatrix} \Delta Ip''_1 \\ \Delta Ip''_2 \\ \cdot \\ \cdot \\ \cdot \\ \Delta Ip''_n \end{bmatrix}$$

(11b)

$$\Delta Ip'' = \sum_{j=1}^{n} \Delta Ip'' \cdot 100$$

The effect on overall prices for state government ($\Delta Ip'''$) is as follows:

(12a)

$$\Delta Ip'''_j = \begin{bmatrix} (1 + \Delta Tc_1) \\ (1 + \Delta Tc_2) \\ \vdots \\ (1 + \Delta Tc_n) \end{bmatrix} \begin{bmatrix} \dfrac{Y'''_1}{\sum_{j=1}^{n} Y'''_j} \\ \dfrac{Y'''_2}{\sum_{j=1}^{n} Y'''_j} \\ \vdots \\ \dfrac{Y'''_n}{\sum_{j=1}^{n} Y'''_n} \end{bmatrix} = \begin{bmatrix} \Delta Ip'''_1 \\ \Delta Ip'''_2 \\ \vdots \\ \Delta Ip'''_n \end{bmatrix}$$

(12b)

$$\Delta Ip''' = \sum_{j=1}^{n} \Delta Ip''' \cdot 100$$

APPENDIX C

ESTIMATING PROCEDURE FOR DERIVING THE CARRIER GROSS IN WEST VIRGINIA 1967-1969

APPENDIX C

ESTIMATING PROCEDURE FOR DERIVING THE CARRIER GROSS IN WEST VIRGINIA 1967-1969

Carriers composed of the following industries: buses, taxis, truckers, telephone, pipelines, steamboats and airlines, and railroads are taxed under the "Annual Tax on Incomes of Certain Carriers." Under this tax statute the tax is levied in two parts:

1. A turnover tax on the gross business from all business activity beginning and ending in West Virginia--intrastate gross.
2. A net income tax on the apportioned net income arising out of multistate operations.

Statistics are available on the gross business conducted within the state (Table 46, Col. 2) but none on that portion of the gross arising out of multistate operations which could be apportioned to the state under the value-added tax. With the exception of railroads, our estimates of the apportionable multistate gross were derived by using the amount of net income apportioned into the state (Col. 3) and dividing this figure by the net/gross ratio for each of the industries as reported by the Internal Revenue Service[1] (Col. 4). The information on the total gross for railroads was obtained from the State Tax Department and is shown in Column 6 along with the estimated total gross for the other carriers.

---

[1]Internal Revenue Service, <u>Statistics of Income--1967, 1968</u> and <u>1969, Corporation Income Tax Returns</u> (Washington, D.C.: Government Printing Office, 1971, 1972, 1973).

TABLE 46

DERIVATION OF CARRIER GROSS FOR VALUE-ADDED TAXATION
WEST VIRGINIA, 1967-1969

Industry	Intra-State Gross	Estimated Net Income Apportioned to West Virginia	Net/Gross Ratio From IRS	Estimated Gross Based on Apportioned Net Income (Col 3/4)	Total Estimated Gross (Col 2 + 5)
1	2	3	4	5	6
		1967			
Buses	6,200,372	200,203	.055736	3,591,987	9,792,359
Taxis	4,888,900	8,316	.055736	149,203	5,038,103
Truckers	19,161,069	303,185	.033352	9,090,459	28,251,528
Telephone	D	D	.199358	D	D
Pipeline	796,167	0	.105728	0	796,167
Steamboats & Airlines	4,158,323	170,902	.058009	2,946,129	7,104,452
Railroads	---	---	---	---	243,819,000
		1968			
Buses	5,749,761	176,622	.050834	3,474,485	9,224,246
Taxis	5,220,479	8,882	.050834	174,725	5,395,204
Truckers	20,263,526	312,987	.037018	8,454,994	28,718,520
Telephone	D	D	.194368	D	D
Pipeline	917,467	0	.121102	0	917,467
Steamboats & Airlines	4,113,321	200,700	.030363	6,610,018	10,723,339
Railroads	---	---	---	---	242,776

TABLE 46--Continued

Industry	Intra-State Gross	Estimated Net Income Apportioned to West Virginia	Net/Gross Ratio From IRS	Estimated Gross Based on Apportioned Net Income (Col 3/4)	Total Estimated Gross (Col 2 + 5)
1	2	3	4	5	6
		1969			
Buses	5,792,823	196,141	.042486	4,616,603	10,409,426
Taxis	5,237,952	898	.042486	21,136	5,259,088
Truckers	26,927,717	436,227	.032830	13,287,450	40,215,167
Telephone	D	D	.173633	D	D
Pipeline	963,507	0	.108055	0	963,504
Steamboat & Airlines	5,943,488	198,543	.022130	8,971,667	14,915,155
Railroads	---	---	---	---	250,235,326

D--Data omitted for disclosure reasons.

APPENDIX D

TURNOVER VERSUS VALUE-ADDED TAX BASE ESTIMATING PROCEDURES AND ESTIMATED CHANGES IN AVERAGE EFFECTIVE TAX RATES BY INDUSTRY, WEST VIRGINIA, 1967

APPENDIX D

TURNOVER VERSUS VALUE-ADDED TAX BASE ESTIMATING PROCEDURES AND ESTIMATED CHANGES IN AVERAGE EFFECTIVE TAX RATES BY INDUSTRY, WEST VIRGINIA, 1967

Although there is no problem in the reporting of the bases and revenues for turnover tax purposes, neither the corporate nor the non-corporate sector reports value added at the state level as such. In order to estimate the value added in various industries, and, thence, the effects of the change from the existing turnover to the proposed value-added tax, arithmetic relationships were assumed which utilized the information provided on existing tax returns. Two returns were used for this purpose--the West Virginia Corporation Net Income Tax Return, 112 (WV 112) and the face of the U.S. Corporation Income Tax Return, 1120 (U.S. 1120) which was required to be filed with the West Virginia corporation return.[1]

The procedure can best be expressed as a series of steps or equations. These are indicated below and are followed by a brief explanation of their meaning. The numbers refer to the line of the U.S. Corporation Tax Return filed with the West Virginia Corporation Net Income Tax Return. In all cases the calculations were performed on each tax entity.[2]

Step 1--Calculate the gross income for tax purposes (GTIA) as follows:

$$GTIA = 11 + 2 - (4 + 6 + 8 + 9 + WAA + WAB)$$

---

[1]Facsimilies of these returns for the period 1967-1969 are on file in the Bureau of Business Research at West Virginia University and may be made available to interested parties.

[2]Unless otherwise indicated all references are to lines on the face of the U.S. Corporation Income Tax Return 1120.

Where: (11 + 2) = Total income of the firm less discounts and allowances.

4 = Dividends

6 = Other Interest

8 = Gross Royalties

9 = Net Gain (losses)

WAA = Interest received on U.S. government obligations from Schedule A, Part 2, line A, WV 112.

WAB = Interest and dividends received on obligations or securities of U.S. instrumentalities from Schedule A, Part 2, line B, WV 112.

The deductions are self-explanatory except for those of line 8 and line 9. Line 8 (gross royalties) is deducted because it refers to royalties received everywhere. The only place to find West Virginia royalties is in Schedule C of the West Virginia 112 and is calculated at a later point because royalty income is not subject to apportionment, being wholly allocable to the state, if received in the state. Line 9 provides for deduction due to capital gains whether positive or negative--since they are not part of current value added.[1]

Step 2--Calculate the entire value-added income (VAIA).

VAIA = GTIA - (2+27) + 16 + 18 + WAC + D2 + 25A + 25B + BOCT

Where: 2 = Cost of Goods Sold

27 = Total Deductions

16 = Rents

18 = Interest

---

[1]This may not, however, be valid in the case of capital gains on fully depreciated capital. See Eldridge, "Fiscal Aspects."

WAC = Income taxes paid from Schedule A, line c of the West Virginia Corporation Net Income Tax Return (WV 112).

D2 = Salaries, wages, and other compensation paid elsewhere from Schedule D, line 2 of WV 112.[1]

25A & B = Pension, profit-sharing, stock bonus, annuity plans, and other employee benefits.

BOCT = Business and Occupation and Carrier Taxes paid.

Since neither the federal nor the state income tax returns contained sufficient detail to use either the addition or subtraction approach to value added, this particular method combines both; first, by deducting from GTIA the cost of goods sold plus all other deductions and then by adding to GTIA those components which were not deductible--rents, interest, income taxes, turnover taxes, salaries and wages, and other employee emoluments, paid in West Virginia.

Step 3--Calculate the Taxable Value-Added Income (TVAI) consisting of apportioned value added (VAIN) and allocated value added (VAIAD)

TVAI = VAIN + VAIAD

Where: VAIN = WC11 + WC21 + WC31

---

[1]Strictly speaking this was only possible for firms which were engaged in multistate operations and were consequently required to furnish information for apportioning their income as in Schedule C of the West Virginia Corporation Net Income Tax Return 112. This schedule contains data relating to property and payrolls everywhere and in West Virginia. For firms who were not multistate, an estimate of their wages and salaries was obtained by taking a percentage of their cost of goods sold. This percentage was derived by calculating an industry, by size, ratio matrix of wage and salary to cost of goods sold for all of the multistate firms. The assumption made was that this was the best proxy indicator of the level of wages and salaries paid by domestic firms. There is an additional caveat that ought to be mentioned, however; royalties paid may be included either in line 16 or line 26. To the extent that they are included in line 16 and arise from operations outside the state, the taxable value added will be overstated. To the extent they are included in line 26, the taxable value added will be understated. Though uncertain, the likelihood is that the bulk will be found in line 26.

Where: WC11 = Rents and royalties received from tangible property in West Virginia and is to be found in Schedule C, line 1, Column 1 of the WV 112.

WC21 = Non-business interest income in West Virginia and is to be found in Schedule C, line 2, Column 1 of the WV 112.

WC31 = Royalties received from patents and copyrights within West Virginia from Schedule C, line 3, Column 1 of the WV 112.

and $\text{VAIAD} = \text{VAIA}\begin{pmatrix}\text{Apportionment}\\ \text{Percentage}\end{pmatrix}$

Where the apportionment percentage is based on the property and payroll factors provided in Schedule D, lines 1, 2, 4, and 5, and is calculated as follows:

$$\left(\frac{\begin{array}{c}\text{Salaries, wages, and}\\ \text{other compensation assigned}\\ \text{to West Virginia}\end{array}}{\begin{array}{c}\text{Salaries, wages, and}\\ \text{other compensation paid}\\ \text{everywhere}\end{array}} + \frac{\begin{array}{c}\text{Average value}\\ \text{of tangible property}\\ \text{in West Virginia}\end{array}}{\begin{array}{c}\text{Average value}\\ \text{of tangible property}\\ \text{everywhere}\end{array}}\right) \div 2$$

This third step yields the estimated value-added income in the state. A number of observations need to be made here: As pointed out in Step 2, rents and royalties were likely to show up in both line 16 of the 1120, which was added and line 26 (1120) which was not; the problem which arises in the allocation and apportionment procedure is that some portion of that amount in line 16 is subject to apportionment and some of it is wholly allocable, but it is not possible to distinguish which part.

A bold assumption was made that the amount of rent and royalty income which could be identified from the WV 112 as income to multistate corporations was equal to the amount of rents and royalties paid by corporations which was wholly allocable to the state. Any residual, if any, which remained was considered subject to apportionment. Recognizing that there is no way to validate this assumption and attempting to make this as conservative as possible, the decision made in building the base of value added was not to add in line 26, since line 26 represents other deductions, some of which are likely to be excluded as part of the value-added base.

The base for measuring the Turnover Tax Base was a direct acquisition from data furnished by the tax department on the Turnover Tax Base and taxes paid by business in West Virginia under the "Business and Occupation Tax" and the "Tax on Income of Certain Carriers" (BOCG). From this data the following identities were established:

BOCG = Turnover Tax Base in West Virginia and equal to the Gross Sales reported under the Business and Occupation Tax,* and Gross Sales reported under the Carrier Tax.**

*The Gross for each business activity was entered alongside the tax due column and totaled to obtain a total gross for that firm.

**The Carrier Tax law only permits the declaration of a gross base from intrastate commerce activities. Gross income from intrastate activity is separately apportioned and taxed from the net income of the business originating in interstate commerce. This income and tax was omitted from consideration in the sample but was included in the revenue estimate.

BOCT = Turnover Taxes Paid = Tax due under the Business and Occupation Tax + the tax due under the Carrier Tax for Intrastate Activity.

Having settled on the procedure for estimating the tax bases under both the turnover and the proposed value-added tax, a sampling scheme[1] was constructed for the universe of firms operating in West Virginia and a series of computer programs were developed for making the

---

[1]See Appendix A for a more detailed description of the sampling design and the results.

calculations.[1] Using the sample data with the estimating methods described above, we calculated the two tax bases in two ways, weighted and unweighted. The weighted procedure was used to give weight to the importance of the large firm in determining taxable bases and revenue potential (dealt with in Chapter VI) as well as impact on various markets (dealt with in Chapter IV). The unweighted procedure gave equal weight to each firm in order to measure excess burden effects in Chapter V and to assess the differential turnover tax treatment of multistate and domestic corporations (see Appendix E).

A comparison of the empirically derived mean turnover tax rates from our stratified sample in Column 3 of Table 47 with those of Table 5 shows significant divergencies from the statutory rates. These differences are a consequence of the fact that firms engage in more than one type of taxable business activity. Coal, for example, in 1967 was taxed at a rate of 1.35 per cent but our estimates show the average rate equal to 1.24 (±0.58) per cent. The lowest average turnover tax rate is 0.42 per cent on the wholesale industry which compares with the 0.25 rate by statute. The highest average turnover tax rate for 1967 was 3.90 (±0.19) per cent on the communication and public utilities industry. Overall the average turnover tax paid is estimated to be 1.24 (±0.09) per cent of gross. Thus, among industries, there is a considerable variation in effective turnover tax rates but not as divergent as the statutes would suggest. Looking at each industry in which we should expect fairly homogenous production or operating methods, we find a considerable

---

[1]These are on file in the Bureau of Business Research at West Virginia University and can be made available for those interested.

TABLE 47

AVERAGE EFFECTIVE TAX RATES ON INDIVIDUAL FIRMS UNDER ALTERNATIVE BUSINESS TAXES
WEST VIRGINIA, 1967

(Rates Expressed as a Per Cent of Gross)

Industry Identification	Number of Firms in Sample	Turnover Tax (Per Cent)	Value-Added Tax (Per Cent)	Change in Rate (Col. 4 - Col. 3)	Per Cent Change in Rate
1	2	3	4	5	6
Coal Mining	125	1.24 0.58[a]	1.00 0.09	-0.24	-19
Crude Petroleum & Natural Gas	35	3.55 1.15	1.06 0.22	-2.49	-70
Contract Construction	182	1.71 0.09	1.01 0.09	-0.70	-41
Manufacturing & Non-Metallic Minerals	346	0.69 0.05	0.95 0.06	+0.26	+38
Transportation[b]	40	2.60 0.31	1.45 0.17	-1.16	-45
Communication & Public Utilities	80	3.90 0.19	1.08 0.13	-2.82	-72
Wholesale Trade	108	0.42 0.10	0.62 0.08	+0.20	+48
Retail Trade	154	0.54 0.10	0.79 0.06	+0.25	+46
Finance	17	1.07 0.07	1.92 0.15	+0.84	+79
Real Estate	9	1.01 0.06	0.89 0.12	-0.12	-12
Services	113	0.93 0.06	1.41 0.12	+0.49	+53
Total	1,209	1.24 0.09	1.00 0.04	-0.24	-19

TABLE 47--Continued

[a]Value represents 3 standard errors of the mean giving a 1 per cent level of significance to the reliability of the data.

[b]This analysis does not include the railroad sector (24 firms) which is included in Chapter VI for the reason that the tax returns did not lend themselves to the standardized treatment required by the method developed for this appendix.

variation in the effective tax rates among firms, as measured by the value of three standard errors--displayed in Table 47, below the mean values for each industry. For example, the coal industry's mean effective turnover tax rate is estimated to lie somewhere between 1.82 and 0.66 per cent.

To provide a comparison of change in effective tax rates by industry between the two taxes, we have recorded in Column 5 of Table 47 the absolute amount of change in rate with the simulated shift to a value-added tax. Here our simulated estimates show that in six industries the average effective tax rate would increase, while in five industries the average effective tax rate would increase. Averaging all of the like-signed changes, there is an average absolute reduction in effective tax rate of 1.26 per cent in six industries as opposed to an average effective tax rate increase of 0.41 per cent in five industries. Overall the shift to a value-added tax is estimated to reduce the effective mean rate from 1.24 to 1.00 per cent and to reduce the value of three standard errors by 56 per cent from 0.09 to 0.04 per cent.

APPENDIX E

ESTIMATE OF DIFFERENCE IN TURNOVER TAX TREATMENT OF DOMESTIC AND MULTISTATE CORPORATIONS WEST VIRGINIA, 1967

APPENDIX E

ESTIMATE OF DIFFERENCE IN TURNOVER TAX TREATMENT OF DOMESTIC AND MULTISTATE CORPORATIONS WEST VIRGINIA, 1967

In Chapter II, we observed that some writers have concluded that the turnover tax in West Virginia gives a tax break to multistate firms because of differences in tax base. Our own analysis, however, suggested that this is an erroneous conclusion and is the result of confusion between turnover tax base definitions and apportioning procedures. Our task here is to see if, in fact, we can estimate the magnitude of difference in the turnover tax treatment, if any, between multistate and domestic firms. Since the argument is couched in value-added terms, we will use the turnover tax as a per cent of value added for the empirical measure, separating multistate firms from domestic firms.

Table 48 shows the average ratio of turnover tax to value added for: (1) all firms in each of the industries (Col. 2); (2) multistate corporations (Col. 4); and (3) domestic corporations (Col. 6). Below each of the ratios is the value of three standard errors of the mean. Below the standard error figures are the number of firms in the sample for that particular cell. Where there are fewer than five firms in the cell, the data has been suppressed for disclosure reasons. The ratios of Table 48 are visually displayed in Figure 8 and identified as (M) multistate, (D) domestic, and (T) total. In addition, we have included ratios for the sub-industries of manufacturing, which for reasons of space were not included in Table 48. Again, where necessary, the data has been suppressed for disclosure reasons: There is indicated, however, the direction of the difference among the three ratios. The line joining

TABLE 48

DOMESTIC VERSUS MULTISTATE CORPORATE TURNOVER TAX RATES
AS A PROPORTION OF VALUE ADDED
WEST VIRGINIA, 1967

Industry Identification	Total Turnover Tax / Value Added	Multistate Turnover Tax / Value Added	Domestic Turnover Tax / Value Added
1	2*	3*	4*
Coal Mining	.04037 .0087 125	.04668 .0278 20	.03917 .0092 105
Crude Petroleum & Natural Gas	.10404 .0436 35	.11015 .0845 17	.09827 .0354 18
Contract Construction	.07336 .0347 182	.13186 .0940 64	.04163 .0064 118
Manufacturing & Non-Metallic Minerals	.02490 .0044 346	.03336 .0085 133	.01977 .0044 213
Motor Freight & Related Services, All Other Transportation	.05222 .0132 40	D	.04848 .0104 36
Communication & Public Utilities	.11517 .0269 80	.12803 .1259 8	.11374 .0272 72
Wholesale Trade	.02292 .0083 108	.03559 .0226 34	.01710 .0055 74
Retail Trade	.01911 .0030 154	.02544 .0076 25	.01788 .0031 129
Finance	.01480 .0014 17	.01672 .0055 5	.01400 .0010 12

TABLE 48--Continued

Industry Identification	Total Turnover Tax / Value Added	Multistate Turnover Tax / Value Added	Domestic Turnover Tax / Value Added
1	2*	3*	4*
Real Estate	.04161 .0310 9	D	.04512 .0481 6
Services	.02068 .0041 113	.03608 .0159 23	.01674 .0021 90
Total	.04153 .0064 1,209	.05915 .0202 336	.03478 .0041 873

*Explanation of data set (Cols. 2, 3, 4)

Coal Mining .04037 = Ratio
.0087 = 3 Standard Errors
125 = Number of firms

D = Data not entered for disclosure reasons (fewer than 5 firms in the sample cell).

FIGURE 8

A GRAPHIC ILLUSTRATION OF DOMESTIC VS MULTISTATE CORPORATE TURNOVER TAX RATES AS A PROPORTION OF VALUE ADDED WEST VIRGINIA, 1967

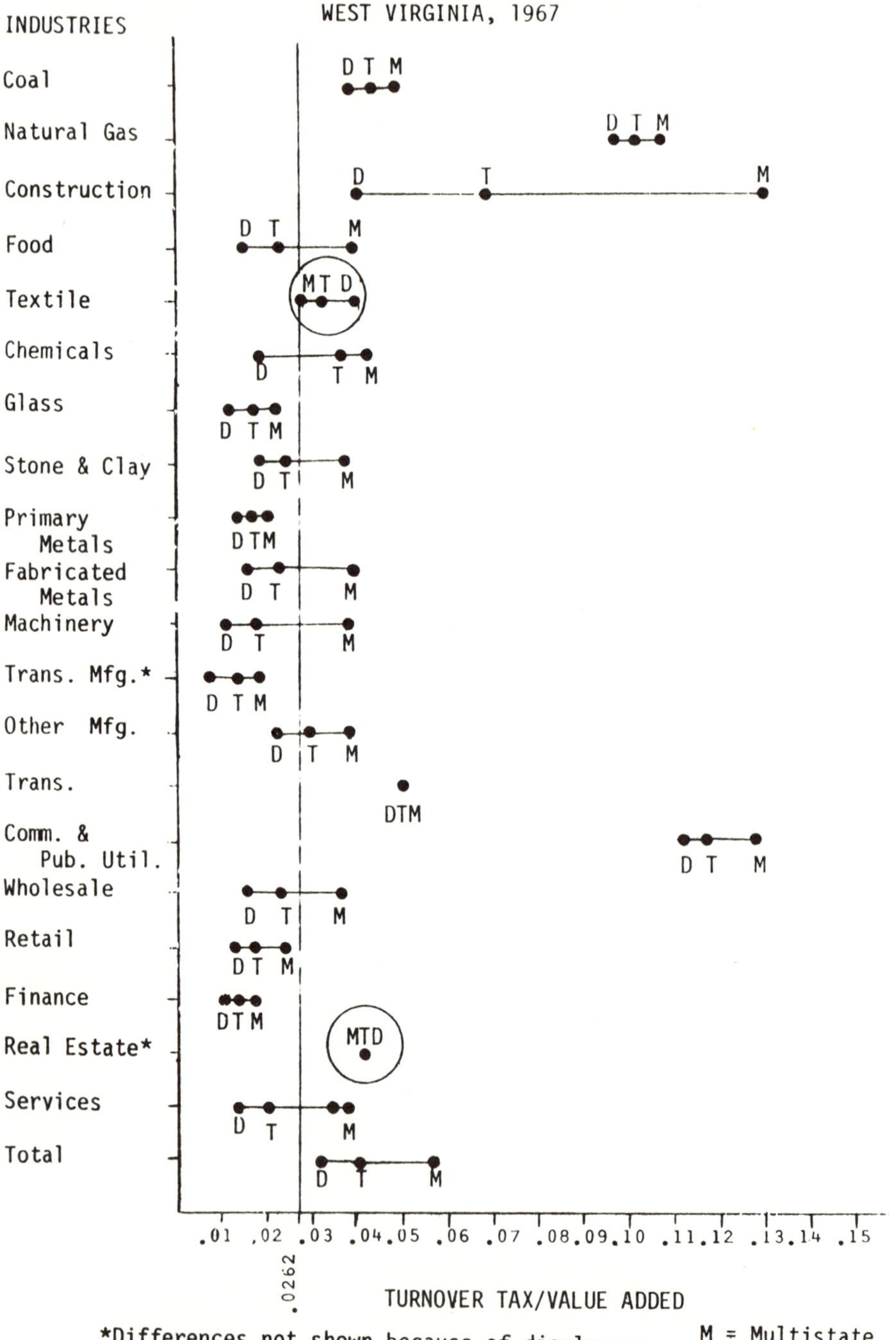

*Differences not shown because of disclosure.

M = Multistate
T = Total
D = Domestic

the three points provides a visual appreciation of the range of difference between multistate and domestic turnover tax rates expressed as a per cent of value added. By contrast, the vertical line running up the graph shows that the shift to an income value-added tax would eliminate not only the difference in tax rates as between domestic and multistate firms, but also the differences which are apparent between industries. What is more striking, however, is that except for the textile and textile products and real estate industries, the domestic firms have lower turnover tax to value-added ratios than their multistate counterparts. It may be, however, that value added declines relative to gross as firms become larger and have more specialized production facilities, and that these firms are more likely to be multistate firms than domestic.

To explore this tack, the data was further disaggregated into four size classes to provide an industry-by-size matrix of turnover tax to value-added ratios for both the domestic and multistate firms in the sample. The domestic matrix was then subtracted from the multistate matrix with a resultant matrix which measured the magnitude and direction of differences of turnover tax treatment of the two types of firms.

This information provided the basis for applying the "Wilcoxon Matched-Pairs Signed Ranks Non-Parametric Test" which takes account of the magnitude of difference between two sets of data and the direction of the difference. It has the effect of giving greater importance to a large difference between pairs than it does to a small difference between pairs.[1]

[1]Siegel, Nonparametric Statistics, pp. 75-83 for a more detailed discussion of the technique which is applied and explained below.

If there are no differences in the treatment of the multistate and domestic firms under the turnover tax, then we should except the sum of the negative ranks to be approximately equal to the sum of the positive ranks. This constitutes the null proposition (Po) of the test.

The test proposition is that there is a difference in treatment between the multistate and domestic firms and that the difference in treatment leads to a lower ratio of turnover tax to value added for multistate than for domestic firms. For purposes of the test, it is called P_1. In light of the evidence presented in Figure 7, however, it appears that there is a more plausible alternative proposition (P_2) namely, that there is a difference in treatment, but that difference provides a lower ratio of turnover taxes to value added for domestic firms than for multistate.

Table 49 shows the derived matrix in which each cell shows the sign and rank of the following operation:

$$\frac{\text{Turnover Tax Multistate}}{\text{Value Added Multistate}} - \frac{\text{Turnover Tax Domestic}}{\text{Value Added Domestic}}$$

The sign will be negative if the multistate ratio is lower than the domestic ratio and positive if the domestic is larger than the multistate. Finally, in the cells where there was no comparison, a mark of "NC" is recorded. The ranking order is based upon the convention that the highest absolute difference without regard to sign is assigned the rank of 1. The sign of that difference is then assigned to the rank. The technique requires that the like-signed difference be summed. These are noted at the bottom of the table along with the number of possible paired differences N. Following this step, the smallest summed rank is declared the "calculated statistic T" and these are circled on the table. For

TABLE 49

DATA FOR TEST OF THE DIFFERENCE IN TREATMENT OF MULTISTATE AND DOMESTIC CORPORATIONS UNDER THE TURNOVER TAX WEST VIRGINIA, 1967

Industry Identification	All Size Classes	Gross ($000) 0-100	100-1,000	1,000-10,000	10,000 & Over
Coal Mining	15	-8	17	16	3
Crude Petroleum & Natural Gas	11	1	- 4	3	NC
Contract Construction	1	3	2	2	-6
Food & Kindred Products	4	NC	3	8	NC
Textile Mill, Apparel & Other Textiles	-16	NC	- 8	7	NC
Chemicals & Allied Products	3	NC	7	6	NC
Glass & Glass Products	18	NC	-12	13	NC
Stone & Clay Products	13	-6	-19	10	2
Primary Metals	20	NC	-13	15	NC
Fabricated Metals	7	NC	5	9	NC
Machinery, Including Electrical	8	5	10	17	NC
Transportation Equipment	17	NC	NC	12	NC
All Other Manufacturing	10	2	-14	4	NC
Transportation	2	-4	6	NC	NC
Communication & Public Utilities	9	NC	1	1	5
Wholesale Trade	6	NC	11	5	1
Retail Trade	14	-9	18	11	4
Finance	19	NC	15	NC	NC
Real Estate	-12	NC	16	NC	NC
Services	5	7	9	14	NC
Number of Possible Paired Differences-N	20	9	19	17	6
Σ Negative Ranks	(28)*	23	(70)	(0)	(6)
Σ Positive Ranks	168	(18)	120	153	15
Critical Value of "T"	43	3	38	28	0

*The calculated value of T is the circled summed rank and represents the lower of the summed negative and positive ranks.

a given alternative proposition to be valid, the smallest summed rank must be opposite in sign to the predicted difference in sign. For P_1 to be valid, therefore, the smallest summed rank must be positive. Thus, only in the case of the smallest size class is this proposition valid. The remaining three classes and the total of all classes admit only to the alternative proposition P_2.

The "calculated statistic T" is compared with the "critical value of T" in a one-tailed test at the 1 per cent level of significance for a given size N-paired comparison. The "critical value of T" for each of the size classes is noted at the bottom of the table.[1] If the "calculated T" is less than or equal to the "critical value of T" then the null proposition is accepted, i.e.:

Accept Po if "T calculated" $\leq$ "T critical"

If the "calculated T" is greater than the "critical T" then accept the alternative proposition, i.e.:

Accept P_1 or P_2 if "T calculated" > "T critical"

Table 50 summarizes the results of the tests. At the aggregate level, the initial inspection of the data is confirmed in that there is only a 1 per cent probability that the magnitude and direction of difference would have occurred by chance. Thus, we conclude that the domestic firms in the aggregate do better than multistate firms with respect to the turnover taxes. When the data is cross-classified by size and each size class tested, the results are less certain. In three of the four classes, the null proposition is accepted, i.e., there is no difference in the turnover tax treatment of multistate and domestic firms. In

---

[1]Ibid., p. 254.

TABLE 50

SUMMARY RESULTS OF THE WILCOXON TEST FOR DIFFERENCE IN TREATMENT OF MULTISTATE AND DOMESTIC CORPORATIONS

Size Class ($000)	N	Critical Value of T[a]	Calculated T	Valid Proposition Set	P_0 D = M	P_1 D > M	P_2 D < M
Total	20	43	-28	$P_0:P_2$	Reject		Accept
0-100	9	3	18	$P_0:P_1$	Accept	Reject	
100-1,000	19	38	-70	$P_0:P_2$	Reject		Accept
1,000-10,000	17	28	- 0	$P_0:P_2$	Accept		Reject
10,000 & Over	6	0	- 6	$P_0:P_2$	Accept		Reject

[a]Level of significance = .01.

the \$100-\$1,000 class, however, the 2nd alternative proposition (P_2) is accepted, i.e., there _is_ a difference, but it is in favor of the domestic firms.

We must conclude from this that there is no case for the argument that under the turnover tax multistate firms are favored over domestic firms, and that in three of the four size classes our conclusion is supported that there is no difference in the tax treatment of these two types of firms. Finally, if there is any case to be made it is that domestic firms are favored over multistate firms under the turnover tax.

NAME INDEX

SUBJECT INDEX